Meet the Presidents

Schiffer Books are available at special discounts for bulk purchases for sales promotions or premiums. Special editions, including personalized covers, corporate imprints, and excerpts can be created in large quantities for special needs. For more information contact the publisher:

Published by Schiffer Publishing Ltd.
4880 Lower Valley Road
Atglen, PA 19310
Phone: (610) 593-1777; Fax: (610) 593-2002
E-mail: Info@schifferbooks.com

For the largest selection of fine reference books on this and related subjects, please visit our website at **www.schifferbooks.com**
We are always looking for people to write books on new and related subjects. If you have an idea for a book please contact us at the above address.

This book may be purchased from the publisher.
Include $5.00 for shipping.
Please try your bookstore first.
You may write for a free catalog.

In Europe, Schiffer books are distributed by
Bushwood Books
6 Marksbury Ave.
Kew Gardens
Surrey TW9 4JF England
Phone: 44 (0) 20 8392 8585; Fax: 44 (0) 20 8392 9876
E-mail: info@bushwoodbooks.co.uk
Website: www.bushwoodbooks.co.uk

Walter Eckman

Meet the Presidents

THE FUN EDUCATIONAL GUIDE TO THE UNITED STATES PRESIDENTS' LIVES

Schiffer Publishing Ltd

4880 Lower Valley Road • Atglen, PA 19310

Independence Hall, Philadelphia, where the Declaration of Independence and the United States Constitution were debated and adopted.

Contents

INTRODUCTION

Did you know that John Quincy Adams skinny-dipped in the Potomac River, that Dwight Eisenhower was an artist and that Franklin Roosevelt collected stamps? Here are some other little-known facts: James Garfield could write Greek in one hand and Latin in the other at the same time; Harry Truman was a skilled classical pianist; Abraham Lincoln never lost a wrestling match; and George H. W. Bush—as captain of the Yale baseball team—accepted Babe Ruth's autobiographical manuscript from the man himself at a ceremony at Yankee Stadium in 1948.

The stories offered here provide an insider's look into the private lives and public journeys of the men who became President of the United States. You may discover similarities in what motivated them to seek the highest office in the land—as well as differences in their lifestyles, personalities, education, and leadership. You will also find that a few didn't want to be president at all! Challenge yourself with "Fun Assignments" and broaden your knowledge with the "Tell Me More" and "Connections" sections. Finally, I invite you to give each president a nickname that describes how you view them. Compare your nicknames to the ones provided for each president.

The presidential sites featured here are located all across this great land. They are divided into three regions: the Northeast, Virginia and Ohio, and the South and West. Most of our presidents had modest beginnings, but a few came from more lofty origins. Their homes, both childhood and adult, reflect their lifestyles and economic status. As you read about them—or even visit them—you will see the following:

- The birthplace of John Quincy Adams, an 18th century New England "salt box" dwelling in Quincy, Massachusetts;
- The 19th century Victorian Gothic home of Martin Van Buren in Kinderhook, New York;
- Theodore Roosevelt's 20th century Queen Ann style mansion in Oyster Bay, New York;
- William Henry Harrison's plantation on the James River in Virginia;
- The only surviving residence of James Polk in Columbia, Tennessee;

- The Lyndon Baines Johnson ranch, which includes his birthplace and home along the banks of the Pedernales River near Johnson City, Texas;
- Bess Truman's fourteen room Civil War Victorian style home in Independence, Missouri;
- The simple, clapboard home of Bill Clinton's grandparents, in Hope, Arkansas;
- Richard Nixon's modest birthplace, surrounded by a lemon grove in Yorba Linda, California.

Learn about these and other presidential sites of yesteryear. This virtual tour allows you

to "walk" in each president's shoes. If you get a chance, visit or take field trips to these places and take advantage of the on-site guided tours for a deeper insight into the homes and those who lived there. If you do visit, be sure to ask a lot of questions (Park Service Rangers and volunteers love questions!). Soak in the environment and search for subtle details such as a time-worn bible, book titles, reading glasses, pen and ink, childhood cradles and toys, and hats of all kinds—Stetson, bowler, stovepipe, and cowboy. Look for not-so-subtle artifacts including chamber pots, spinning wheels, dinnerware, saddles, and even a moose head. Explore the grounds, gardens, and outhouses. Be adventurous. Even visit their burial grounds. You may be surprised at the clues you will find to the true nature of our country's leaders. The cemeteries themselves may be simple or ostentatious, the tombstones plain or elaborate, and the inscriptions humble or self-serving. You be the judge.

I recommend that you select a small group of favorite presidents and delve further into

their lives and their presidencies. The men who took on the presidential mantle were quite human and faced many and varied challenges. Nonetheless, they often rose to levels greater than even they could dare to imagine. You are about to meet the architects of the great experiment we call America. Enjoy what you see, savor what you learn, and explore the varied journeys of the leaders who found their way to 1600 Pennsylvania Avenue.

FOREWORD

The presidents: Very few subjects have a more natural affinity to the American people than these individuals. Forty-two have occupied the highest office of the land since George Washington, who refused to be called "His Majesty" or "King George." However, most of us have only a thimble-full of knowledge about the men behind this elevated title. Grappling with the concept of "the presidency," I realized that each of our country's leaders defined "presidency" on their own terms and so I naturally wondered, who *are* these men?

I was introduced to the presidents at home, where my family, like many others across the country, "watched" and listened to the radio as Franklin Delano Roosevelt reassured us with his "fireside chats." I was fortunate that my grandfather had dragged me to our local railroad station to see Harry S. Truman, then on a whistle-stop campaign for reelection. I saw Dwight D. Eisenhower at a horse show, Ronald Reagan stumping for votes at a gentleman's farm in Chester County, Pennsylvania, and George W. Bush doing likewise at a local college. How fortunate I feel. Brian Lamb's series on the presidents drove my curiosity — and now I am a self-admitted presidential junkie!

To share all I have learned about the presidents, I went on the stump myself, talking to groups of all ages from ten-year-old students to ninety-year-old youngsters. The enthusiasm I saw across the board was rewarding and proof perfect that the topic has an "ageless" appeal. I decided to go outside the classroom and into your car and homes. This book is not only educational, but it can serve as a travelogue—a guide to prod you to "meet" the presidents by visiting their homes, libraries, museums, and gravesites. It also can be a primer to the presidents, an introduction to forty-three top executives and a supplement to American history studies. By any name, though, it is fun and factual, light and non-political, and uncomplicated yet informative. My intent is to "whet your appetite," so that you will want to seek more details and insights. There may be self-learning lessons in-between these pages as well. The true stories of our presidents may inspire you to try harder, believe in the impossible, even entice you to consider a career in public service, politics, or maybe the presidency! For those readers who are older, these stories will give you the opportunity to reminiscence on an era long gone and provide great coffee clatch conversation. I encourage you to visit these presidential sites, or sit in your cozy chair and turn the key to your imagination. Either way, have a great trip!

DEDICATION

To *Editor* Bill Cannon and *Designer* Dave Beverage whose enthusiasm, encouragement, and professionalism are very much appreciated, and to my wife JoAnne.

JOHN ADAMS

2nd President of the United States

POLITICAL PARTY: Federalist
ELECTION OPPONENTS:
Thomas Jefferson, Democratic-Republican
Thomas Pinckney, Federalist
Aaron Burr, Democratic-Republican
Samuel Adams, Federalist
TERM OF OFFICE: March 4, 1797 to March 3, 1801
VICE PRESIDENT: Thomas Jefferson

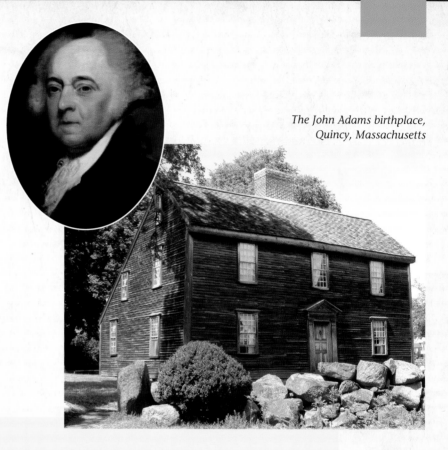

The John Adams birthplace, Quincy, Massachusetts

Tell me more!

What was a Democratic-Republican?
The Democratic-Republican Party was founded around 1792 by Thomas Jefferson and James Madison. It was the dominant political party in the United States from 1800 to 1824.

Personal Profile

BORN: October 30, 1735
Quincy, Massachusetts
SIBLINGS: First of three brothers
RELIGION: Unitarian
EDUCATION: Harvard College; graduated 1755
CAREER: Lawyer

MILITARY: None
MARRIAGE: Abigail Smith, October 25, 1764
Weymouth, Massachusetts
OFFSPRING: Two daughters, three sons
DIED: July 4, 1826, Quincy, Massachusetts

Visiting the President

BIRTHPLACE/HOMESTEAD/LIBRARY:
Adams National Historic Park
1250 Hancock Street, Quincy, Massachusetts
GRAVESITE: United First Parish Church
1306 Hancock Street, Quincy, Massachusetts

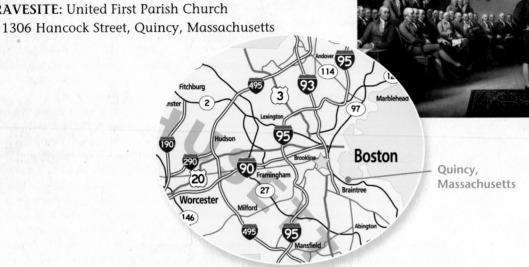

John Adams was one of the signers of the Declaration of Independence.

Quincy, Massachusetts

Political Profile

- Representative of the Massachusetts Legislature
- Representative to First and Second Continental Congress
- Commissioner to Paris
- Delegate to Massachusetts Constitutional Convention

- Envoy to France, the Netherlands, England
- Minister to Great Britain
- Vice President of the United States
- President of the United States

1798
Edward Jenner publishes the results of his vaccinations
against smallpox with cow virus

The Adams Administration Highlights

- XYZ Affair (1797)
- Naturalization, Alien and Sedition Act (1798)
- Creation of Navy Department and Marine Corps (1798)
- U.S. Government moves from Philadelphia to Washington, D.C. (1800)
- Library of Congress established (1800)

The Adams Administration officially created the Navy and Marine Corps in 1798

John Adams, one of the founding fathers of this country, was the consummate patriot and leader at home in Massachusetts and throughout the colonies. His political career started with his series of essays provoked by the British-imposed Stamp Act of 1765. In 1770, he was harshly criticized for publicly defending British soldiers who opened fire on protesters. Nonetheless, Adams was elected to the Massachusetts legislature that same year and then to the First Continental Congress in 1774. He continued his literary protests for colonial rights and liberties in the face of unreasonable British demands.

At the Second Continental Congress, Adams spoke aggressively for independence from Britain, headed the Board of War, recommended naming George Washington as Commander of the Continental Army, and sat on the committee to prepare the Declaration of Independence.

In his home state, Adams single-handedly wrote the new state constitution, which included provisions for three independent branches of government (executive, legislative, and judicial), two legislative

Fun Assignment!

The first United States Capitol was in Philadelphia, Pennsylvania. You might think that the iconic Independence Hall was the first U.S. Capitol building, but it wasn't...do you know what it was?

Congress Hall, Philadelphia, PA

houses, and appointed judges for the Supreme Court.

As a foreign envoy, Adams' blunt, caustic, and determined style made him an unpopular emissary. However, he did manage to obtain French naval aid, secure a $5 million loan from Dutch financiers, a commerce treaty with the Dutch Republic, and a trade agreement with Prussia. Adams was in Europe from 1778 to 1787. He was joined by his wife Abigail during a portion of these years. In 1789, Adams became the first Vice President of the United States after receiving the second highest number of votes from the presidential electorate. Adams described his eight-year term as Vice President to George Washington as "the most insignificant office that ever the invention of man contrived..."

Adams succeeded the two-term George Washington by three electoral votes over Thomas Jefferson who, in turn, became Vice President. Adams' administration was consumed by the French Revolution and in particular the growing conflict between France and Great Britain. Adams pursued the diplomatic route with both countries to avoid U.S. involvement. He sent an envoy

John Adams' life was driven by love of country. He and his family made a variety of sacrifices to help secure freedom for the colonies. Throughout his marriage and frequent and extended absences, he and his wife Abigail exchanged numerous letters filled with tenderness and political fervor. By all accounts Abigail was her husband's perfect match, intellectually and emotionally.

Adams was a short and rotund man who preferred to dress in the fashion of European gentry and carry himself in a somewhat imperial manner. This went along with his sometimes abrasive and relentless style of interaction with his colleagues. Unfortunately, his manner of dealing with people and issues sometimes overshadowed his many accomplishments. Adams' somewhat pretentious style led to a letdown when he left the White House after his presidency. He apparently felt betrayed in some ways and under-appreciated thereafter.

Abigail Adams

Back at home in Massachusetts, Adams nonetheless continued his interest in politics. One of his greatest joys during this period was seeing his son, John Quincy Adams, follow in his footsteps and become a U.S. president. However, his "retirement" years also brought much tragedy, as he lost his son Charles, his daughter "Nabby," and his wife of fifty-four years, Abigail.

The timing of John Adam's death is ironic. On the fiftieth anniversary of the signing of the Declaration of Independence, July 4, 1826, John Adams, one of the signers of the historic document, died at the age of ninety. Only hours before, Thomas Jefferson, fellow founding father and author of the document, had also died.

What is the Library of Congress?

The Library of Congress, established by the Adams administration in 1800, is the national library of the United States, the oldest federal cultural institution in the United States, and the largest library in the world. Today it occupies four buildings in Washington, D.C. The Library was housed in the U.S. Capitol for most of the 1800s, until the Library's first dedicated building was completed in 1897.

The Thomas Jefferson Building is the first building of the Library of Congress.

to France. Three agents of the French government demanded a bribe before the envoy would be received by the French foreign minister. Informing Adams of the situation in coded messages, the envoy referred to the three agents as X, Y, and Z. The news of the "XYZ Affair" inflamed the United States and Adams prepared for war. In response to the war scare, Congress passed—and Adams signed—the Alien and Sedition Acts that gave the federal government the power to imprison aliens and citizens who opposed the government. These acts were used by the Adams Administration to shut down newspapers and silence opponents. Adams' inability to quickly acquire a diplomatic solution with France and his inability to escape the negative civic response to the Acts, which were widely criticized as violations of the First Amendment guarantee of free speech, culminated in his losing his bid for a second presidential term.

My 2 cents

What would you nickname this president?

The Author's Idea: Mr. Independence

United States Capitol, Washington, D.C.
John Quincy Adams is the only president to serve in the House of Representatives after leaving office.
He served from 1831 until his death in 1848.

JOHN QUINCY ADAMS

6th President of the United States

POLITICAL PARTY: Federalist
ELECTION OPPONENTS:
 Andrew Jackson, Democratic-Republican
 Henry Clay, Democratic-Republican
 William H. Crawford, Democratic-Republican
TERM OF OFFICE: March 4, 1825 to March 3, 1829
VICE PRESIDENT: John C. Calhoun

The John Quincy Adams birthplace, Quincy, Massachusetts.

Fun Assignment!

Who else was in the unique father and son category as being president of the United States?

George Herbert Walker Bush and George W. Bush

Personal Profile

BORN: July 11, 1767, Quincy, Massachusetts
SIBLINGS: Second of five children
RELIGION: Unitarian
EDUCATION: Harvard College, graduated 1787
CAREER: Lawyer, Professor of Rhetoric and Oratory, Harvard College

MILITARY: None
MARRIAGE: Louisa Catherine Johnson July 26, 1797, London, England
OFFSPRING: Three sons
DIED: February 23, 1848, Washington, D.C.

Louisa Catherine Johnson Adams

1825
Previous president:
James Monroe

1826
James Fennimore Cooper publishes
The Last of the Mohicans

Visiting the President

BIRTHPLACE/HOMESTEAD/LIBRARY:

Adams National Historic Park

1250 Hancock Street, Quincy, Massachusetts

GRAVESITE: United First Parish Church

1306 Hancock Street, Quincy, Massachusetts

The impressive Stone Library is part of the original family home of John Quincy Adams. It was added by Adam's son Charles Francis and consists of books, papers, and other possessions of the family. The oak library table is rich with historic meaning, as many generations of this famous political family studied and wrote at it through the years.

Fun Assignment!

John Quincy Adams was honored twice by the U.S. government after his death. First was with a memorial U.S. postage stamp in 1938. What was the second way President Adams was honored in 2008?

Adams was honored with a one-dollar coin in 2008.

Quincy, Massachusetts

Political Profile

- Minister to the Netherlands, Prussia, Russia, and Great Britain
- State and federal senator for Massachusetts
- Peace Commissioner, Treaty of Ghent (War of 1812)
- Secretary of State
- President of the United States
- House of Representatives for Massachusetts

The Adams Administration Highlights

- Erie Canal completed (1825)
- Reciprocal trade treaty with Central America (1825)
- John Adams (father) and Thomas Jefferson die, July 4, 1826
- Restitution of property damages incurred during the War of 1812 (1826)
- Agreement for joint occupation of the Oregon Territory with Great Britain (1827)
- Trading agreements with Sweden, Denmark and Norway (1824-1828)
- Baltimore & Ohio Railroad chartered (1827), ground-breaking in 1828

CONNECTIONS

You've seen the Baltimore & Ohio Railroad on the Monopoly® *game board: the **B&O Railroad**.*

O f all the presidents, the resume of John Quincy Adams reads like a 'Who's Who' in the world of national and international politics. Interestingly, his "resume" before and after his presidency overshadows his four years in the White House. For example, from a young age, Adams was literally in the fray of the Revolutionary War and the diplomatic missions that followed. At the age of 8, he and his mother Abigail watched the start of the war at Bunker Hill from nearby Penn's Hill. When Adams was 12, he joined his father John, a founder of the new country, on a diplomatic mission to Europe, the first of several between 1778 and 1816. He dined with Benjamin Franklin and strolled with Thomas Jefferson in Paris, traveled to Sweden, Denmark, and Germany and served as Minister to the Netherlands, Prussia, Russia, and Great Britain. At the age of 14, Adams' father sent him to Russia as a member of the American emissary. While there, he taught French to other members of the group. Later, he would graduate from Harvard (1787), practice law, marry, serve in both the state and federal senates (1803 to 1808), and become a professor of Rhetoric and Oratory at Harvard.

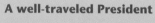

A well-traveled President

John Quincy Adams visited more countries than any previous President.

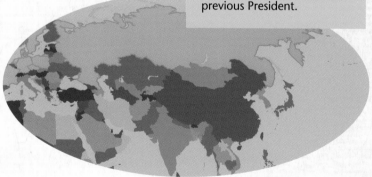

1828
Noah Webster publishes
An American Dictionary Of The English Language in two volumes

John Quincy Adams was a somewhat short (5 foot, 7 inches) and stocky New Englander with an austere personality. He walked and swam to control his weight and liked to play billiards. He began a journal at the age of 11, which he kept most of his life. He was a biblical scholar and an avid bibliophile, particularly of the Roman authors, whom he could read in the original Latin. He owned the largest private library in the country. Adams spoke fluent French and was comfortable with German and Italian. John Quincy Adams' unwavering selflessness and love of country was his greatest contribution to the new republic. He is the only former president to return to Washington as an elected member of the House of Representatives. He died of a stroke on the floor of the House of Representatives at the age of 80.

John Quincy Adams returned to his homeland for good in 1817. He served honorably as Secretary of State under James Monroe. In concert with Monroe, he implemented broad policies through negotiations and treaties. He authored much of the Monroe Doctrine, an instrument discouraging European influence in North and South American borders and policies.

In 1824, Adams was elected president, succeeding the two-term James Monroe under a cloud of "corrupt bargaining." None of the four presidential candidates had the necessary majority of electoral votes, so his election was determined by the House of Representatives. Many of the domestic policies of the Adams administration were met with rejection, but they had some successes with trade initiatives. A very significant day for John Quincy Adams was July 4, 1826. Sadly, on the 50th anniversary of the signing of the Declaration of Independence, Adams mourned the death of his father—former president John Adams—and another of the greatest founding fathers, Thomas Jefferson. John Quincy Adams would make a bid for a second presidential term, but this attempt failed. Andrew Jackson succeeded Adams in the White House after the election of 1828; he won with a resounding victory. Adams then returned to his ancestral home in Quincy, Massachusetts.

My 2 cents

What would you nickname this president?

_____

The Author's Idea: Boy Wonder

FRANKLIN PIERCE

14th President of the United States

POLITICAL PARTY: Democrat
ELECTION OPPONENT: Winfield Scott, Whig
TERM OF OFFICE: March 4, 1853 to March 3, 1857
VICE PRESIDENT: Rufus King
 • Rufus King died without serving; Pierce completed his term without a Vice President

Pierce Manse in Concord, New Hampshire

THE PIERCE MANSE
Home of the 14th President of the United States
Franklin Pierce
1804 -1869

WIKI, Craig Michaud

Fun Assignment!

1. Franklin Pierce was honored with a postage stamp in 1938. What denomination was this stamp?
2. Pierce was also honored with the creation of a gold dollar. What year was this coin minted?

The Pierce gold dollar coin was minted in 2010.
The Pierce stamp was 14 cents.

Personal Profile

BORN: November 23, 1804
    Hillsborough, New Hampshire
SIBLINGS: Sixth of eight children
RELIGION: Episcopalian
EDUCATION: Bowden College, graduated 1824
CAREER: Lawyer
MILITARY: Brigadier General, Mexican War

MARRIAGE: Jane Means Appleton, November 10, 1834, Amherst, New Hampshire
OFFSPRING: Three sons
 • None lived past the age of 12
Died: October 8, 1869, Concord, New Hampshire

Jane Appleton Pierce

1853
Previous president:
Millard Fillmore

1853
The U.S. Postal Service issues
the first stamped envelopes

Visiting the President

BIRTHPLACE: The Franklin Pierce Homestead
   Routes 9 and 31, Hillsborough, New
   Hampshire
HOMESTEAD/MUSEUM:
   The Franklin Pierce Manse
   14 Horseshoe Pond Lane
   Concord, New Hampshire
GRAVESITE: Old North Cemetery, State Street
   Concord, New Hampshire

This 1856 map explains the Kansas-Nebraska Act, showing slave states (tan), free states (pink), U.S. territories (green), and Kansas in center (white).

Hillsborough,
New Hampshire

Tell me more!

What was the Kansas-Nebraska Act?

The 1854 Kansas–Nebraska Act created the territories of Kansas and Nebraska, repealed the Missouri Compromise of 1820, and allowed settlers to determine if they would allow slavery in their territories. Opponents denounced the act as a concession to slaveholders in the South. The Republican Party (created in 1854), formed in opposition to the act, attempted to stop the expansion of slavery, and soon emerged as the dominant force throughout the North.

Political Profile

- State Representative, New Hampshire
- U.S. House of Representatives for New Hampshire
- United States Senator for New Hampshire

- New Hampshire Democratic Party State Chairman
- U.S. District Attorney for New Hampshire
- President, New Hampshire State Constitution Convention
- President of the United States

1854
Alfred, Lord Tennyson publishes
The Charge Of The Light Brigade

1854
The U.S. Postal Service issues the first
postal directory

The Pierce Administration Highlights

- The Gadsden Purchase (1853)
- Opening of Japanese-American trade (1854)
- Kansas-Nebraska Act (1854)
- Formation of the Republican Party (1854)
- The John Brown Affair (1856)
- State of Disunion Convention in Massachusetts (1857)
  (to discuss peaceful separation of the North and South)

CONNECTIONS
You've probably read **The Scarlet Letter**. *Its author, Nathaniel Hawthorne, was the closest friend of Franklin Pierce.*

General Franklin Pierce mounted on a horse during the Mexican War.

Franklin Pierce is a lost man in American presidential history and perhaps the most tragic figure to occupy the White House. Early in his life though, all one would have seen was a promising future. Although Pierce initially struggled with his studies at Bowden College, he soon improved and graduated in the top tier of his class in 1824. Of note are two of his classmates, Nathaniel Hawthorne, who remained a lifelong friend, and Henry Wadsworth Longfellow.

Pierce was admitted to the bar in 1827. He established his law practice in his hometown and quickly became involved in politics. Over a thirteen-year period he was elected to the state legislature, the U.S. House of Representatives, and the U.S. Senate. Pierce never lost an elected seat that he sought, including the presidency.

He married Jane Means Appleton in 1834. Jane was a religious, introspective, shy, and frail woman with a tendency toward depression. She disliked politics, life in Washington, and her husband's drinking. Jane even persuaded Pierce to resign from the Senate in 1842. After that decision, Pierce returned to New Hampshire. Their first

1856
The first kindergarten in America is
established in Watertown, Wisconsin

1856
Remains of a prehistoric man
are found in Germany

21

son died after three days of life in 1836. Now, with the arrival of two more sons, the couple focused on family life. However, tragedy struck again with the loss of their 4-year-old son to typhus in 1843. In 1847, Pierce turned his efforts in a new direction by enlisting in the Army during the Mexican War, and he rose to the rank of Brigadier General. Then, in 1852, despite promising his wife that he would not seek the presidency, he schemed to obtain the Democratic nomination. On the forty-ninth ballot, Pierce emerged as the "dark horse." His wife collapsed at the news and son Bennie hoped he would not be elected, but elected he was in November 1852. Tragedy struck again in January 1853. President-Elect Pierce, his wife Jane, and their 12-year old son Bennie were traveling by train when it derailed, killing Bennie before their eyes. Jane later made the surprising claim that Bennie's death was actually an act of God's will. She reasoned that God was trying to keep Pierce from being distracted from his presidential duties. In 1853, tragedy came calling on Franklin Pierce yet again when his vice-president, who had taken the oath of office in Cuba, died there having never served in his elected role. Pierce would not replace him, but rather served out his term without a second in command.

The Pierce Administration was marred by two events: the Kansas-Nebraska Act (1854), which outraged Northern anti-

The Franklin Pierce grave at the Old North Cemetery, Concord, New Hampshire.

WIKI, George Money

Franklin Pierce was a handsome man, popular with his peers and completely faithful to his wife. With typical New England frugality, he saved money from his law practice and half of the $25,000 yearly salary he received as president. This money allowed him to travel abroad with his wife Jane for several years in an effort to improve her health, but to no avail; she died in 1863. The remaining six years of his life were a downward spiral. His closest friend and college classmate, Nathaniel Hawthorne, died while the two were vacationing in the White Mountains of New Hampshire. He saw his beloved union disintegrate and his friends imprisoned for opposing the war. Finally, he was considered a security risk by the federal government because of his Southern sympathies. Rejected, alone, and almost friendless, Pierce turned to alcohol. However, at the end of his life, he returned to religion and seemed to find a personal peace that had eluded him for many years.

1856
Big Ben, the bell in Parliament Tower in London, is installed

1857
The U.S. Postal Service issues the first perforated postage stamps

Tell me more!

Why was Pierce's oath of office unique?

Pierce is the only president who took the oath of office using the word affirm (not swear), presumably because of a religious reason; the choice of the two words is offered in the Constitution.

slavery Democrats and precipitated violence in Kansas; and the Ostend Manifesto (1854), the end result of frustrated efforts to purchase Cuba in an attempt to further slavery. On a brighter note, however, Pierce did successfully purchase land from Mexico, which defined the border between the United States and our neighbor to the south; favored land grants to railroads; federally funded construction on the Atlantic cable to improve communications with Europe, and negotiated far-reaching trade treaties with Japan.

When his party met in Cincinnati in June 1856, Pierce fully anticipated re-nomination. However, the nomination went to James Buchanan. After Pierce left office, he and Jane stayed in Washington for a number of weeks. He was reluctant to return to New Hampshire, fearing the kind of reception he would receive in his abolitionist home state.

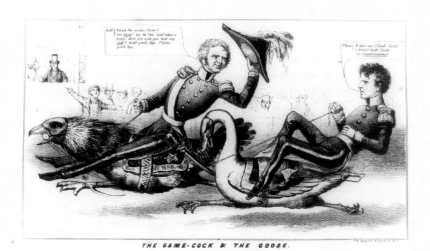

THE GAME-COCK & THE GOOSE.

An 1852 Whig Party cartoon favoring Winfield Scott, Pierce's main opponent.

My 2 cents
What would you nickname this president?

_____

The Author's Idea: Mr. Obscure

Built in New York City between 1902 and 1907 by the federal government, this building served as the U.S. Customs House for the duty collection operations for the port of New York. It is now the home of the New York branch of the National Museum of the American Indian.

24

CHESTER A. ARTHUR

21st President of the United States

POLITICAL PARTY: Republican
ELECTION OPPONENTS: None
TERM OF OFFICE: September 19, 1881 to March 3, 1885
VICE PRESIDENT: None

Chester A. Arthur statue, Madison Square, New York City

Fun Assignment!

What is the name of the kidney disease that Chester Arthur suffered from? This disease caused Arthur to have the second shortest post-presidency in history. At the time of his diagnosis, there was no successful treatment for it. Today, this disease is referred to as Glomerulonephritis and is treatable.

Bright's Disease, named for English physician Richard Bright.

Personal Profile

BORN: October 5, 1829 in Fairfield, Vermont
SIBLINGS: Fifth of nine children
RELIGION: Episcopalian
EDUCATION: Union College, Schenectady, New York; graduated 1848
CAREER: Teacher, school principal, lawyer

MILITARY: Quartermaster General for New York State
MARRIAGE: Ellen Lewis Herndon October 25, 1859, New York, New York
OFFSPRING: Two sons, one daughter
DIED: November 18, 1886, New York, New York

Ellen Lewis Herndon Arthur

1881
Previous president:
James A. Garfield

1881
The Boston Symphony Orchestra
gives its first concert

25

Visiting the President

BIRTHPLACE: Chester Arthur Historic Site
455 Chester Arthur Road, Fairfield, Vermont
• A 1953 recreation of the second house in
which Arthur lived as an infant

HOMESTEAD: 123 Lexington Avenue, New York,
New York (bronze plaque inside building)

MUSEUM/LIBRARY: Union College (includes statue of Arthur)
Schenectady, New York

GRAVESITE: Albany Rural Cemetery,
Cemetery Avenue, Menands, New York

Fun Assignment!

Chester Arthur taught at North Pownal Academy in Vermont. What
other future president taught penmanship at the Academy?

James A. Garfield

Fairfield, Vermont

Tell me more!

What is a "Customs House"?

Before becoming President, Chester Arthur served in the powerful
position of Collector at the Customs House at the Port of New York from 1871 to
1878. A Customs House was a building housing the offices for the government
officials who processed the paperwork for the import and export of goods into
and out of the country. Today's equivalent is the Port Authority of New York and
New Jersey.

Political Profile

• Collector of the Port of New York
• Vice President of the United States
• President of the United States

1881	1881	1882
The Gunfight at the OK Corral occurs	The American Federation of Labor (AFL) is founded	Jesse James is shot and killed

The Arthur Administration Highlights

- Use of census to determine U.S. congressional representation results in increase of house members to 325 (1882)
- Senate ratifies Geneva Convention of 1864 that sets standards for the care of the wounded during war and the neutrality of medical personnel (1882)
- The Pendleton Act establishes a bipartisan Civil Service Commission (1883)
- France presents the United States with the Statue of Liberty (1884)
- Dedication of the Washington Monument (1885)
- Arthur signs bill for the construction of a new steel Navy ship (1883)

ANOTHER PRESIDENT WHO HAD A RISE IN THE WORLD.

"FROM THE TOE-PATH TO THE WHITE HOUSE."

1881 cartoon from Puck magazine depicting Chester Arthur kicked out of New York Customs House.

Chester Arthur was the son of a Baptist minister and abolitionist who helped found the New York Anti-Slavery Society. He attended local schools in towns in New York State where his father preached. He entered Union College in Schenectady, New York, at the age of fifteen and was one of six in his class of one hundred admitted to the National Honor Fraternity. After graduating, Arthur began to study law. In 1854, he was admitted to the New York Bar and was made a partner in a New York law firm. Arthur was engaged in two cases involving the civil rights of African-Americans. Both were settled in favor of the plaintiffs.

Arthur entered the political arena in 1856, attending his state's first Republican Convention and campaigning for the party's presidential candidate. As a reward, he was appointed honorary post of state engineer-in-chief. At the outbreak of the Civil War, he was named Quartermaster General of the State of New York.

When a democratic governor was elected, Arthur returned to his successful law practice. He maintained his ties with the New York Republican Party machine headed by the ruthless, shrewd U.S. senator from New York, Roscoe Conkling. Through Conkling's influence, President Ulysses Grant appointed Arthur to the post of Collector of the Port

1882
The Knights of Columbus
is founded

1883
The Brooklyn Bridge
is completed

1883
Robert Louis Stevenson publishes
Treasure Island

27

of New York in 1871. This was considered the most important federal job in the city. In keeping with the political patronage system of the era (the Spoils System), Arthur placed members of his party in New York Customs House positions and collected a portion of their salaries for use by the party. After eight years, President Rutherford Hayes, who was determined to dismantle the system, removed him from office. Nonetheless, Arthur became known as the "Gentleman Boss" of the Republican Party in New York City and continued to build the party machine.

Arthur married Ellen Herndon in 1859 and they had two sons and a daughter; however, the eldest boy died in infancy. In 1880, after twenty years of marriage and the year before her husband would become president, Ellen died

Chester A. Arthur was a tall, stout figure who took pleasure in dressing and living well. He socialized with glamorous and cultured people and entertained lavishly, earning the moniker "Elegant Arthur."

Arthur was a widower president; his younger sister performed hostess duties. In memory of his wife Ellen he donated a stained glass window to St. John's Episcopal Church across from the White House.

As president, Arthur earned the respect of the nation, but the ire of his party. One of those admiring Arthur was Mark Twain who said: "...it would be hard to better President Arthur's administration."

At the end of his presidency, Arthur, a dying man, returned to 123 Lexington Avenue in New York City, the home he shared for many years with his beloved wife. Arthur once said: "I may be President of the United States, but my private life is nobody's damn business." Prior to his death, he had all his personal papers burned.

1883
The Orient Express makes its first run

1884
Construction begins in Chicago on the world's largest skyscraper

of pneumonia. Arthur attended the Republican National Convention in June of that year as part of the "Stalwart" faction of the party. The "Stalwarts" supported the nomination of Ulysses S. Grant for a third term. In the end, Garfield became the compromise candidate for president on the Republican ticket and Arthur, the concession vice presidential candidate. Arthur, who had never run for political office before, became Vice President of the United States.

On September 19, 1881, Arthur became the nation's fourth "accidental" president following the death of James Garfield from an assassin's bullet. There was consternation in many quarters when Arthur became president, as he was a product of the questionable Conkling political machine and had been charged with corruption, but he confounded his critics, because, as president, Arthur was an honest, upright, efficient political servant. He vetoed "pork-barrel" legislation, ignored special interest groups, defied party bosses, and prosecuted illegal acts in government. Most importantly, he pushed for civil service reform. He did all this despite only partial support from Congress. After his first year in office, Arthur was diagnosed with a fatal kidney disorder. He kept his illness a secret and placed himself in the running for the 1884 presidential nomination so as not to appear politically weak. However, because he had alienated many of his supporters, he was not nominated.

Chester A. Arthur's grave
Albany Rural Cemetery, Menands, New York

Postdlf, GNU

My 2 cents

What would you nickname this president?

_____

The Author's Idea: The Spoilsman

Grace Goodhue Coolidge
A vivacious and charming First Lady, as White House hostess, she planned unpretentious but dignified soical events. In 1931, she was voted one of America's twelve greatest living women.

CALVIN COOLIDGE
30th President of the United States

POLITICAL PARTY: Republican
ELECTION OPPONENTS:
   John W. Davis, Democrat
   Robert M. LaFollette, Progressive
TERM OF OFFICE: August 3, 1923 to March 3, 1929
VICE PRESIDENT: Charles Gates Dawes

Coolidge homestead in Plymouth, Vermont

Fun Assignment!

President Coolidge was the only president to have his portrait on a coin in his lifetime. What coin was this and what was the year it was minted?

Sesquicentennial of American Independence half dollar, minted in 1926.

Grace Goodhue Coolidge

Personal Profile

BORN: July 4, 1872, Plymouth, Vermont
SIBLINGS: Younger sister
RELIGION: Congregationalist
EDUCATION: Amherst College; graduated 1895
CAREER: Lawyer

MILITARY: None
MARRIAGE: Grace Goodhue, October 4, 1905, Northampton, Massachusetts
OFFSPRING: Two sons
DIED: January 5, 1933 Northampton, Massachusetts

1923
Previous president:
Warren G. Harding

1924
Nellie Taylor Ross of Wyoming becomes the
first woman to be elected governor of a state

Visiting the President

BIRTHPLACE/HOMESTEAD/GRAVESITE:
President Calvin Coolidge State Historic Site
Route 100 A, Plymouth, Vermont
LIBRARY: Calvin Coolidge Library and Museum
20 West Street, Northampton, Massachusetts

Fun Assignment!

Calvin Coolidge was administered the oath of office twice; first in Vermont by his father, a justice of the peace, and then in Washington by a former president. Who was he?

Chief Justice William Howard Taft

Tell me more!

Embracing the Media

President Coolidge was the first president to have his presidential inauguration broadcast on radio. In December 1923 he was the first president whose address to Congress was broadcast on radio. In February 1924, he was the first president to deliver a political speech on the radio. Coolidge assured radio regulation by signing the Radio Act of 1927.

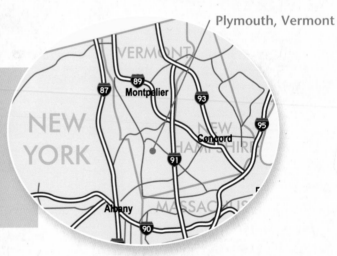

Plymouth, Vermont

Political Profile

- State Representative, Massachusetts
- Mayor of Northampton, Massachusetts
- State Senator, Massachusetts
- Lieutenant Governor, Massachusetts
- Governor of Massachusetts
- Vice President of the United States
- President of the United States

1924
Herman Melville publishes
Billy Budd

1924
Edna Ferber publishes
So Big

1925
F. Scott Fitzgerald publishes
The Great Gatsby

The Coolidge Administration Highlights

- Indian Citizenship Act (1924)
- Revenue Acts (1926, 1928)
- Immigration Act of 1924
- Military presence in Nicaragua (1926)
- Federal Radio Commission created to grant licenses to radio stations (1927)
- Dedication of Mount Rushmore (1927; project completed 1941)
- Kellogg-Briand Act: Fifteen nations agree to renounce war as solution to international controversies (1928)

Calvin Coolidge was the son of a Vermont farmer and store keeper. He learned early the importance of hard work and frugality, traits that would follow him into adulthood. When he was twelve, his mother, an invalid, died. He carried her picture in the back of his pocket watch the rest of his life. Between the ages of thirteen and seventeen, Coolidge attended an academy in Ludlow, Vermont, later going on to Amherst College in 1891. Although shy, he developed a reputation for being a wit, and learned to debate and make speeches. He graduated cum laude in 1895. With the help of a friend, he got a job as a law clerk in Northampton, Massachusetts. Two years later he was admitted to the Massachusetts Bar. Coolidge set up his own law practice in Northampton and began to take an active part in Republican politics. On the local level, he was city councilman, city solicitor, clerk of courts, chairman of the Republican Committee, and mayor. He also held a number of state offices, eventually becoming governor. As governor, he gained national attention during the Boston Police Strike of 1919. Coolidge regarded the strike action as unlawful since the right to unionize had not been granted. He called out the state militia and declared: "There is no right to strike against the public safety by anybody, anywhere, anytime." Seen as fearless and forthright, Coolidge easily won re-election to the Governor's mansion. When Coolidge went to the 1920 Republican National Convention, he was the "favorite son" of the Massachusetts delegation.

Coolidge first gained national attention while Governor of Massachusetts during the Boston Police Strike. This photo shows Massachusetts militia as they try to keep order in Scollay Square, September 9, 1919.

The convention revolted against their party leaders' choice for Warren Harding's running mate and nominated Coolidge. He received 674 out of 820 votes. At the age of forty-eight, Coolidge became Vice President of the United States. At first, he was little noticed, but all that changed on August 3, 1923 when Coolidge, vacationing with his father in Plymouth Notch, Vermont, became president following the death of Warren Harding; the sixth accidental president, or president by fate, not election. He returned to Washington and the brewing scandals of the Harding Administration. Coolidge, naturally tight-lipped, tight-fisted, and almost colorless, was a peculiar character in the "roaring twenties" world around him, where bootleg booze, a changing morality, and get-rich-quick schemes prevailed.

President Harding and Vice-President Coolidge with their wives, 1921.

Now in the White House, Coolidge wanted to restore some of the dignity lost under Harding, which meant no more drinking and no more card parties. He appointed a bipartisan counsel to investigate allegations of wrongdoing by members of the Harding Administration and to restore confidence.

At the Republican National Convention in 1924, Coolidge received the presidential nomination on the first ballot. With a prevailing sense of national peace and prosperity, Coolidge won the election handily. In his first full term as president, Coolidge advocated tax cuts, reduced spending,

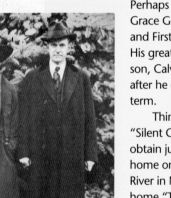

Calvin Coolidge, the only president born on the fourth of July, was an unassuming man and essentially a quiet farm boy who was somewhat uncomfortable in the national spotlight, but popular with his constituents.

Perhaps his best personal decision was to court and marry Grace Goodhue. An attractive, outgoing, and gracious wife and First Lady, she counterbalanced Coolidge's stiff persona. His greatest personal tragedy was the loss of his 16-year-old son, Calvin, Jr. in 1926 from blood poisoning, one month after he obtained his party's nomination for a full presidential term.

Thin and 5'10", Coolidge liked to fish and walk his dogs. "Silent Cal" sought peace and tranquility in retirement. To obtain just that, he and his wife purchased a gated single home on nine acres of land on the banks of the Connecticut River in Northampton, Massachusetts. They called their home "The Beeches." Coolidge died there from heart failure at the age of sixty ... three years and 308 days after leaving the White House.

An irreverent, well-known pundit inquired: "How can they tell?"

1927	1927	1928
Babe Ruth hits 60 home runs	First Ryder Cup Golf Tournament	Amelia Earhart becomes the first woman to fly across the Atlantic Ocean

The Coolidge Cabinet in 1924 (outside the White House). Front row (left to right): Harry Stewart New, John W. Weeks, Charles Evans Hughes, Coolidge, Andrew Mellon, Harry M. Daugherty, Curtis D. Wilbur; Back row (left to right): James J. Davis, Henry C. Wallace, Herbert Hoover, Hubert Work.

CONNECTIONS

Have you heard of the **Roaring Twenties**? *Coolidge was in office through much of this era. These were years of dynamic growth and optimism in the U.S. The period was known for the emergence of jazz music, women's suffrage, and the distinctive Art Deco style of architecture, art, and design. Ironically, the 1920s also encompassed the era of Prohibition, which saw the ban on the manufacture, sale, and transportation of alcoholic beverages. The Roaring Twenties came to an abrupt halt with the Wall Street Crash of 1929 and the beginning of the Great Depression.*

and increased business prosperity. In contrast to his famous close-mouth nature, he held frequent press briefings and made use of the new medium of radio to talk to the nation. In 1928, Coolidge declined to run for a second full term. Herbert Hoover, Secretary of Commerce, won on the first ballot at the Republican National Convention. Coolidge and Grace, his wife of twenty-four years, left by train for Massachusetts on the evening of the inauguration of President Herbert Hoover.

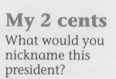

My 2 cents
What would you nickname this president?

The Author's Idea: Born on the 4th of July

1929
St. Valentine's Day
Massacre

1929
Successor president:
Herbert Hoover

35

JOHN FITZGERALD KENNEDY spoke eloquently at his inaugural address on January 20, 1961. His immortal words — "Ask not what your country can do for you...ask what you can do for your country" — continue to live in the American spirit.

Kennedy also spoke eloquently on peace and freedom. Here are just some of the quotes from our thirty-fifth president:

"Peace does not rest in charters and covenants alone. It lies in the hearts and minds of all people."

"However close we sometimes seem to that dark and final abyss, let no man of peace and freedom despair."

"Wherever we are, we must all, in our daily lives, live up to the age-old faith that freedom and peace walk together."

"Difficult days need not be dark. I think these are proud and memorable days in the cause of peace and freedom... We have every reason to believe that our tide is running strong."

"Our goal is not the victory of might, but the vindication of right; not peace at the expense of freedom, but both peace and freedom, here in this hemisphere."

However, Kennedy's humility really shone in these illuminating words:

"... our most basic common link is that we all inhabit this planet. We all breathe the same air. We all cherish our children's future. And we are all mortal."

JOHN FITZGERALD KENNEDY

35th President of the United States

POLITICAL PARTY: Democratic
ELECTION OPPONENT: Richard M. Nixon, Republican
TERM OF OFFICE: January 20, 1961 to November 22, 1963
VICE PRESIDENT: Lyndon B. Johnson

The John Fitzgerald Kennedy birthplace, Brookline, Massachusetts.

Tell me more!

First Televised Presidential Debate

The first televised presidential debate was in 1960 between John F. Kennedy and Richard M. Nixon. TV was black-and-white in those days. Nixon refused to use makeup and looked pale and sickly, in addition to sweating profusely under the studio lights. In contrast, Kennedy appeared tan and confident. This was the turning point of the campaign.

Personal Profile

BORN: May 29, 1917, Brookline, Massachusetts
SIBLINGS: Second of nine children
RELIGION: Roman Catholic
EDUCATION: Harvard University; graduated 1940
CAREER: Author, newspaper reporter

MILITARY: Lieutenant Senior Grade, United States Navy
MARRIAGE: Jacqueline Lee Bouvier, September 12, 1953 Newport, Rhode Island
OFFSPRING: Daughter and Son
DIED: November 22, 1963, Dallas, Texas

Jacqueline Lee Bouvier Kennedy

Visiting the President

BIRTHPLACE: 83 Beale Street, Brookline, Massachusetts
LIBRARY/MUSEUM: Columbia Point, Boston, Massachusetts
GRAVESITE: Arlington National Cemetery, Arlington, Virginia

Brookline, Massachusetts

Fun Assignment!

While visiting West Berlin, Germany, in June 1963, President Kennedy gave a notable speech criticizing communism. What is the famous phrase from this speech?

"Ich bin ein Berliner" or in English "I am a Berliner."

Political Profile

- United States Representative from Massachusetts
- United States Senator from Massachusetts
- President of the United States

1961	1961	1961
Russian astronaut Yuri Gagarin is first human to be rocketed into orbital space	First patent filed for an integrated circuit (a computer chip)	Roger Maris hits 61 home runs, breaking the 1927 record set by Babe Ruth

The Kennedy Administration Highlights

- Executive Order establishing the Peace Corps (1961)
- Invasion of Cuba at the Bay of Pigs (1961)
- First American launched into space (Alan Shepard, 1961)
- Established Alliance for Progress to fight poverty, establish democratic governments, and combat communism (1961)
- Naval blockade of Cuba to prevent missile deliveries from the Soviet Union (1961)
- Discontinued trade between Cuba and the United States (1962)
- First American orbited Earth (John Glenn, 1962)
- Initial United States presence in Vietnam (1963)
- Nuclear Test Ban Treaty (1963)

With Kennedy's enthusiastic support of space exploration, Alan Shepard was the first American astronaut in space in 1961. In 1971, Shepard was the fifth person to walk on the moon.

John Fitzgerald Kennedy was the second son of a wealthy and politically connected family that grew to eight children, all of whom were encouraged by their parents to be competitive, athletic, and keen for every challenge, but also to be attuned to the events of the day. Jack, as he was called, overcame numerous physical maladies. In addition to a number of childhood diseases, Jack developed colitis, Addison's disease, and serious back problems.

President Kennedy greeting Peace Corps volunteers in 1961.

While growing up, Jack moved from school to school, eventually graduating from Harvard University in 1940. Following graduation, he expanded his thesis on the rise of Nazi Germany and Britain's efforts to avoid war with Germany. His book, *Why England Slept*, became a best seller.

During World War II, Jack had difficulty getting into the service due to his poor health, but was allowed to enlist in the Navy in 1941, largely through

1961
Joseph Heller publishes *Catch 22*

1962
Philadelphia Warrior's Wilt Chamberlain scores a record breaking 100 points

1962
Launching of Telstar, one of the first communications satellites

39

his father's connections. He was eventually placed in command of a PT (Patrol Torpedo) boat, the *PT 109*. When his boat was rammed by a Japanese destroyer, he and his surviving crew were rescued. During this ordeal, Kennedy displayed leadership and courage.

After discharge from the service, Kennedy tried his hand as a reporter for the Hearst newspapers, but quickly dropped the work to enter politics. Ignoring the Democratic Party machine, he relied on his family, friends, and Navy buddies to help him campaign for the U.S. House of Representatives in 1946. After serving three terms in the House, he successfully ran for the Senate in 1952 and 1958. In 1953, he married Jacqueline Lee Bouvier, a woman of wealth and privilege. While recuperating from back surgery in 1955, he wrote *Profiles in Courage*, which won the Pulitzer Prize in 1957.

Kennedy set his sights on the presidency and easily won his party's nomination in 1960. He and his Republican opponent, Richard Nixon, made history by holding the first televised political debates. Kennedy won the presidency by 118,550 popular votes and 303 electoral votes.

Fun Assignment!

At age forty-three, John F. Kennedy was the youngest man elected president, although not the youngest to serve. What president was?

Theodore Roosevelt succeeded to the presidency after the assassination of President William McKinley six weeks before his forty-third birthday.

"Backstage" at the Kennedy household

Joseph Kennedy Sr., the power behind the Kennedy dynasty

There is an intriguing story behind the Kennedy presidency. The key figure is the family patriarch—Joseph Patrick Kennedy, Sr. He was a ruthless, driven millionaire who aspired to be president. Joe was a major contributor to the Democratic Party and served on the Securities and Exchange Commission. In 1938, President Franklin Roosevelt appointed him Ambassador to Great Britain. His performance as ambassador was unsatisfactory. Out of step with the times, he appeared to accept the rise of fascism and believed in Germany's military might and ability to win the war against Great Britain, regardless of whether America would aid the English or not.

As a result, he resigned under a cloud in 1940. Joe Sr. then transferred his presidential ambition to his eldest son, Joseph, Jr., who would serve as a Navy pilot during World War II. In 1944, Joe Jr. volunteered to fly a secret military mission over the English Channel. Tragically, his plane exploded during the flight and he was killed instantly. Once again, Joe, Sr. passed his presidential ambition on to another son, John Fitzgerald, also called Jack. Joe Sr. was rich enough, determined enough, and wise enough to accomplish the goal. The plan was put into action when Jack ran for the House of Representatives in 1946.

Every member of the family plunged in to help campaign under

1962
Boxer Sonny Liston knocks out Floyd Patterson to become heavyweight champion of the world

1962
Anthony Burgess publishes *A Clockwork Orange*

1962
First single by the Beatles is released "Love Me Do" with "P.S. I Love You" on the flip side

Kennedy's presidency was often focused on foreign affairs including the Cuban Bay of Pigs invasion (1961), the Berlin Wall, the Cuban nuclear missile crisis, increased U.S. presence in Vietnam, and the Nuclear Test Ban Treaty (1963)

Soviet Premier Nikita Khrushchev and President Kennedy in 1961, before the Cuban Missile Crisis

between the U.S., Great Britain, and the Soviet Union. On the domestic front, Kennedy created the Peace Corps, pressed the space program into action and enforced existing desegregation laws, sending a Civil Rights bill to Congress in 1963.

the watchful eye of Joe, Sr. Jack Kennedy was successful and served six years as the U.S. Representative from Massachusetts, followed by election to the U.S. Senate in 1952. That win has been credited to his father's financial support, receptions for influential people, and "old-fashioned" knocking on doors by family members to get out the vote. With an eye on the 1960 Democratic Convention, the family concentrated this time on winning the presidential nomination for Jack, which may not have been successful without the nearly obsessional wish of Joe Sr. to see a Kennedy in the White House. In that role, he served as the campaign chairman, the strategist, the financier, and the undisputed decision-maker.

John (Jack) Fitzgerald Kennedy was the first president born in the twenteith century, the youngest elected president, and the first Roman Catholic to hold the office. He was an excellent communicator, an inspiring orator, and a potentially great president. Nonetheless, what some have come to call the "Kennedy Curse" would strike this young president down in the prime of his office and his life. For the superstitious, note that every president since 1840 who was elected in a year ending in a zero died before his term was up. Kennedy was aware of this before he decided to run. On the morning of November 22, 1963, Jack Kennedy was quoted as saying, "You know last night would have been a hell of a night to kill a president." Little did he or the world know it, but at the moment he made that observation, he had just three hours to live.

John Fitzgerald Kennedy was a charismatic and engaging man who captured the imagination of the nation's youth with his idealistic "New Frontier" program. Two years and ten months into his presidency, he was cut down by a bullet—the fourth President of the United States to be assassinated.

My 2 cents
What would you nickname this president?

_____

The Author's Idea: Joe's Boy

1963
Michael DeBakey implants first artificial heart

1963
Dr. Martin Luther King, Jr. delivers his "I have a dream" speech

1963
Successor president: Lyndon B. Johnson

41

HAIL TO THE CHIEF

"Hail to the Chief" is the official anthem of the President of the United States and is played at many White House functions. The music was written by English songwriter James Sanderson; the inspiration for the song came from a poem, "The Lady of the Lake," written by Sir Walter Scott, and the words, rarely sung, were written by Albert Gamse. The song was first published in the United States in 1812.

The first time "Hail to the Chief" was played to honor an American president was in 1815 during the commemoration of George Washington's birthday. In 1828, the song was performed for John Quincy Adams and it is believed to have been played during the administrations of Andrew Jackson, Martin Van Buren, John Tyler, and James Polk. In 1954, The Department of Defense made the song the official tune to announce the arrival of a United States president during official events and ceremonies.

Hail to the Chief we have chosen for the nation
Hail to the Chief! We salute him one and all
Hail to the Chief, as we pledge cooperation
In proud fulfillment of a great, noble call

Yours is the aim to make this grand country grander
This you will do, that's our strong, firm belief
Hail to the one we selected as commander
Hail to the President! Hail to the Chief!

MARTIN VAN BUREN

8th President of the United States

POLITICAL PARTY: Democrat

ELECTION OPPONENTS:

William Henry Harrison, Whig; Hugh L. White, Whig; Daniel Webster, Whig; W.P. Mangum, Whig

TERM OF OFFICE: March 4, 1837 to March 3, 1841

VICE PRESIDENT: Richard M. Johnson

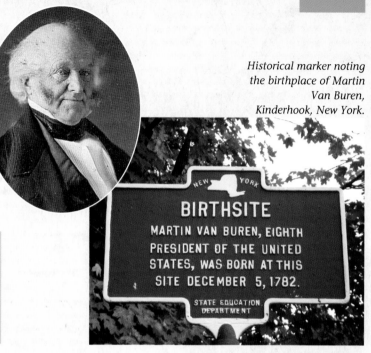

Historical marker noting the birthplace of Martin Van Buren, Kinderhook, New York.

NEW YORK

BIRTHSITE
MARTIN VAN BUREN, EIGHTH
PRESIDENT OF THE UNITED
STATES, WAS BORN AT THIS
SITE DECEMBER 5, 1782.

STATE EDUCATION
DEPARTMENT

Fun Assignment!

Martin Van Buren had a U.S. postage stamp issued in his honor. What year was this stamp issued, and what was the stamp's value?

1938, 8 cents.

Personal Profile

BORN: December 5, 1782, Kinderhook, New York

SIBLINGS: Third of five children

RELIGION: Dutch Reformed

EDUCATION: Kinderhook Academy; graduated 1796

CAREER: Lawyer

MILITARY: None

MARRRIAGE: Hannah Hoes, February 21, 1807, Catskill, New York

OFFSPRING: Four sons

DIED: July 24, 1862, Kinderhook, New York

Hannah Hoes Van Buren

Visiting the President

BIRTHPLACE: 47 Hudson Street, Kinderhook, New York
(There is a marker at this site -- the original location of
Van Buren's father's tavern -- where Van Buren was
born)

MUSEUM: Martin Van Buren National Historic Site
1013 Old Post Rd., Kinderhook, New York

GRAVESITE: Kinderhook Reformed Cemetery
Albany Avenue, Kinderhook, New York

Fun Assignment!

Martin Van Buren's daughter-in-law, Angelica Singleton, served
as hostess in the White House. What famous former First Lady
was she related to?

Dolley Madison

Tell me more!

What was the 1838 "Trail of Tears"?

This is an event you may not know about. You may not have even heard of
it, but it's something you should know about. The Trail of Tears refers to the
forced relocation of five Native American tribes (tens of thousands of people)
from their home territories throughout the southern U.S. to a huge Indian
Territory (reservation) in present-day Oklahoma. Although voted for in the
President Jackson administration, it was imposed by President Van Buren
during his administration.

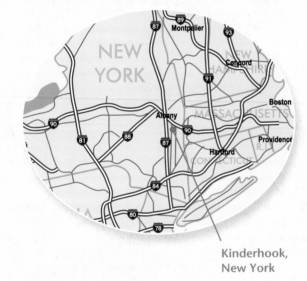

Kinderhook,
New York

Political Profile

- New York State Senator
- New York Attorney General
- U.S. Senator for New York
- Governor of New York
- U.S. Secretary of State
- Minister to England
- Vice President of the United States
- President of the United States

1837
King William IV dies and his niece, Victoria
becomes Queen of Great Britain and Ireland

1837
Charles Dickens publishes
Oliver Twist

The Van Buren Administration Highlights

- Number of Supreme Court justices increased from seven to nine (1837)
- The United States House of Representatives adopts the "Gag Rule" prohibiting the discussion of petitions from abolitionists to limit or end slavery (1837)
- Trail of Tears (1838)
- The Amistad Case (1841)

Martin Van Buren grew up in the Old Dutch community of Kinderhook, New York, where he attended local schools. He graduated from Kinderhook Academy in 1796 at the age of fourteen. Van Buren then studied law, first under a local attorney and then in New York City. He was admitted to the New York Bar in 1803 and joined his half-brother in his practice.

In 1807, Van Buren married Hannah Hoes, a distant cousin. Over the next twelve years she bore him five sons, one of whom died in infancy. Hannah contracted tuberculosis and died in 1819.

As a youth Van Buren had heard frequent political conversations in his father's tavern, which, no doubt, were the seeds from which his political appetite grew. He was nominated for and narrowly won a seat in the New York senate at the age of thirty. He simultaneously served as New York's Attorney General. During these state senate years, Van Buren formed political alliances, eventually building a political machine that emphasized party loyalty and domination of state government. In 1821, he was elected

The rejected Minister,
*We never can make him President,
without first making him Vice President*

This 1832 lithograph depicts Van Buren being carried into office on Andrew Jackson's back. The Democratic Party nominated Van Buren as Jackson's Vice Presidential candidate.

1839
Audubon publishes
Birds of North America

1839
Canadian Samuel Cunard establishes the first steamship line
with scheduled transatlantic crossings

45

to the United States Senate, serving two terms. He was elected Governor of New York State in 1828. He resigned in 1829 when President Andrew Jackson appointed him Secretary of State. Van Buren's nemesis during this time was Vice President John C. Calhoun, as the two vied for Jackson's favor. Van Buren ingratiated himself to Jackson and took up horseback riding so he could accompany Jackson on daily rides. With Jackson's support, Van Buren won the 1836 Democratic nomination for president and won the presidency easily against a divided opposition. Martin Van Buren was the first president born after the signing of the Declaration of Independence and, as such, is the first president born a United States citizen. He is also the first president of non-British descent. His ancestors came from the Netherlands as indentured servants. Van Buren continued many of Jackson's policies including a war against the Seminole Indians in the south and the forced removal of many Native Americans west along the "Trail of Tears," during which thousands of Native Americans died. His biggest

Angelica Singleton Van Buren assumed the role of White House hostess. This painting is from 1842.

Martin Van Buren was a man of small stature, but he had large political aspirations. He became known over his career as the "Little Magician" and the "Red Fox" because of his ability to successfully manipulate and maneuver his political peers and opponents. He was also occasionally called "Old Kinderhook" in reference to his hometown of Kinderhook, New York. The use of "OK" during his second presidential campaign stands today as a common expression for "all right." During his political career, Van Buren was obsessed with his personal appearance and was known to be something of a "dandy." Van Buren was a widower of twenty years when he entered the White House. He relied on his eldest son's wife, Angelica Singleton, to serve as hostess.

After the White House, Van Buren returned to his roots in Kinderhook, New York, with two goals in mind. The first was the perpetuation of his public image. Some former presidents had large estates with names that became significant in the public mind like Mount Vernon, Monticello, and the Hermitage. He felt a similar residence would endear him to the people. His answer was Lindenwald, a magnificent estate near Kinderhook. This luxurious home would be used to promote his second goal: a return to the White House. His guests, however, were nonplussed at the juxtaposition of the rural setting and the lavish lifestyle. Van Buren made two unsuccessful attempts to reclaim the White House, but the magician had lost his magic. Martin Van Buren died at Lindenwald on July 24, 1862 at the age of seventy-nine.

46

1840
The census of 1840 shows a U.S. population
of more than 17 million people

This 1858 painting of President Van Buren is on display at the White House.

domestic issue was the financial crisis that began in 1837 and led to a nationwide depression that lasted most of his term. In foreign affairs, Van Buren averted a full-scale war along the Canadian border using political compromise, resolving the dispute through diplomatic channels. In 1840, Van Buren was unanimously chosen by his party for a second presidential term. His opponent's party portrayed their candidate, William Henry Harrison, as a simple man of the people and Van Buren as a luxury-loving aristocrat. Their campaign strategy worked. Van Buren lost.

Daguerreotype of Martin Van Buren, probably from 1855.

My 2 cents
What would you nickname this president?

_____

The Author's Idea: The "OK" Dandy

The Library of Congress, Jefferson Building, Washington, D.C.
Millard Fillmore's wife Abigail initiated the White House Library. Previously, each president would bring his own books to the White House and take them with him when he left office.

MILLARD FILLMORE
13th President of the United States

POLITICAL PARTY: Whig
ELECTION OPPONENT: None
TERM OF OFFICE: July 10, 1850 to March 3, 1853
VICE PRESIDENT: None

This East Aurora, New York, house is the only surviving Fillmore residence, which Fillmore helped to build in 1825. He lived here until 1830.

WIKI, Yoho2001

Tell me more!

What was the Whig political party?

The Whig Party was formed in 1833 in opposition to the policies of President Andrew Jackson and the Democratic Party. Whigs supported programs of modernization, economic protectionism, and the supremacy of Congress over the presidency. The party dissolved in 1856.

Personal Profile

Born: January 7, 1800, Locke, New York
Siblings: Second of nine children
Religion: Unitarian
Education: Common school
Career: Lawyer
Military: None

Marriages: Married twice
• Abigail Powers, February 5, 1826 Moravia, New York
• Caroline Carmichael McIntosh, February 10, 1858, in Albany, New York
Offspring: one son, one daughter
Died: March 8, 1874, Buffalo, New York

Abigail Powers Fillmore

1850
Previous president:
Zachary Taylor

1851
Gail Borden announces the invention of evaporated milk

1851
The first American YMCA is organized in Boston

Visiting the President

BIRTHPLACE: Locke (Summerhill), New York
- There is a marker at the birthplace site; Fillmore Glen State Park in Summerhill has a replica of the Fillmore birthplace

MUSEUM: Millard Fillmore Museum
24 Shearer Avenue, East Aurora, New York

GRAVESITE: Forest Lawn Cemetery
1411 Delaware Avenue, Buffalo, New York

Tell me more!

What was the Know-Nothing Party?

The Know-Nothing Party, also known as the American Party, was prominent in the late 1840s and early 1850s. Its members strongly opposed immigrants and followers of the Catholic Church. It was a secret organization. Members responded to questions about their beliefs with, "I know nothing."

Locke, New York

Fun Assignment!

Millard Fillmore was one of six presidents who were born in log cabins. Who were they?

Andrew Jackson, Abraham Lincoln, Ulysses S. Grant, Millard Fillmore, James Buchanan, and James Garfield.

Political Profile

- Commissioner of Deeds for East Aurora, New York
- Member, New York State Legislature
- United States Representative from New York
- Comptroller of New York State
- Vice President of the United States
- President of the United States

1851	1851	1851
Artist Emanuel Gottlieb Leutze paints "Washington Crossing the Delaware"	Fires in May and June destroy much of San Francisco	The *New York Times* begins publication

The Fillmore Administration Highlights

- Compromise of 1850
- Brigham Young named Governor of Utah Territory (1850)
- California becomes a state (1850)
- Commodore Matthew Perry opens two Japanese ports to American trade (1852)
- Oregon Territory is divided and Washington territory is formed (1853)
- Transcontinental rail survey authorized (1853); railway is completed in 1869

Millard Fillmore was born in a log cabin in a frontier village in New York State. He was the second of nine children of a transient tenant farmer. Fillmore helped to clear land and raise crops. There was little time for school. His father wanted more of a vocational direction for his children. He arranged an apprenticeship with several businesses, but Millard did not like the work. Having a strong desire to learn about the world, he purchased his first book, a dictionary, which he studied while working at the mill. When a private high school opened in nearby New Hope, New York, he enrolled; he was nineteen. Eventually, Fillmore developed a relationship with his teacher and they were married in 1826. Benefitting from the recommendation his father made to a judge, Fillmore performed clerical duties for that judge and paid his way through law school. However, following a disagreement with the judge, he quit and returned to his family, now living in Aurora, New York. Fillmore accepted a clerkship with a local law firm, teaching to support himself, and studied law. He was admitted to the New York Bar in 1823 and became active in local politics. He served as a New York legislator for three terms and then as New York's representative in the United State House of Representatives for four terms. He made an unsuccessful run for New York governor in 1844. In 1848, his party

Daguerreotype of Millard Fillmore, March 1849.

1851	1851	1851
Herman Melville publishes *Moby Dick*	Nathaniel Hawthorne publishes *The House of Seven Gables*	The yacht America wins the race around the Isle of Wight; the first "America's Cup"

51

Fillmore/Donelson campaign poster.

Millard Fillmore had a difficult time adjusting to private life. In 1854, only a year after losing his wife, his daughter Mary died of cholera at the age of 22. He was reluctant to practice law, believing it inappropriate for a former president to oppose little-known lawyers. His personal finances would not allow him to take a place among the country's prominent citizens. Loneliness may have led him into politics again. In 1856, he ran for president on the Know-Nothing party ticket. He came out a poor third. Fillmore removed himself from the political stage. Fortunately, in 1858 Fillmore met and married a wealthy widow, Caroline Carmichael McIntosh from Albany, New York, thirteen years his junior. They bought and renovated a spacious mansion in Buffalo, New York. She endeared herself to Buffalo society and Millard became Buffalo's "first citizen." His list of accomplishments as first citizen is more impressive than those as president: he developed a library, created the University of Buffalo, opened an art museum, organized a YMCA, constructed a hospital, and helped American-Indians in the area. Millard Fillmore was a six-foot tall, blue-eyed, handsome politician who, with limited ability, obtained the highest office of the land. He remains one of our more obscure, less regarded presidents. Millard Fillmore suffered a stroke and died in Buffalo on March 3, 1874.

selected him as Zachary Taylor's running mate for the White House. Taylor was a southerner and a slave owner. Fillmore was nominated to balance the ticket.

On July 9, 1850, Zachary Taylor died, probably of cholera. Fillmore took the oath of office the day after, becoming the nation's second accidental president. The most significant event during Fillmore's presidency was the raging debate in Congress over the disposition of territories acquired in the Mexican-American War and the delicate balance of power between slave and free states, which was evenly divided. The solution came in the form of a group of measures that made up the Compromise of 1850. During Fillmore's

1852	1852	1852
Uncle Sam makes his debut as a cartoon character in the *New York Lantern*	Harriet Beecher Stowe publishes *Uncle Tom's Cabin*	Peter Mark Roget publishes his first *Roget's Thesaurus*

Millard Fillmore's gravesite, Forest Lawn Cemetery, Buffalo, New York. The obelisk is surrounded by the graves of his two widows and children.

stay at the White House, a bathtub and kitchen stove were installed. Abigail Fillmore asked her husband to request funds from Congress for a White House library and also selected the core of books for it. Abigail accomplished this despite the fact that her health was frail for most of her husband's presidency. Their daughter Mary often filled in for her mother as the White House hostess.

In 1852, Fillmore lost his party's nomination for a full presidential term. He was known as the "last of the Whigs." The National Whig Convention was irretrievably torn by dissension. The party had alienated the antislavery northern Whigs, suffered the deaths of two of their major party leaders—Henry Clay and Daniel Webster—and had seen their presidential candidate go down to defeat in the 1862 election. All of this contributed to the demise of the Whig Party. Millard and Abigail Fillmore attended the inauguration of his successor, Franklin Pierce. Abigail died in Washington less than a month later. The bereaved Fillmore returned to Buffalo, New York.

Statue of Fillmore at City Hall Buffalo, New York.

My 2 cents
What would you nickname this president?

_____

The Author's Idea: Know-Nothing

The first one dollar bill was issued in 1862 as a legal tender note with a portrait of Salmon P. Chase, the Secretary of Treasury under President Abraham Lincoln. The current design dates to 1913. The most recognizable element of the "modern" bill is the portrait of George Washington, painted by Gilbert Stuart.

JAMES BUCHANAN
15th President of the United States

POLITICAL PARTY: Democrat
ELECTION OPPONENTS:
   John C. Fremont, Republican
   Millard Fillmore, Know-Nothing
TERM OF OFFICE: March 4, 1857 to March 3, 1861
VICE PRESIDENT: John C. Breckinridge

A stone pyramid marks the site of President Buchanan's log-cabin birthplace in Buchanan's Birthplace State Park, near Cove Gap, Pennsylvania.

WIKI, Clint

Fun Assignment!

James Buchanan had a U.S. postage stamp issued in his honor. What year was the stamp issued, and what was the stamp's value?

1938, 15 cents.

Personal Profile

BORN: April 23, 1791, near Mercersburg, Pennsylvania
SIBLINGS: Second of eleven children
RELIGION: Presbyterian
EDUCATION: Dickinson College, Carlisle, Pennsylvania; graduated 1809

CAREER: Lawyer
MILITARY: Volunteer, War of 1812
MARRIAGE: None
OFFSPRING: None
DIED: June 1, 1868, Lancaster, Pennsylvania

Harriet Rebecca Lane Johnston, Buchanan's niece, served as First Lady.

Visiting the President

BIRTHPLACE: Buchanan's Birthplace State Park
   Cove Gap, Pennsylvania
MUSEUM/ADULT RESIDENCE: Wheatland
   1120 Marietta Avenue, Lancaster, Pennsylvania
GRAVESITE: Woodward Hill Cemetery
   South Queen Street, Lancaster, Pennsylvania

Fun Assignment!

Lancaster, Pennsylvania is known for "Wheatland," the home of James Buchanan. It briefly served as what else in American history?

Lancaster was the interim Capitol of the colonies in 1777 during the Revolutionary War.

Tell me more!

What was the Dred Scott Decision?

Handed down by the Supreme Court only two days after Buchanan took office, the Dred Scott Decision stated that Congress had no constitutional power to exclude slavery in the U.S. territories. Buchanan had hoped that territorial expansion would be a road block to the expansion of slavery. However, the Dred Scott Decision allowed the expansion of slavery.

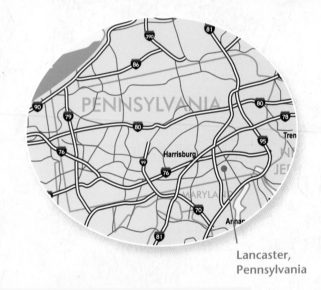

Lancaster, Pennsylvania

Political Profile

- Pennsylvania State Representative
- United States House of Representatives for Pennsylvania
- United States Senator for Pennsylvania
- Secretary of State
- Minister to Great Britain
- President of the United States

1857
First issue of *Atlantic Monthly* appears

1857
First Mardi Gras parade of floats in New Orleans occurs

The Buchanan Administration Highlights

- Brigham Young is removed as governor of the Utah Territory (1857)
- Minnesota becomes a state (1858)
- Oregon becomes a state (1859)
- Kansas becomes a state (1861)

*Vice President
John C. Breckinridge*

James Buchanan was born in 1791 in a tiny one-room log cabin in central Pennsylvania near Mercersburg. In 1796, the family moved to the center of town, with part of their home becoming a store. As a young boy, Buchanan worked for his father and learned arithmetic and bookkeeping. Buchanan attended Old Stone Academy in Mercersburg and then Dickinson College in Carlisle, Pennsylvania. Although a good student, he showed a rebellious streak, smoking and drinking. His classmates sometimes found him to be unbearably conceited. After his first year, the college expelled him for disorderly conduct and insubordination. He was reinstated when he pledged to settle down and work hard. He graduated a year later and began to study law. He was admitted to the Pennsylvania Bar in 1812 and set up his law practice in Lancaster, Pennsylvania. He proved to be an able attorney.

In 1814, Buchanan won a seat in the Pennsylvania House of Representatives as a Federalist. Following Andrew Jackson's defeat for the presidency in 1824, Buchanan worked diligently to build the Democratic Party in Pennsylvania and to support Jackson's bid for the presidency in the 1828 race. Jackson won and rewarded Buchanan by appointing him minister to Russia where he succeeded in negotiating the first trade

Buchanan's inauguration, March 4, 1857. It was the first inauguration to be recorded photographically.

treaty between the United States and Russia. Following his return, Buchanan was elected to the United States Senate where he served for ten years. He then served as President James Polk's Secretary of State. In 1849, Buchanan retired to his home, Wheatland, in Lancaster, Pennsylvania, where he unsuccessfully sought his party's presidential nomination for the 1852 election. President Franklin Pierce appointed Buchanan minister to Great Britain in 1853. At the 1856 Democratic National Convention Buchanan's three-year absence from the country stood him in good stead. His two chief rivals, President Pierce and Stephen A. Douglas, were

The Buchanan Cabinet, from left to right: Jacob Thompson, Lewis Cass, John B. Floyd, James Buchanan, Howell Cobb, Isaac Toucey, Joseph Holt, and Jeremiah S. Black.

James Buchanan was a tall, sturdy, handsome man with a good career; as such, he attracted interest as an eligible bachelor. He was far-sighted in one eye and near-sighted in the other, causing him to cock his head to compensate his vision. In 1818, he became engaged to Ann Coleman, the daughter of a wealthy Lancaster iron mill owner. Ann's father questioned Buchanan's intent: was it love or was it money. Ann broke off the engagement believing Buchanan was flirtatious with other women. She later died and suicide was suspected, but never proven.

Buchanan didn't marry after that and became the only

Wheatland, the Buchanan estate in Lancaster, Pennsylvania.

bachelor-president. While in office, Buchanan's unmarried niece, Harriet Lane served as hostess. Buchanan had a peerless resume, but was unable to rise above the role of "politician" to become a leader and statesman. He privately expressed his dislike of slavery, but did nothing to halt it, claiming he had to adhere to the Constitution and that it would not be possible to end slavery without destroying the Union. Buchanan died June 1, 1868 at the age of seventy-seven, showing that the years bore heavily upon him. The day before his death he believed that "history will vindicate his memory." History has not.

1859
Charles Darwin publishes *On the Origin of Species by Means of Natural Selection*

1859
Edwin Drake drills first oil well in Pennsylvania

Buchanan memorial at the southeast corner of Washington, D.C.'s Meridian Hill Park.

tainted by their espousal of the pro-slavery cause in Kansas, where a bitter war had broken out. Unconnected with "bleeding Kansas," Buchanan won the nomination. Buchanan carried only five free states and all but one slave state.

The 65-year-old Buchanan took office in a firestorm. In his inaugural address, he announced that he would not seek re-election in 1860, inadvertently sacrificing his leadership in his own party. The conflict over slavery continued to burn. His support of a bill to allow slavery in Kansas, a deepening recession, and the Republican Party's control of the House of Representatives all opened the door to Abraham Lincoln's victory over Buchanan in 1860.

When James Buchanan relinquished the presidency to Abraham Lincoln, he declared: "If you are as happy in entering the White House as I shall feel in returning to Wheatland, you are a happy man indeed."

My 2 cents
What would you nickname this president?

_____

The Author's Idea: Buch the Bachelor

1861
Successor president:
Abraham Lincoln

The quarter has been around since 1796. The George Washington quarter was initially issued as a commemorative, but was made a regular issue coin in 1934. The reverse featured an eagle prior to the 1999 "50 State Quarters Program."

The dime was authorized by the Coinage Act of 1792. The term "dime" comes from the old French "disme," meaning "the tenth part." The obverse underwent several changes until 1945, when Franklin Delano Roosevelt's image replaced the Mercury design. The reverse elements of a torch, olive branch, and oak branch symbolize liberty, peace, and victory.

The nickel design has featured the portrait of Thomas Jefferson on the obverse since 1938. From 1938 to 2003, Monticello was featured on the reverse. For 2004 and 2005, nickels featured designs of the Louisiana Purchase and the Lewis and Clark expedition; in 2006, Monticello returned to the reverse.

The Lincoln cent was adopted in 1909, replacing the Indian Head cent. Its reverse was changed in 1959 from a wheat stalks design, which includes the Lincoln Memorial to celebrate Lincoln's sesquicentennial, and replaced again in 2009 with four new designs to commemorate Lincoln's bicentennial.

GROVER CLEVELAND
22nd and 24th President of the United States

POLITCAL PARTY: Democrat
ELECTION OPPONENTS:
- 1884 James Blaine, Republican
  Benjamin Butler, Monopolist/Greenback
  John St. John, Prohibition
  Anson Streeter, Union Labor
- 1892 Benjamin Harrison, Republican
  James Weaver, Populist
  John Bidwell, Prohibition

TERMS OF OFFICE:
March 4, 1885 to March 4, 1889
March 4, 1893 to March 4, 1897
VICE PRESIDENTS:
1885 Thomas Hendricks
1893 Adlai E. Stevenson

The Grover Cleveland birthplace in Caldwell, New Jersey, houses Cleveland artifacts and political memorabilia.

Fun Assignment!

Grover Cleveland's image appears on one denomination of U.S. paper money. On what bill is Cleveland pictured?

$1,000 bill

Personal Profile

BORN: March 18, 1837, Caldwell, New Jersey
SIBLINGS: Fifth of nine children
RELIGION: Presbyterian
EDUCATION: Did not attend college
CAREER: Lawyer
MILITARY: None

MARRIAGE: Frances Folsom, June 2, 1886
Blue Room of the White House Washington, D.C.
OFFSPRING: Three daughters, two sons
DIED: June 24, 1908, Princeton, New Jersey

Frances Folsom Cleveland

Visiting the President

BIRTHPLACE/MUSEUM: The Grover Cleveland Birthplace
State Historic Site, 207 Bloomfield Avenue, Caldwell,
New Jersey

HOMESTEAD: 15 Hodge Road, Princeton, New Jersey
(privately owned, not open to the public)

GRAVESITE: Princeton Cemetery
29 Greenview Avenue, Princeton, New Jersey

Fun Assignment!

After retiring from the White House, Grover Cleveland
became a trustee of Princeton University. What future
president was the president of the university at the same
time?

Woodrow Wilson

Tell me more!

**Although Cleveland was president twice, he was
actually elected _three_ times. How was this possible?**

Cleveland was the winner of the _popular_ vote for president three times: 1884,
1888, and 1892. However, he did not win the _Electoral College_ vote in 1888. It
is the Electoral College vote that actually elects the president. At the same time a person
votes for president, they also vote for local individuals called "presidential electors"
who have pledged to vote for particular candidates. The electors cast their votes for
president in December after the November national election, and it is these electors'
votes that actually elect the president. This system was developed by the authors of
the Constitution to give more equal representation to smaller less-populated states.

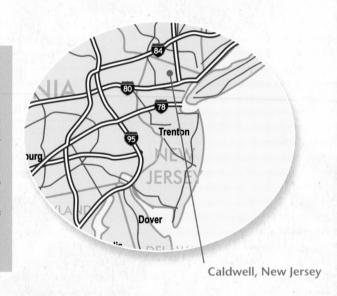

Caldwell, New Jersey

Political Profile

- Assistant District Attorney, Erie
  County, New York
- Sheriff, Erie County, New York
- Mayor, Buffalo, New York
- Governor of New York
- President of the United States

1886	1886	1886
Dr. John Stith Pemberton develops a cola drink that is named Coca-Cola	Statue of Liberty is dedicated	Robert Louis Stevenson publishes _The Strange Case of Dr. Jekyll and Mr. Hyde_

The Cleveland Administration Highlights

- Haymarket Riot, a labor strike for an 8-hour workday escalates, leaving 12 dead (1886)
- Edmunds-Tucker Act of 1887 seizes the property of the Mormon Church that is not used exclusively for worship, requires loyalty oaths for voter eligibility, disenfranchises women, and declares women to be competent witnesses
- Scott Act of 1888 bans Chinese laborers from immigrating or returning to the United States
- Congress creates the Department of Agriculture (1889)
- The Panic of 1893 sets off a depression after a run on gold and the failure of railroads, banks, and businesses; unemployment hits 18 percent
- A cancer is removed from Cleveland's jaw without the public's knowledge (1893)
- In Debs vs. the United States, the Supreme Court affirms the use of injunctions to break strikes (1895)
- Utah becomes a stage (1896)
- The Supreme Court hands down the decision that sets the precedent for "separate but equal" facilities for whites and African Americans (1896)

Stephen Grover Cleveland was the son of a Yale graduate and Presbyterian minister who went from pastorate to pastorate. The family moved from Caldwell, New Jersey, to Fayetteville, New York, to Clinton, New York, over the first fourteen years of Cleveland's life. Several years later, Cleveland was working toward admission to Hamilton College, but his father died, forcing Cleveland to forgo college. He then began work as an assistant at the New York Institution for the Blind, and regularly sent his pay to his mother. At the age of eighteen, Cleveland decided to head west to make his fortune. On his way he stopped to visit relatives in Buffalo, New York, and decided to stay for awhile. Through the influence of his uncle, Cleveland was able to clerk and study law at a local law firm. He was admitted to the New York Bar in 1859. During the Civil War, Cleveland was the assistant district attorney of Erie County, New York. Because he provided the main financial support of his family, he paid for a substitute to fulfill his military obligation, a permitted practice at the time. In 1870, Cleveland was elected sheriff of Erie County. He gained the reputation as an honest public official. He also served

An 1884 cartoon depicted the rumor that Cleveland had fathered an illegitimate child. Cleveland opponents chanted "Ma, Ma, where's my Pa?"

1888
George Eastman introduces the first
Kodak camera for amateurs

1888
The National Geographic Society
is founded

1889
Successor president:
Benjamin Harrison

63

as the public executioner, springing the trap on the gallows himself, saying he would not ask his deputies to do a job just because he did not want to do it himself. In 1881, Cleveland ran for mayor of Buffalo as a reform candidate to clean up corruption in city government. He won and set about proving himself, putting in place cost-effective services and vetoing bills he deemed fiscally irresponsible or catering to special interests. At the 1884 Democratic National Convention, Cleveland, with his reputation as an honest, civic-minded politician, obtained the presidential

Grover Cleveland was the only president married in the White House

When **Grover Cleveland** entered the White House in 1885, the 48-year-old was a single, six-foot, 285-pound, blue-eyed portly man known as "Uncle Jumbo." He was accustomed to the bachelor life. He worked long, hard hours and enjoyed fishing trips, Sunday evening poker games, and eating and drinking with his buddies. Following the death of his law partner, Oscar Folsom, Cleveland gave financial advice to Oscar's widow, Emma, and guided Oscar's daughter, Frances, whom he called "Frank," on her education. Romance blossomed, not with the widow Emma as the press had speculated, but with the daughter, Frank, twenty-seven years his junior. He proposed to Frank by letter and the upcoming wedding became front-page news. Grover and Frank married June 2, 1886 in the Blue Room of the White House. It is the only wedding of a sitting president held in the White House itself.

When the Clevelands returned to the White House

in 1893, as predicted by Frank, they brought their daughter, Ruth, who was born in 1891. Two more daughters followed: Esther, born in 1893, and Marion, born in 1895.

When the Clevelands left after the presidential term, they moved to Princeton, New Jersey. In 1904, their eldest child, Ruth, died at the age of thirteen from diphtheria. Ruth's name is perpetuated by the candy bar "Baby Ruth®."

Historically neglected, Grover Cleveland never intended to be a politician. Although a calm, methodical, confident, honest, and hard-working public servant, he is perhaps remembered only for two things: his two non-consecutive presidential terms and his wedding at the White House.

Cleveland died June 14, 1908 at the age of seventy-one at his home in Princeton, New Jersey. His last words were: "I have tried so hard to do right."

1893
The first Stanley Cup
is won

1894
Congress makes Labor Day
a national holiday

Members of Grover Cleveland's first cabinet. Sitting, left to right: Thomas F. Bayard, Cleveland, Daniel Manning, Lucius Q. C. Lamar; Standing, left to right: William F. Vilas, William C. Whitney, William C. Endicott, and Augustus H. Garland

nomination on the fourth ballot and became the first Democrat to be elected president in a quarter of a century.

Cleveland continued his legacy of honesty, hard work, and vetoing. He also signed an act that created the Interstate Commerce Commission and an act that authorized the apportioning of land to individual Native Americans rather than to entire tribes. Cleveland also was instrumental in helping create the United States Department of Labor. After he left office in 1889, Cleveland practiced law in New York City, but remained involved in politics. He again became a presidential candidate in 1892 and was elected. This time, Cleveland presided over a country in a depression. He did not believe in heavy federal intervention; he believed the economy should play out naturally. On foreign affairs, Cleveland resisted efforts to annex Hawaii, enforced the Monroe Doctrine over a border dispute between Venezuela and Great Britain, and avoided United States involvement in the Cuban revolt against Spain. After leaving the White House, the Cleveland family settled in Princeton, New Jersey, in a home they labeled "Westland."

Grover Cleveland in 1892

My 2 cents
What would you nickname this president?

_____

The Author's Idea: Two-Timer

1895
Wilhelm Conrad Röntgen
discovers x-rays

1896
The first modern Olympics
are held in Athens, Greece

1897
Successor president:
William McKinley

65

Located in Montezuma County, Colorado, the Mesa Verde was established as a United States National Park in 1906. The park occupies 81.4 square miles and is best known for its cliff dwellings, built by the Ancestral Puebloan people in the late 12th century.

THEODORE ROOSEVELT
26th President of the United States

POLITICAL PARTY: Republican
ELECTION OPPONENT:
1904 Alton B. Parker, Democrat
TERM OF OFFICE: September 14, 1901 to March 4, 1909
VICE PRESIDENT:
1901 None
1905 Charles W. Fairbanks

Roosevelt's birthplace, New York City

WIKI, Beyond My Ken

Fun Assignment!

President Roosevelt was the first president to invite an African-American to dinner as a guest. Who was this auspicious guest, who also was the first leader of the Tuskegee Institute in Alabama?

Booker T. Washington

Personal Profile

BORN: October 27, 1858, New York, New York
SIBLINGS: Second of four children
RELIGION: Dutch Reformed
EDUCATION: Harvard College; graduated 1880
CAREER: Writer, Rancher
MILITARY: Army Colonel

MARRIAGES:
• Alice Hathaway Lee, October 27, 1880 Brookline, Massachusetts
• Edith Kermit Carow, December 2, 1886 London, England
OFFSPRING: Four sons, two daughters
DIED: January 6, 1919 at Sagamore Hill; Oyster Bay, New York

Alice Hathaway Lee Roosevelt

1901	1901	1903
Previous president: William McKinley	The first Nobel Prizes are awarded	The first "teddy bear" is introduced in America

Visiting the President

BIRTHPLACE: 28 East 20th Street, New York, New York
MUSEUM/RESIDENCE:
Sagamore Hill National Historic Site
Cove Neck Road, Cove Neck, New York
GRAVESITE: Young's Memorial Cemetery
Oyster Bay, New York

Fun Assignment!

Theodore Roosevelt and his son, Theodore, Jr., each received the Congressional Medal of Honor posthumously for bravery in combat. Can you name the wars?

Theodore Roosevelt fought in the Spanish-American War; his son fought in World War II

Tell me more!

Why was Theodore Roosevelt called a conservation president?

Roosevelt signed legislation creating a remarkable 150 National Forests, 18 national monuments, and five national parks (Crater Lake, Oregon; Wind Cave, South Dakota; Sullys Hill, North Dakota (later redesignated a game preserve); Mesa Verde, Colorado; and Platt, Oklahoma (now part of Chickasaw National Recreation Area). No other president has had such a huge effect on conservation.

New York, New York

Political Profile

- Member, New York State Legislature
- Member, United States Civil Service Commission
- President, New York City Police Board
- Assistant Secretary of the Navy
- Governor, State of New York
- Vice President of the United States
- President of the United States

1903	1903	1903
The first Tour de France bicycle race is held	The first World Series is held	Orville and Wilbur Wright fly the first powered heavier-than-air craft at Kitty Hawk, North Carolina

The Roosevelt Administration Highlights

- Hay-Pauncefats Treaty which gave the United States control of proposed Panama Canal (1901)
- Anti-trust suits filed against J.P. Morgan (Northern Securities) and John D. Rockefeller (Standard Oil Company) (1902)
- United Mine Workers Strike (1902)
- National Forest Service established (1905)
- Treaty of Portsmouth signed, ending the Russo-Japanese War (1905)
- The Pure Food and Drug Act (1906)
- The Meat Inspection Act (1906)
- Roosevelt awarded the Noble Peace Prize (1906)
- The Panic of 1907 following stock market crashes
- Oklahoma becomes a state (1907)
- National Conservation Commission established (1908)

CONNECTIONS

*The famous **Maxwell House Coffee** trademark "Good to the Last Drop®" was first spoken by Theodore Roosevelt at the Maxwell House Hotel in Nashville, Tennessee.*

Theodore Roosevelt was the son of a wealthy New York philanthropist. He was near-sighted, frail, and suffered from asthma attacks. With the encouragement of his father and a vigorous exercise program, Roosevelt determined to improve his body. He and his siblings were tutored at home and traveled in Europe. When he was eighteen, he entered Harvard College. In 1880, he graduated magna cum laude and was a member of Phi Beta Kappa. That same year he married Alice Hathaway Lee, the daughter of a socially prominent Boston family. He then entered Columbia Law School, only to drop out within a year, finding legal studies dull. He joined a local Republican Club and it was from there that he was propelled into the political world. He served three terms in the New York legislature. On February 12, 1884, his daughter Alice was born. When he

The Roosevelt family, 1903.

1904
The New York subway begins operation

1905
Albert Einstein publishes his theory of relativity

1906
Mount Vesuvius erupts

returned home from Albany after receiving an urgent telegram, he was hit with a double blow: both his wife and mother were gravely ill. On the same day, February 14, 1884, his wife died of Bright's disease and his mother of typhoid fever. Devastated, he completed his term as state legislator and left for the Badlands of Dakota to restore his spirit. He left his infant daughter in the care of his sister. Roosevelt returned three years later and renewed his relationship with his childhood friend Edith Carow. They married in 1886. He also renewed his ties with the Republican Party. Roosevelt approached every political appointment with alacrity, unbounded vigor, and a reforming spirit. Just two of his many appointments included serving as Assistant Secretary of the Navy and Colonel in the Spanish-American War. During that conflict, in 1898, Roosevelt served with the first volunteer Calvary Regiment. His war exploits catapulted him onto the national political stage. Roosevelt easily won his

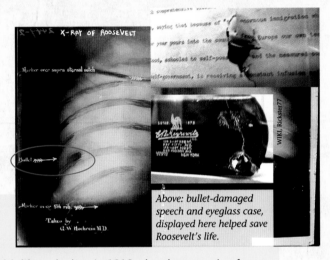

Above: bullet-damaged speech and eyeglass case, displayed here helped save Roosevelt's life.

Theodore Roosevelt was 50 years old when he left the White House. He returned to his beloved home, Sagamore Hill in Oyster Bay, New York. Independently wealthy, his time was spent traveling, writing and speechmaking. He safaried in Africa, and explored the River of Doubt, exhibiting his fearlessness and physical endurance. He was short in stature but tall in vitality. This man with the Harvard accent, the bushy mustache, and the toothy smile never met a challenge he would not accept. With high spirit and great oratory skills he coined the terms: good to the last drop, bully pulpit, trust buster, muckraker, Bull Moose and square deal. He is the origin of the famous "Teddy Bear" stuffed animal. He was a prolific writer, penning over forty books. One of the most amazing incidents in

Roosevelt's life took place in 1912 when he was vying for the Republican presidential nomination. While campaigning in Milwaukee, he was shot in the chest by a would-be assassin. He insisted on giving a 90-minute speech before receiving medical attention.

That near tragedy was followed by a worse one in 1918 when Roosevelt's fighter pilot son, "Q" was shot down and killed over France. Teddy Roosevelt was never quite the same after that, and he died in January 1919 at the age of sixty. His son, Archie wired his brother: "The lion is dead."

1906
Earthquake occurs in San Francisco, killing 6,000

1907
The first Montessori School opens in Rome

1908
First *Scouting for Boys* is published beginning the Boy Scout movement

WIKI, Dean Franklin

Mount Rushmore National Monument.

bid for Governor of New York. Eager to get rid of a governor they could not control, the Republican Party bosses pushed his nomination as Vice President to President William McKinley. They believed that post would sideline him from reform efforts; little did they know. On September 14, 1901, Roosevelt was sworn in as the youngest President of the United States following the death of William McKinley from an assassin's bullet. Roosevelt became the nation's fifth "accidental" president, reaching the presidency through the loss of a sitting president. He conducted his presidency with a bold hand through both his terms. Several significant events were carried out without the knowledge of his Cabinet including an anti-trust suit against the Northern Securities Company and the "taking" of Panama following its struggle for independence from Columbia. The Panamanian revolt, encouraged by Roosevelt, led to the building of the Panama Canal. Roosevelt's farthest-reaching impact was in the area of conservation. He was the first conservation president. Through his efforts, *230 million acres of wilderness* were preserved in the form of dams, irrigation projects, five national parks, fifty-one federal bird reservations, the National Forest Service, and 150 national forests.

WIKI, GK tramrunner

Sagamore Hill National Historic Site Oyster Bay, New York.

My 2 cents
What would you nickname this president?

_____

The Author's Idea: Colonel Rushmore

1908
Henry Ford introduces
the Model T

1909
The National Association for the Advancement
of Colored People (NAACP) is formed

1909
Successor president:
William Howard Taft

71

The United States Holocaust Memorial Museum in Washington, D.C.
Dedicated April 22, 1993, the museum has had nearly 30 million visitors.

FRANKLIN DELANO ROOSEVELT
32nd President of the United States

POLITICAL PARTY: Democrat
ELECTION OPPONENTS:

1932 Herbert Hoover, Republican; Norman Thomas,
      Socialist; William Foster, Communist
1936 Alfred Landon, Republican; William Lemke, Union
1940 Wendell Wilkie, Republican
1944 Thomas Dewey, Republican

TERM OF OFFICE: March 3, 1933 to April 12, 1945
VICE PRESIDENTS:

1932 John Nance Garner
1936 John Nance Garner
1940 Henry A. Wallace
1944 Harry S. Truman

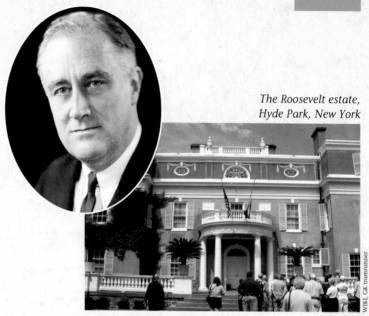

*The Roosevelt estate,
Hyde Park, New York*

WIKI, GK tramrunner

Personal Profile

BORN: January 30, 1882
   Dutchess County, Hyde Park, New York
SIBLINGS: Half-brother
RELIGION: Episcopalian
EDUCATION:
   Harvard College; graduated 1903
   Columbia Law School, 1905 to 1907

CAREER: Lawyer
MILITARY: None
Marriage: Anna Eleanor Roosevelt
   March 17, 1905, New York, New York
OFFSPRING: One daughter, five sons
DIED: April 12, 1945, Warm Springs,
   Georgia

*Anna
Eleanor
Roosevelt*

1933
Previous president:
Herbert Hoover

1933
Wiley Post completes the first solo flight
around the world (7 days, 19 hours)

1934
Clyde Barrow and Bonnie Parker are shot
and killed by police in Louisiana

Visiting the President

BIRTHPLACE/MUSEUM/LIBRARY/GRAVESITE:
The Franklin D. Roosevelt Library and Museum
4079 Albany Post Road, Hyde Park, New York

Fun Assignment!

FDR was the first president to appear on television. What year did this occur, and what was the occasion?

Roosevelt appeared on TV for the opening session of the New York World's Fair, April 30, 1939.

Tell me more!

What was the Great Depression?

The Great Depression began with the stock market crash of 1929 and continued through the 1930s. It was a severe worldwide economic downturn resulting in a huge loss of jobs. Unemployment hit 25% of the United States population. Complicating this situation was the Dust Bowl, a massive drought that destroyed thousands of acres of farmland in Colorado, Kansas, Nebraska, New Mexico, Oklahoma, and Texas. Government spending on World War II stimulated the economy and helped the U.S. emerge from the Great Depression in the 1940s.

Hyde Park, New York

Political Profile

- New York Senator
- Assistant Secretary of the Navy
- Governor of New York
- President of the United States

1935	1935	1935
Parker Brothers introduce new board game, Monopoly	Richter Scale introduced for measuring the magnitude of earthquakes	Babe Ruth hits his record 714th home run in his final season of baseball

The Roosevelt Administration Highlights

- 21st Amendment to the Constitution repealing the prohibition of alcohol enacted by the 18th Amendment is passed by Congress (1933)
- Bill is signed to establish the last Thursday in November as Thanksgiving Day, a national holiday (1941)
- The United States declares war on Japan on December 8, 1941
- Germany and Italy declare war on the United States on December 11, 1941
- Office of Censorship is established December 19, 1941
- Executive Order 9066 is signed February 19, 1942; it leads to the detention and interment of Japanese-Americans
- Jefferson Memorial is dedicated on the 200th anniversary of Jefferson's birth (1943)
- GI Bill of Rights is signed June 22, 1944

Franklin Delano Roosevelt was born into aristocracy. His father, James, was a railroad executive and his mother, Sara, twenty-six years younger than her husband, was the daughter of a wealthy merchant. At the age of fourteen, he was enrolled at a private preparatory school in Massachusetts, a natural step to Harvard University. After Harvard, Roosevelt entered Columbia Law School in 1905. That same year he married Anna Eleanor Roosevelt, his fifth cousin once removed. He dropped out of law school after he passed the New York State Bar examination in 1907.

Roosevelt entered politics at the age of twenty-eight. After serving as state senator, his party nominated him for Vice President in 1920. He and the presidential candidate—James Cox—lost by a landslide, but Roosevelt won national recognition. While vacationing with his family at their summerhouse on Campobello Island, Canada, in August 1921, Roosevelt was struck with polio and his legs were paralyzed. Over the next several years, he underwent rehabilitation and eventually he was able to walk with the aid of a cane, leg braces, and the arm of a strong bodyguard. With the support of his wife and Louis Howe, a most trusted political adviser and

President Roosevelt and predecessor President Hoover on Inauguration Day, March 4, 1933.

1935
Baseball Hall of Fame names its first honorees, including Ty Cobb and Babe Ruth

1937
The German airship Hindenburg bursts into flames at Lakehurst, NJ

1937
Amelia Earhart vanishes while attempting an around-the-world flight

strategist, he returned to the political stage, first at the 1924 and then at the 1928 Democratic National Conventions. His visibility there helped him win the governorship of New York in 1928. His popularity as governor then gave him a strong standing at the 1932 Democratic National Convention. Roosevelt was nominated as the party's presidential candidate on the fourth ballot; he won by a landslide.

When the 51-year-old paraplegic president took office, the nation was in a deep depression. He immediately laid the foundation for his "New Deal," pushing programs and legislation that resulted in a multitude of new federal agencies known by their initials. These agencies included the CCC (Civilian Conservation Corps) to provide work for unemployed youth, for example. On March 12, 1933, Roosevelt initiated his "fireside chat" radio broadcasts to bolster the stricken country. Roosevelt was re-elected in 1936 and then broke the two-term tradition,

This is one of two known photos of Roosevelt in a wheelchair (1941).

Franklin Delano Roosevelt, elected President of the United States for an astounding four terms, could be described as the right person at the right time. In the face of a depression of monumental proportions and a ferocious World War, he led the country he loved with determination, ingenuity, confidence, and charisma, but, as is usually the case, there is a story behind the story.

This was a man whose mother, Sara, could not let go of, as he was her only child. She was overindulging and a domineering, intrusive, and near constant presence. Without consulting Franklin and his wife, she built adjoining townhouses: one for the couple and one for herself, with connecting doors; she visited frequently. She also sat at the head of her son's table. Sara wanted her paraplegic son to be a country gentleman at her Hyde Park Estate rather than a politician. She controlled the family fortune and it was not until her death, four years before her son's, that Franklin managed his own money.

This was a man who had an affair with his wife's personal secretary, Lucy Mercer. Eleanor discovered love letters after Franklin contracted polio. She confronted him and offered to divorce him, something he did not want. Neither did his mother, who threatened to cut him off financially if he did not agree to stop seeing Lucy. Eleanor and Franklin remained married, but their marriage was forever changed.

This was a man who could not walk, but who overcame his disability--both physically and emotionally. The country did not see the cane and braces and the media agreed to ignore them. This was a man who was unable to walk on his own, but who stood by his country and guided her through the nightmare of the greatest crises of his century.

1938	1938	1939
E.I. du Pont de Nemours, Inc. announces the invention of nylon, the first synthetic fiber	The first *Superman* comic book is published	The Baseball Hall of Fame opens in Cooperstown, New York

Roosevelt signs the declaration of war against Japan, December 8, 1941.

successfully running for a third term. On December 7, 1941, Japan attacked Pearl Harbor in Hawaii, a day famously described by Roosevelt as "a day that will live in infamy." The United States declared war on Japan on December 8, 1941. In his remaining presidential years, Roosevelt was immersed in mobilizing the country and developing military strategies with Allied partners.

Winston Churchill, Franklin Roosevelt, and Joseph Stalin at the Yalta Summits in 1945, discussing Europe's post-war reorganization.

In 1944, Roosevelt was elected to an unprecedented fourth term of office, but the war and poor health had taken its toll on him. On April 12, 1945, at approximately 1:15 P.M. in the living room of the "Little White House", as his Warm Springs, Georgia, home had become known, Roosevelt put his hand to his head, murmured "I have a terrific headache" and collapsed into unconsciousness. He was pronounced dead at 3:35 P.M. that day. Roosevelt was sixty-three years of age.

My 2 cents
What would you nickname this president?

_____

The Author's Idea: The Charmer

1942	1943	1945
Scientists of the Manhattan Project create an atomic bomb	The Pentagon building in Washington, D.C. is completed	Successor president: Harry S. Truman

Professor's Gate, leading to Monroe Court and Kogan Plaza, on the campus of George Washington University, Washington, D.C.

GEORGE WASHINGTON

1st President of the United States

POLITICAL PARTY: Federalist
ELECTION OPPONENT: None
TERM OF OFFICE: April 30, 1789 to March 3, 1797
VICE PRESIDENT: John Adams

George Washington Birthplace National Monument, Westmoreland County, Virginia. A foundation outline indicates the location of Washington's boyhood home, which burned down in 1779.

WIKI, James G. Howes

Fun Assignment!

Washington is the only president inaugurated in two different cities. Can you name the cities?

New York City in 1789 and Philadelphia in 1793

Personal Profile

BORN: February 22, 1732, Pope's Creek, Virginia
SIBLINGS: 3 stepbrothers, 1 stepsister; eldest of six children by father's second wife
RELIGION: Episcopalian
EDUCATION: Limited formal schooling
CAREER: Surveyor, planter

MILITARY: Major in the Virginia Militia; General and commander-in-chief of the Continental forces during the Revolutionary War
MARRIAGE: Martha Dandridge Custis January 6, 1759, New Kent County, Virginia
OFFSPRING: No biological children; two stepchildren
DIED: December 14, 1799 Mount Vernon, Virginia

Martha Dandridge Custis Washington

Visiting the President

BIRTHPLACE: George Washington Birthplace National Monument
Virginia State Route 204, off Virginia State Route 3
Westmoreland County, Virginia
MUSEUM/LIBRARY/GRAVESITE: Mount Vernon, Fairfax County, Virginia

Mount Vernon, Fairfax County, Virginia.

Tell me more!

Did George Washington really have wooden teeth?

George Washington did wear false teeth; but they weren't made of such materials as hippopotamus ivory.

Westmoreland County,
Virginia

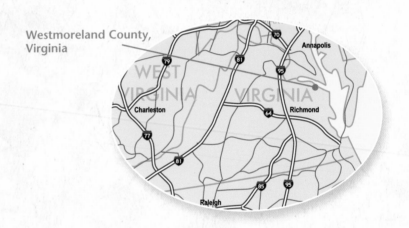

Political Profile

- Member, Virginia House of Burgesses
- Justice of Peace, Fairfax County, Virginia
- Delegate, Williamsburg Convention
- Delegate, First Continental Congress
- Delegate, Second Continental Congress
- Delegate and President of the Constitutional Convention
- President of the United States

1790
First U.S. census estimates
population at 4 million

1792
The New York Stock Exchange
is organized

The Washington Administration Highlights

- Congress creates the Departments of State, War and Treasury (1789)
- Congress authorizes creation of the Supreme Court and the federal judicial system (1789)
- Vermont becomes a state (1791)
- Bill of Rights ratified (1791)
- Kentucky becomes a state (1792)
- Cornerstone of the U.S. Capitol is laid (1793)
- The Naturalization Act (1795) requires a residency of five years for U.S. citizenship
- Tennessee becomes a state (1796)

CONNECTIONS
Folklore has George Washington sleeping in nearly every old colonial home in the eastern United States. This claim is so common it was even reflected in a 1942 movie titled "George Washington Slept Here," starring Jack Benny and Ann Sheridan.

George Washington was the eldest child of a second marriage. His father died when he was only eleven. Nonetheless, he grew up enjoying hunting, fishing, and horseback riding. One person with whom Washington had a close relationship was his stepbrother Lawrence. When Lawrence died in 1752, Washington acquired Lawrence's handsome mansion, Mount Vernon, named for a British admiral under whom Lawrence served. After Lawrence died, Washington decided to follow in his military footsteps, initially serving as a major in the Virginia militia. He gained fame in the colonies, but was resentful toward the British who refused to put colonial officers on the same footing as their British counterparts, so Washington resigned at the end of the French and Indian War.

In 1759, Washington married the widow Martha Dandridge Custis. She brought to the marriage a fortune in land and money, as well as two

Depiction of Washington crossing the Delaware River on December 25, 1776.

1793
Eli Whitney invents the cotton gin

1794
Robert Burns composes "Auld Lang Syne"

children by her first marriage. Washington entered colonial politics as a member of Virginia's House of Burgesses, attending the Continental Congress in 1774. At the Second Continental Congress in 1775, John Adams nominated Washington as leader of the colonial military forces. Washington accepted, but refused payment for his services. The Revolutionary War against Great Britain was put into motion. Over the next several years Washington and his troops endured hardships, deprivations, and a number of retreats. Eventually though, Washington's

George Washington was a towering figure both in physique and accomplishments. Calm and noble in demeanor, the six foot-two inch, two hundred pound Washington was an idol among his contemporaries and the first American icon. He enjoyed the company of women, card playing, dancing and fine horses. During his long military career, Washington demonstrated steadfastness and courage, gaining admiration and loyalty among his troops. As president, he guided the fledgling country with determination and integrity, setting precedents and traditions that would be followed by his successors. After giving most of his life to the service of his country, the sixty-five year old Washington settled into the life of a private citizen and set about improving his plantation, enjoying his family and socializing with friends. On the snowy morning of December 14, 1799 Washington awoke with a throat so sore he could hardly speak; by ten o'clock that night the first president of the United States was dead. At a memorial service held at the nation's capital, Philadelphia, Washington's former officer, Henry Lee made the now famous statement in his eulogy: "First in war, first in peace, first in the hearts of his countrymen."

General George Washington addresses Congress to resign his commission as Commander-in-Chief of the Army.

1796
English physician Edward Jenner uses cowpox
to create an inoculation against smallpox

brilliance as a general and better training of the troops led to the ultimate victory at Yorktown.

At the close of the war, the victorious and popular general resigned his commission and returned to his beloved Mount Vernon. Over time it became evident to Washington that the neophyte Congress could not solve national problems because of its lack of authority under the Articles of Confederation. Washington left Mount Vernon for Philadelphia in 1787 to preside over the Constitutional Convention. Within nine months the country ratified the new Constitution. Following the procedures outlined in the constitution, the Electoral College unanimously elected Washington the first president of the United States. He was keenly aware that he would be setting precedents for his successors. The main departments of the federal government were established (during his second term this group would be referred to as the "cabinet"), the location of the new capitol was determined, the Bill of Rights was ratified, and the presidential veto was first invoked. Washington intended to retire at the end of his first term, but Thomas Jefferson persuaded him otherwise when he said, "North and South will hang together if they have you to hang on."

*Washington's tomb,
Mount Vernon, Virginia.*

Washington was unanimously elected to a second term--one that would turn out to be vastly different from his first. The excitement of forming the new government was over, and political invectives began to be directed at Washington himself for various policies. For example, Washington issued the Neutrality Proclamation Act (1793) and signed the Jay Treaty (1795) with Great Britain, both unpopular with the opposition party. Washington also was forced to send militia during the Whiskey Rebellion in Pennsylvania (1794) to prove that the federal government could enforce its power of taxation. As Washington approached the end of his second term, efforts were underway to persuade him to accept a third term. This time, though, he was firm in his desire to leave the presidency and have the next president chosen as the Constitution stipulated. John Adams was elected to be the second president of the United States.

My 2 cents
What would you nickname this president?

_____

The Author's Idea: # 1 Patriot

The Declaration of Independence, 4th of July 1776.

THOMAS JEFFERSON

3rd President of the United States

POLITICAL PARTY: Democratic Republican
ELECTION OPPONENTS:

1800: John Adams, Federalist
Charles Pinckney, Federalist
Aaron Burr, Democratic-Republican
John Jay, Federalist

1804: Charles Pinckney, Federalist

TERM OF OFFICE: March 4, 1801 to March 4, 1809
VICE PRESIDENT:

1801: Aaron Burr
1805: George Clinton

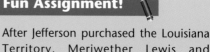

Fun Assignment!

After Jefferson purchased the Louisiana Territory, Meriwether Lewis and William Clark led an expedition across the continent. The team included one woman. Can you name her?

Sacagawea of the Shoshone tribe

Personal Profile

BORN: April 13, 1743, Shadwell Plantation, Goochland County, Virginia
SIBLINGS: Third of ten children
RELIGION: No affiliation
EDUCATION: College of William and Mary; graduated 1762
CAREER Planter, lawyer
Military: None

MARRIAGE: Martha Wayles Skelton January 1, 1772, The Forest (the Wayles family estate), Williamsburg, Virginia
OFFSPRING: Five daughters, one son
• The son died at birth; only two daughters survived into adulthood
Died: July 4, 1826 at Monticello Charlottesville, Virginia

Visiting the President

BIRTHPLACE: Shadwell, Albemarle, Virginia
   Route 250, two miles from Interstate 64
   • Marker at site, home burned to the ground in 1770
MUSEUM/LIBRARY/GRAVESITE:
   Monticello, Charlottesville, Virginia

Monticello, Charlottesville, Virginia.

Tell me more!

Perspective on the Speed of Travel

Today we can fly from New York to Los Angeles in only 5 hours. We can travel by train from New York to Atlanta in 18 hours. By contrast, in 1807, Robert Fulton's steamboat, the Clermont, traveled up the Hudson River from New York to Albany. It took 32 hours to complete the trip.

Albemarle, Virginia

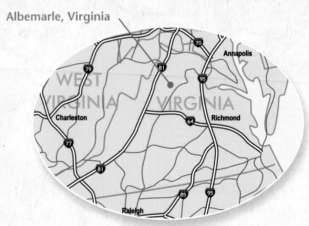

Political Profile

- Member, Virginia House of Burgesses
- Delegate, Continental Congress
- Delegate, Virginia House of Delegates
- Governor of Virginia
- Minister to France
- Secretary of State
- Vice President of the United States
- President of the United States

1801
Beethoven composes *Piano
Sonata in C Sharp Minor*

The Jefferson Administration Highlights

- Congress establishes the United States Military Academy at West Point (1802)
- Ohio becomes a state (1803)
- The United States purchases the Louisiana Territory (828,000 square miles) from France for $15 million (1803)
- Lewis and Clark lead an expedition from St. Louis to the Pacific Ocean (1804-1806)
- 12th Amendment to the Constitution provides that voters will vote separately for president and vice president (1804)
- Congress prohibits the importation of African slaves, effective January 1, 1808

Thomas Jefferson was born at Shadwell, a modest estate on the Rivanna River in Goochland, Virginia. His father was more than a planter; he also was a surveyor, a mapmaker, a colonel in the colonial militia, a member of the Virginia House of Burgesses, and a justice of the peace. His mother came from a wealthy and powerful Virginia family. Jefferson was tutored in his early years and took easily to learning, including subjects such as Greek, Latin, French, and music. When Jefferson was fourteen, his father died. As the eldest son, Jefferson, following the tradition of primogeniture, was the sole heir to his father's estate. He attended William and Mary College, and then studied law. In 1767, he was admitted to the Virginia Bar. Jefferson married Martha Wayles Skelton, a well-to-do widow whose fortune almost doubled Jefferson's sizable estate. Over the following ten years, the couple lost four of their six children. These tragedies were compounded for Jefferson in 1782 when Martha died as well. During these years, Jefferson entered politics, steadily adding to his reputation for patriotic views and skill in expressing them in writing.

Statue of Thomas Jefferson in the Jefferson Memorial in Washington, D.C. Excerpts from the Declaration of Independence on the wall in background.

He was elected to the Continental Congress in 1775. Jefferson's skill as a writer and his southern roots made him the obvious choice to write the Declaration of Independence. In his various governmental positions, Jefferson accomplished the following: mandated the complete separation of church and state; recommended the dollar as the main currency and the decimal system as the basis for the currency; and served in France as a trade commissioner and then as minister to France for five years. In 1790, Jefferson was appointed the country's first Secretary of State. During the three years he served in the position, he was at odds with the ruling political party, the Federalists, who favored a strong national government, while Jefferson's party,

The Jefferson Memorial in Washington, D.C.

Thomas Jefferson was an urbane and sophisticated man. The 6'2", slender redhead was the most versatile of all American chief executives. He was a statesman, diplomat, and political scientist, but also a philosopher, architect and builder, inventor, author, bibliophile, biologist, geographer, and educator. After the death of his wife Martha, he did not remarry. When Jefferson retired from politics, he devoted his life to his plantation, his family, and his intellectual pursuits. However, he was in debt and made a meager living off his crops. Jefferson sold his large personal library at a loss to the United States Congress to keep his estate. These books became the nucleus of the Library of Congress.

One of Jefferson's greatest accomplishments, and one he wished to be remembered for, was the founding of the University of Virginia, near Monticello. In 1817, at the age of 74, Jefferson began designing the school's buildings, planning the curriculum, recruiting the academic staff, and, at the age of 83, acting as the head of the governing body of the school. He died just months after the school opened.

Jefferson died on the fiftieth anniversary of the signing of the Declaration of Independence. John Adams, his fellow founding father, died several hours later.

In 1962, nearly a century and a half after Jefferson's death, President John F. Kennedy addressed a group of Noble laureates at the White House: "I think this is the most extraordinary collection of talent and human knowledge that has ever gathered at the White House—with the possible exception of when Thomas Jefferson dined alone."

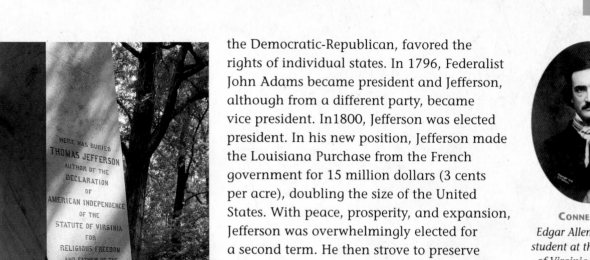

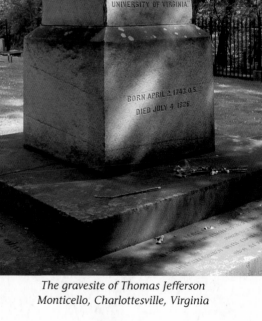

*The gravesite of Thomas Jefferson
Monticello, Charlottesville, Virginia*

the Democratic-Republican, favored the rights of individual states. In 1796, Federalist John Adams became president and Jefferson, although from a different party, became vice president. In 1800, Jefferson was elected president. In his new position, Jefferson made the Louisiana Purchase from the French government for 15 million dollars (3 cents per acre), doubling the size of the United States. With peace, prosperity, and expansion, Jefferson was overwhelmingly elected for a second term. He then strove to preserve neutrality in the face of the continuing conflict between Great Britain and France. Refusing all pleas to run for a third term, Jefferson supported his political disciple, good friend, and Secretary of State, James Madison, as his successor. Jefferson wrote: "Never did a prisoner released from his chains feel such relief as I shall on shaking off the shackles of power." He returned to his beloved Monticello to live as a farmer-philosopher.

CONNECTIONS
Edgar Allen Poe was a student at the University of Virginia from 1826 to 1827. Jefferson invited him and other students to Sunday dinners at Monticello. Poe attended Jefferson's funeral in 1826.

My 2 cents
What would you nickname this president?

_____

The Author's Idea: Mr. Cosmopolitan

The United States Constitution, authored and adopted in Philadelphia in 1787.

JAMES MADISON

4th President of the United States

POLITICAL PARTY: Democratic-Republican
ELECTION OPPONENTS:
    1808: Charles Pinckey, Federalist
        George Clinton, Democrat-Republican
    1812: DeWitt Clinton, Federalist
TERM OF OFFICE: March 4, 1809 to March 4, 1817
VICE PRESIDENT: 1809, George Clinton; 1813,
    Elbridge Gerry

Historical marker indicates the location of Madison's birthplace in Port Conway, Virginia

BIRTHPLACE OF MADISON

WIKI, Clariosophic

Fun Assignment!

The frigate USS Constitution defeated two British frigates during the War of 1812. As a result, the Constitution earned a nickname. What was it?

"Old Ironsides"

Personal Profile

BORN: March 16, 1751, Port Conway,
    King George County, Virginia
SIBLINGS: Eldest of twelve children
RELIGION: Episcopalian
EDUCATION: College of New Jersey (today
    Princeton University); graduated 1771
CAREER: Lawyer, planter

MILITARY: Commissioned colonel in the
    county militia
MARRIAGE: Dolley Dandridge Payne Todd
    September 15, 1794 at Harewood
    Jefferson County, Virginia
OFFSPRING: None
DIED: June 28, 1836 at Montpelier
    Orange County, Virginia

Dolley Dandridge Payne Todd Madison

1809
Previous president:
Thomas Jefferson

1810
The Yale Medical School
is established

Visiting the President

BIRTHPLACE: Belle Grove Plantation, Port Conway, Virginia
* It no longer exists; marker at site on Route 30

MUSEUM: The James Madison Museum
129 Caroline Street, Orange, Virginia

HOMESTEAD/GRAVESITE: Montpelier
11407 Constitution Highway, Orange County, Virginia

Port Conway, Virginia

James and Dolley Madison temporarily lived in The Octagon House in Washington, D.C. after The White House was burned by the British in 1814.

WIKI, Aude

Tell me more!

An Era of Firsts

There were many firsts during the Madison administration: the first inaugural ball, the first White House wedding, the first Easter egg roll, the first personal message using the Morse telegraph, and the introduction of ice cream.

Political Profile

* Member, Virginia Constitutional Convention
* Member, Continental Congress
* Member, Virginia Legislature
* Member, Constitutional Convention
* Member, United States House of Representatives
* Secretary of State
* President of the United States

1810
U.S. census shows
population of 7.2 million

1811
Jane Austen publishes
Sense and Sensibility

The Madison Administration Highlights

- Louisiana becomes a state (1812)
- War against England is declared (1812)
- Washington, D.C. is captured, the White House and the Capital are burned (1814)
- The "Star Spangled Banner" is written by Francis Scott Key (1814)
- The Treaty of Ghent ends the war (1814)
- The Capitol and White House are rebuilt (1815)
- Indiana becomes a state (1816)

CONNECTIONS

Inspired by the sight of the United States flag during a battle at Fort McHenry, Baltimore, in 1814, Francis Scott Key wrote The Star Spangled Banner.

James Madison was born into a well-connected family and was related on both sides to many prominent Virginians, including future president Zachary Taylor. He was born at the home of his maternal grandmother and grew up at his father's plantation, Montpelier. His father was a planter, but also a justice of the peace, vestryman of the church, and commander of the county militia. Madison was called "Jemmy" to distinguish him from the elder James. He was sent to boarding school and attended the College of New Jersey (Princeton University), graduating in two years. The future president plunged into politics when Virginia declared itself independent of Great Britain in 1776. As a state legislator, he met Thomas Jefferson--and a lifelong friendship and political alliance began between the two men. In 1786, at the Annapolis Convention, Madison and fellow delegate Alexander Hamilton proposed a constitutional convention of states to revise the Articles of Confederation. As a delegate to the Convention, Madison drafted a complete plan advocating a federal government with three main branches to provide checks and balances of power, a legislature with proportional representation based on population and procedures for admitting new states into the union. This "Virginia Plan" was adopted as the Constitution of the United States. To explain the new Constitution to the people, Madison and others wrote a series of essays, called the Federalist Papers. From 1789 to 1797, Madison served as a member of the House of Representatives. He drafted the Bill of Rights, prepared much of the legislation forming various government departments, and wrote George Washington's Inaugural and Farewell Addresses. He was Secretary of State during both of Thomas Jefferson's presidential terms.

1812
Jacob and Wilhelm Grimm publish *Grimm's Fairy Tales*

1813
Jane Austen publishes *Pride and Prejudice*

As Jefferson's choice to succeed to the presidency, Madison easily won the election of 1808. Madison inherited the nation's continuing difficulties with France and Great Britain, and on June 1,1812, Madison asked Congress for a declaration of war on Great Britain. The culmination of the War of 1812 was the capture of Washington, D.C. and the burning of the Capitol and White House by British troops. However, subsequent U.S. victories on land and sea, and a peace agreement that left the country intact, spurred national pride. The War of 1812 was seen as a second war for independence. Madison was decisively elected to a second presidential term. Following the war, he concentrated on domestic affairs including protective tariffs and infrastructure. On March 3, 1817 Madison left the presidency in the hands of his former Secretary of State, James Monroe. He retired a popular and respected man.

James Madison was a five-foot, four-inch, one hundred-pound man. To make himself appear taller, he walked on the balls of his feet. He was shy around women, but managed to woe a vivacious, charming young widow, Dolley Todd. Madison, forty-three years old, and Dolley, seventeen years his junior, married in 1794. They had no children, but Madison reared Dolley's son by her previous marriage. Dolley was attractive and witty, the perfect hostess. During the War of 1812, Dolley was forced to flee Washington as British troops approached the city. She saved what she could, most importantly, the famous portrait of George Washington.

The retired couple returned to Montpelier after living many years in Washington. Madison had a difficult time remaining financially solvent. Dolley's son, Payne Todd, had accumulated gambling debts and Madison paid to keep him out of prison. Over time, he was forced to sell his land.

Nonetheless, Madison continued his interest in his native state. He worked with Thomas Jefferson in the founding of the University of Virginia at Charlottesville, assuming the presidency of the university after Jefferson's death. Madison's last public service came in 1829, when he was elected a delegate to the Virginia State Convention.

James Madison, the Father of the Constitution and the Bill of Rights, had an eminent career before reaching the White House, but less than outstanding terms as the country's chief executive. When he died on June 28, 1836, at the age of eighty-five, he was the last of the Founding Fathers to become president and the last of all his old colleagues of the Constitutional Convention. Had he lived another year, he would have died in the fiftieth year after the framing of the Constitution.

My 2 cents
What would you nickname this president?

_____

The Author's Idea: Little Big Man

1816
Rossini's opera *The Barber of Seville* is first performed

1817
Successor president: James Monroe

JAMES MONROE

5th President of the United States

POLITICAL PARTY: Democratic-Republican
ELECTION OPPONENTS:
   1816: Rufus King, Federalist
   1820: John Quincy Adams, Federalist
TERM OF OFFICE: March 5, 1817 to March 4, 1825
VICE PRESIDENT: Daniel Tompkins

Fun Assignment!

James Monroe was a member of the Masonic Order.
What previous president was also a freemason?

George Washington

*The marker indicating the site
of James Monroe's birthplace
in Monroe Hall, Virginia.*

WIKI, COACH 1.0

Personal Profile

BORN: April 28, 1758
   Westmoreland County, Virginia
SIBLINGS: Eldest of five children
RELIGION: Episcopalian
EDUCATION: College of William and Mary
   • Left in the spring of 1776
CAREER: Lawyer

MILITARY: Lieutenant in Continental Army;
   Military Commissioner of Virginia
   with rank of lieutenant colonel
MARRIAGE: Elizabeth Kortright
   February 16, 1786, New York, New York
OFFSPRING: Two daughters, son died in
   infancy
DIED: July 4, 1831, New York, New York

*Elizabeth
Kortright
Monroe*

Visiting the President

BIRTHPLACE: Westmoreland County, Virginia
(Route 205, east towards Oak Grove; marker at site)

MUSEUM/LIBRARY: James Monroe Museum and Memorial Library
908 Charles Street, Fredericksburg, Virginia

HOMESTEAD:
- Ash Lawn-Highland, 1000 James Monroe Parkway
Charlottesville, Virginia

- Oak Hill, Loudon County, Virginia
(eight miles south of Leesburg; private
residence, not open to the public)

GRAVESITE: Hollywood Cemetery
412 South Cherry Street
Richmond, Virginia

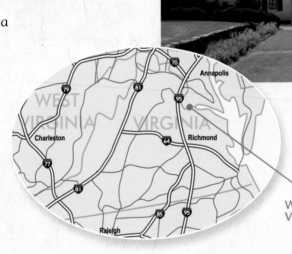

The Monroe homestead, Ash Lawn-
Highland, in Charlottesville, Virginia.
The original house is the white section
in the middle of the photograph.

Westmoreland County,
Virginia

Political Profile

- Member, Continental Congress
- United States Senator from Virginia
- Minister to France
- Governor of Virginia
- Minister to France and England
- Secretary of State
- Secretary of War
- President of the United States

1817
Construction begins on the Erie Canal
(Canal completed 1825)

1818
Mary Shelley writes
Frankenstein

The Monroe Administration Highlights

- Mississippi becomes a state (1817)
- Illinois becomes a state (1818)
- Congress establishes thirteen stripes for the U.S. flag to honor the original thirteen colonies and decrees that a new star will be added for each new state that joins the Union (1818)
- Alabama becomes a state (1819)
- Maine becomes a state (1820)
- Missouri becomes a state (1821)
- The General Survey Bill provides for improvements to the nation's roads and waterways (1824)

Statue of James Monroe at Ash Lawn-Highland, Charlottesville, Virginia.

James Monroe was the eldest son of a respectable family of modest means. In 1774, at the age of sixteen, he entered the College of William and Mary. That same year his father died. With the outbreak of the Revolutionary War, Monroe quit college in 1776 to join a Virginia regiment of the Continental Army, receiving a commission as lieutenant. Monroe saw battle in New York and was seriously wounded in 1776. The war ending, Monroe became a protégé of Thomas Jefferson. He reentered the College of William and Mary, and read law under Jefferson's direction. Monroe was elected to the United States Congress as formed under the Articles of Confederation in 1783. While serving in Congress, he married Elizabeth Kortright, the daughter of a New York businessman. Monroe did not take part in the Constitutional Convention of 1787; he opposed ratification of the new Constitution, believing that too much power had been given to the federal government at the expense of the states. Nonetheless, Monroe served as a United States senator as formed by the new Constitution. During his term, Monroe became a leading figure in the Democratic-Republican Party formed in opposition to the Federalist Party of George Washington and John Adams. Despite this fact, Monroe was appointed minister to France by President Washington in 1794. Viewed as sympathetic to the French, he was recalled in 1796. He returned to France in 1803 during the Jefferson presidency to negotiate the

1820
Washington Irving publishes *The Sketch Book*, including *Rip Van Winkle*

1822
Clement Moore writes *Twas the Night Before Christmas*

Purchase of the Louisiana Territory from Napoleon. In 1811, Monroe was appointed Secretary of State under President Madison. Monroe won his party's presidential nomination by a narrow margin, but went on to win the 1816 presidential election by a 183 to 34 electoral vote. Monroe's popularity remained strong throughout his two presidential terms. In foreign affairs, he formulated the doctrine that bears his name. The Monroe Doctrine warned European powers that the Americas were not available for colonization and that any interference by European powers in North or South America would be considered an unfriendly act. In domestic affairs, Monroe essentially followed the precepts of Jefferson and Madison; less federal involvement in states' affairs was preferable. The Missouri Compromise of 1820 maintained the balance between slave and free states. Missouri was admitted to the Union as a slave state and Maine as a free state, thus prolonging a solution to the "slavery problem." After four years in military service and forty-three years in public service, James Monroe turned the country over to the newly elected president, his former Secretary of State, John Quincy Adams. Monroe and his wife went home to Virginia.

James Monroe was the last of the revolutionary leaders to become president. He was tall and rawboned and had a quiet, natural dignity. Although the style had changed, he continued to wear knee breeches and shoes with buckles. He enhanced his popular support with months-long tours of the country; everywhere he went he was greeted with cheering crowds. As a result, Monroe's presidency came to be known as the "Era of Good Feeling." In his reelection bid in 1820, Monroe received 231 of the Electoral College's 232 votes. One elector cast his ballot for John Quincy Adams, supposedly to preserve for George Washington the honor of having received the only unanimous vote by the College. In 1825, Monroe returned to Oak Hill in Virginia. Thomas Jefferson had helped him design the mansion in the grandeur of Mount Vernon, Monticello, and Montpelier. In retirement, though, Monroe suffered financial distress. To keep solvent, he sold all his land except his plantation at Oak Hill. He then applied to Congress for reimbursement of monies he spent during his long public service. Congress acted on his claim in a partial payment, but the money came just weeks before his death.

Elizabeth Monroe died in 1830. After her death, Monroe sold Oak Hill and moved to New York City to live with his daughter Maria and her husband. Eight years later, he died on the 4th of July, the third president to die on the anniversary of independence. A public eulogy was held in New York City Hall. Following a seventy-three gun salute for each year of his life, Monroe's body was placed in his son-in-law's family burial vault. On the centenary of his birth, April 1858, the Virginia legislature ordered that all deceased Virginians who had been president of the United States should rest in Virginia soil. Monroe's body was removed to Richmond, Virginia, and placed in a tomb befitting a chief executive. James Monroe came home for the last time.

My 2 cents
What would you nickname this president?

_____

The Author's Idea: Jefferson's Neighbor

WILLIAM HENRY HARRISON
9th President of the United States

POLITICAL PARTY: Whig
ELECTION OPPONENT: Martin Van Buren, Democrat
TERM OF OFFICE: March 4, 1841 to April 4, 1841
VICE PRESIDENT: John Tyler

Berkeley Plantation in Charles City County, Virginia, was the birthplace of William Henry Harrison

Fun Assignment!

At age sixty-eight, Harrison was the oldest man to become president. Who was elected president that passed that record?

Ronald Reagan, at the age of sixty-nine

Personal Profile

BORN: February 9, 1773, Berkeley Plantation, Charles City County, Virginia
SIBLINGS: Youngest of seven children
RELIGION: Episcopalian
EDUCATION: Hampden-Sydney College 1787-1790, did not graduate
CAREER: Politician

MILITARY: Ensign, United States Army, assigned to Ohio Territory (1791); rose to major general and commander in the Northwest (1812)
MARRIAGE: Anna Tuthill Symmes November 25, 1795, North Bend, Ohio
OFFSPRING: Four daughters, six sons
DIED: April 4, 1841, Washington, D.C.

Anna Tuthill Symmes Harrison

Visiting the President

BIRTHPLACE: Berkeley Plantation
   12602 Harrison Landing Road, Charles City, Virginia
HOMESTEAD/MUSEUM: Grouseland
   3 West Scott Street, Vencennes, Indiana
GRAVESITE: Harrison Tomb State Memorial
   Cliff Road (off Route 50), North Bend, Ohio

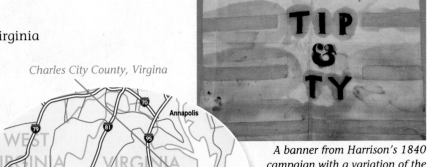
Charles City County, Virginia

A banner from Harrison's 1840 campaign with a variation of the famous slogan "Tippecanoe and Tyler Too."

Tell me more!

What is the Tenskwatawa curse?

American folklore has long circulated the story of a curse put on United States presidents by Tecumseh or his half-brother, Tenskwatawa. The curse is on presidents elected in years ending with a zero. Harrison was its first victim, elected in 1840, followed by Lincoln (1860), Garfield (1880), McKinley (1900), Harding (1920), Franklin Roosevelt (1940), and Kennedy (1960).

Political Profile

- Northwest Territory delegate to Congress
- United States Representative from Ohio
- Member, Ohio state senate
- United States senator from Ohio
- Minister to Columbia
- President of the United States

This statue of Harrison as a General is in Cincinnati, Ohio.

1841
The first U.S. steam fire engine
is tested in New York City

The Harrison Administration Highlights

- The Supreme Court affirms that the black slaves who had seized the slave ship Amistad were free and need not be returned to the Spanish in Cuba who claimed them as property (1841)

Harrison's memorial and tomb North Bend, Ohio.

William Henry Harrison was born at Berkeley, a plantation on the James River in Virginia. His father, Benjamin Harrison V was a wealthy planter and a signer of the Declaration of Independence. Harrison attended college for three years and briefly studied medicine under Benjamin Rush in Philadelphia. When his father died in 1791, the eighteen-year-old Harrison joined the United States Army. He was assigned to duty on the northwest frontier and fought in a number of battles against Indian tribes. He was made commander of Fort Washington in the Ohio Territory in 1795 at the age of twenty-two. While there he met Anna Symmes, the daughter of a judge who opposed their courtship, fearing frontier life would be too difficult for his daughter. The couple eloped in 1795. Bored with garrison duty, Harrison resigned from the Army and moved his family from Fort Washington to North Bend, Ohio. That same year Harrison was appointed secretary of the Northwest Territory.

Over the next fourteen years, twelve of which he served as territorial governor of Indiana, Harrison acquired land from Native Americans through various treaties. In 1811, the famous Chief Tecumseh took a stand against further white expansion and amassed his followers on the banks of the Tippecanoe River in Indiana. Harrison led 1,000 soldiers against Tecumseh. The Battle of Tippecanoe was bloody with heavy casualties on both sides, but Harrison's troops prevailed. The battle made Harrison famous and led to his appointment as brigadier general and commander of the Army in the northwest during the War of 1812.

Harrison resigned his commission in 1814 and sought political office. He held various state and federal government positions, culminating as the first United States minister to Columbia. In 1840, at its first national presidential convention, the newly formed Whig Party united behind Harrison and his running mate, John Tyler. The new type of campaigning used by the Whigs reached the masses and involved a large segment of the population in the election. Drawing from Harrison's nationally known military victory at the Battle of Tippecanoe, the party introduced the slogan, "Tippecanoe and Tyler too." When the Democrats made fun of Harrison, saying he belonged in a log cabin with a barrel of hard cider, the Whigs turned the tables, using the log cabin as a symbol and holding rallies in large log cabins built for the occasion. Hard cider became the popular drink at these rallies.

Harrison's Democratic opponent, sitting president Martin Van Buren, was portrayed as a luxury-loving decadent while Harrison was portrayed as a frontiersman and self-made man. In reality, Harrison was a pedigreed aristocrat born in Virginia. The Harrison/Van Buren presidential election was the first in which any candidate received over one million votes. Harrison won the popular vote by a narrow margin, but captured 234 electoral votes to Van Buren's 60. President-elect Harrison traveled by riverboat, carriage, and train to Washington. Along the way, he was greeted by large, enthusiastic crowds. At one stop he made a prophetic statement: "… perhaps this may be the last time I may have the pleasure of speaking to you on earth or seeing you; I will bid you farewell, if forever, fare thee well."

Inauguration Day, March 4, 1841 was cold and blustery. **William Henry Harrison** stood before the crowd hatless and coatless. The 68-year-old newly elected president delivered an 8,445-word, 105-minute address. Briefly after, he came down with a cold that developed into pneumonia and within days he died, a mere month into his presidency. The Harrison presidency is riddled with dubious distinctions. He was the first president-elect to arrive in Washington by train; he was the oldest elected president to enter the White House (until Ronald Reagan in 1981); he delivered the longest inaugural address in presidential history; and he was the first president to die in office, hence serving the shortest term in presidential history.

Harrison and his Whig Party introduced an entirely new way of campaigning: bands, torchlight parades and political songs, banners and floats, the first campaign slogan, and a slang expression still in our lexicon: "Keep the ball rolling." The Party virtually turned politics into entertainment--a game everybody could play. Almost a million more persons went to the polls in 1840 than in 1836. The president, who had been elected in the most spectacular political campaign to date, died in office with little to show that he had ever been there…except 8,455 words.

My 2 cents
What would you nickname this president?

_____

The Author's Idea: Tippecanoe

JOHN TYLER
10th President of the United States

POLITICAL PARTY: Whig
ELECTION OPPONENT: None
TERM OF OFFICE: April 6, 1841 to March 3, 1845
VICE PRESIDENT: None

Fun Assignment!

John Tyler was born in 1790, during George Washington's presidency; his youngest daughter died in 1947. Who was president that year?

Harry Truman

CONNECTIONS
P. T. Barnum purchased the American Museum in New York City in 1841 and began exhibiting unusual people, starting with one he called "Tom Thumb." This character represents a fictional hero in English folklore as far back as the 16th century. The name is often applied to people or objects of small stature.

Personal Profile

BORN: March 29, 1790, Greenway Plantation Charles City County, Virginia
SIBLINGS: Sixth of eight children
RELIGION: Episcopalian
EDUCATION: College of William and Mary; graduated 1807
CAREER: Lawyer
MILITARY: Captain, Charles City County Company, War of 1812

MARRIAGES:
• Letitia Christian, March 29, 1813 Cedar Grove, New Kent County, Virginia
• Julia Gardiner, June 26, 1844 Church of the Ascension New York, New York

OFFSPRING:
• With Letitia: 8 children (one died at 3 mos.)
• With Julia: seven children

DIED: January 18, 1862, Richmond, Virginia

Letitia Christian Tyler

Julia Gardiner Tyler

1841
Previous president:
William Henry Harrison

1841
James Fenimore Cooper publishes *The Deerslayer*

Visiting the President

BIRTHPLACE: Greenway, John Tyler Memorial Highway (Virginia Route 5), Charles City, Virginia (privately owned, closed to public, marker at site)

RESIDENCE: Sherwood Forest Plantation 14501 John Tyler Memorial Highway, Charles City, Virginia

GRAVESITE: Hollywood Cemetery 412 South Cherry Street, Richmond, Virginia

Charles City, Virginia

Tell me more!

Hail to the Chief

The custom of playing *Hail to the Chief* whenever a president arrives at a state function was begun by Tyler's second wife, Julia.

Tyler's grave at Hollywood Cemetery, Richmond, Virginia.

Political Profile

- Member, Virginia House of Delegates
- Member, United States House of Representatives
- Governor of Virginia
- Member, United States Senate
- Vice President of the United States
- President of the United States

1841
Horace Greeley begins publication of the *New York Tribune* newspaper

1842
The New York Philharmonic Society is founded

1842
P.T. Barnum purchases the American Museum in New York City

The Tyler Administration Highlights

- The Preemptive Act of 1841 stipulated that settlers on land that had been surveyed by the government had the first right to buy the land after a 14-month residence on it. (1841)
- Florida becomes a state (1845)
- For the first time, Congress overrides a presidential veto (1845)

John Tyler was born in Charles City County, Virginia. He was the son of a distinguished planter-politician and graduated from the College of William and Mary in 1807 at the age of seventeen. He then read law under his father's tutelage. Tyler was admitted to the Virginia Bar at the age of nineteen. He launched his political career by winning election to the Virginia legislature. On his twenty-third birthday, he married Letitia Christian. In 1816, Tyler was elected to the United States House of Representatives.

While serving in the House, he resisted attempts by the federal government to restrict slavery and voted against the Missouri Compromise. Disgruntled, he declined to run for a second term in the House. However, by 1823 he was again in politics, first in the Virginia state legislature, then in the Virginia governor's seat, and finally in the United States Senate in 1826. Tyler was elected to these positions as a Democratic-Republican. He objected to some of President Jackson's policies and was the only senator to vote against the Force Bill that gave the president authority to use military force, if necessary, to collect federal revenues. When the Senate censured Jackson, Tyler voted with the majority. When a resolution was put forward to expunge Jackson's censure, Tyler was instructed to vote for the resolution. He would not comply and resigned in 1836.

Tyler then joined the newly formed Whig party. In 1840, at the Whig National Convention, Tyler was

TYLER RECEIVING THE NEWS OF HARRISON'S DEATH.

Vice President Tyler receives news of President Harrison's death from Chief Clerk of the State Department Fletcher Webster.

1843
Charles Dickens publishes
A Christmas Carol

1844
Samuel Morse transmits the first telegraph message from Washington to Baltimore

1844
Charles Goodyear patents the process for vulcanizing rubber

nominated for Vice President as the running mate for William Henry Harrison. They subsequently won the election. However, on April 5, 1841, Tyler learned the startling news of President Harrison's death. Tyler was the first "accidental" president, having come to office due to the death of a president under which he served. This set the precedent for succession on the death of a sitting president. As president, Tyler ignored the Whig platform, twice vetoing legislation. His Whig counterparts were outraged and officially expelled Tyler from the party.

Nonetheless, Tyler was able to claim some accomplishments. For example, he oversaw a treaty with Great Britain delineating the border between the United States and British-held Canada. Also, a treaty was negotiated with China, opening trade at Chinese ports. His pro-slavery stance, though, influenced other decisions. In 1844, the Republic of Texas applied for admission to the Union as a slave state. Despite objections, Tyler signed the resolution that sanctioned the annexation, one of his last acts as president. The election year of 1844 found Tyler in the odd position of having no party willing to nominate him for a full term. Unsuccessful in his bid to retain the White House, Tyler relinquished the presidency to the Democrat, James Polk, on March 4, 1845. Tyler, the president without a party, immediately left Washington for his beloved Virginia.

John Tyler was a good-looking, courteous, soft-spoken gentleman who appeared younger than his age. He wrote poetry and played the violin. In 1813, Tyler married Letitia Christian. Between 1815 and 1830, the couple had eight children. When Tyler entered the White House, Letitia was ill, having suffered a stroke. She died in 1842. Tyler was the first president whose wife died while he was in office. In 1842, Tyler met Julia Gardiner, a New York socialite thirty years his junior. Allegedly, Tyler proposed quickly, but she declined until tragedy struck. In 1844, Julia's father was killed in an accidental gun explosion. Tyler and Julia married several months later. Julia was young, beautiful, and wealthy. It is said that in the final days of Tyler's presidency she held a lavish party in his honor, saying, "They can't say the president doesn't have a party." Tyler and Julia had seven children.

At home in Virginia, Tyler continued to support states' rights and slavery. When Virginia joined the other seceding states, Tyler was elected to the House of Representatives of the Confederate Congress. He went to Richmond to join the new government. He died on January 18, 1862, at the age of seventy-one, without ever taking his seat in Congress. His body lay in state in Richmond. The Virginia House of Delegates paid tribute. No official notice of his death was taken by the United States government, his allegiance to the Confederacy regarded as subversive to the Union. Outlaw to the end, John Tyler loved his country, but he loved his native state more.

My 2 cents

What would you nickname this president?

_____

The Author's Idea: All in the Family

1845
Successor president:
James Polk

ZACHARY TAYLOR

12th President of the United States

POLITICAL PARTY: Whig
ELECTION OPPONENTS:
Lewis Cass, Democratic
Martin Van Buren, Free Soil
TERM OF OFFICE: March 5, 1849 to July 9, 1850
VICE PRESIDENT: Millard Fillmore

Fun Assignment!

Taylor's daughter, Sarah married the future president of the Confederacy. Can you name him?

Jefferson Davis

Zachary Taylor's childhood home, Springfield, in Louisville, Kentucky.

Personal Profile

BORN: November 24, 1784
Montebello, Barboursville, Virginia
SIBLINGS: First of nine children
RELIGION: Episcopalian
EDUCATION: Common school
CAREER: Planter
MILITARY: Appointed first lieutenant (1808); rose to brigadier general (1846)

MARRIAGE: Margaret Mackall Smith
June 21, 1810, Jefferson County, Kentucky
OFFSPRING: 6 children, 4 lived into adulthood
DIED: July 9, 1850, Washington, DC

Daguerreotype photo of Margaret Mackall Smith Taylor

1849
Previous president:
James Polk

1849
Harriet Tubman escapes
from slavery

Visiting the President

BIRTHPLACE: Montebello, Highway 33,
   Virginia (privately owned, marker at site)
HOMESTEAD: Springfield, 5608 Apache Road
   Louisville, Kentucky (privately owned)
GRAVESITE: Zachary Taylor National
   Cemetery
   4701 Brownsboro Road, Louisville, Kentucky

Barboursville, Virginia

1848 portrait of Zachary Taylor
by artist Joseph Henry Bush.

Tell me more!

A Frugal Man

Taylor was mailed notification of his nomination for president, but refused to accept it because there was postage due on the letter.

Political Profile

- President of the United States

1850	1850	1850
The first medical school for women opens in Pennsylvania	Nathaniel Hawthorne publishes *The Scarlet Letter*	The U.S. census of 1850 reports a population of 23.1 million

The Taylor Administration Highlights

- The Clayton-Bulwer Treaty with Great Britain guarantees access to the future Panama Canal to all nations (1850)
- Senator Henry Clay proposes the Compromise of 1850; provides for the admission of California into the union as a free state, formation of New Mexico as a territory with the option of slavery if admitted to the union, and harsher fugitive slave laws (1850)

Zachary Taylor's mausoleum in the Zachary Taylor National Cemetery in Louisville, Kentucky.

Zachary Taylor was born at Montebello, a plantation owned by a close relative. His parents came from established and prosperous families. When less than a year old, Taylor's family moved from Orange County, Virginia to the frontier post of Louisville, Kentucky. They moved to a parcel of land granted to his father, a lieutenant colonel in the Continental Army, as a bonus for his service. Taylor had limited education. However, in May 1808, through the influence of his cousin (Secretary of State James Madison), the 23-year-old Taylor received a commission as a first lieutenant in the Army.

In 1810, Taylor married Margaret Smith from Maryland. While stationed at Fort Harrison, Indiana, in 1812, Taylor organized the successful defense of the fort against an attack by Native Americans, resulting in his promotion to the rank of major. Over the next two decades, Taylor served at various garrisons and led forces in Indian campaigns, including the Black Hawk War (1832) and the Second Seminole War (1835). Taylor earned the name, "Old Rough and Ready." He was unkempt, used colorful language, and was willing to be in the thick of the battle. Taylor's national fame came during the Mexican-American War. After winning significant victories, President James Polk realized Taylor's growing popularity with the public and began to view him as a potential political foe. Polk ordered Taylor to remain in northern Mexico. Instead, Taylor engaged Mexican troops at the Battle of Buena Vista in February 1847. With his regulars significantly stripped by Polk, Taylor gallantly withstood an attack by a 20,000-member Mexican force. However, with the escalating tension between himself and Polk, Taylor resigned from the Army.

At this time, Taylor's standing as a military hero convinced the Whig Party that he would be an excellent presidential candidate. He was nominated at the Whig Convention in 1848 with Millard Fillmore as his running mate. In the first presidential election in which the entire nation voted on the same day, Taylor won by a narrow margin. Immediately,

1850	1850	1850
Levi Strauss makes his first pair of blue jeans	The first modern safety pin is designed by Walter Hunt	Elizabeth Barrett Browning publishes *Sonnets from the Portuguese*

a controversy erupted over the new territories acquired from Mexico. The issue was not only slavery, but also the potential disturbance to the balance of power between slave and free states. When California sought admission to the union as a free state, southern leaders called for a secession movement. With military bluntness, Taylor declared: "I will command the army in person and hang any man taken in treason." Although a Southern slave owner himself, Taylor opposed the spread of slavery into the new territories. A proposed Compromise of 1850 suggested California enter the Union as a free state and New Mexico as a United States territory, to decide the slavery issue at a later date. Taylor objected to the Compromise.

On July 4, 1850, the 65-year-old Taylor attended a ceremony at the Washington Monument in the sweltering heat. After sitting hours in the blazing sun, he returned to the White House. He consumed a large quantity of cherries and a considerable amount of ice-cold milk. Within hours, he became seriously ill. Taylor sensed the end, saying: "I am about to die." Four doctors tried, but could not save him. Within five days, Taylor was gone.

Zachary Taylor grew up in a frontier environment. He learned to ride, shoot and hunt. He followed in his father's footsteps, joining the Army at the age of twenty-three. Short and stocky, he had unusually short legs, needing assistance from an orderly to mount his horse. He was a forty-year career officer and moved often. His wife, Margaret, endured the hardships of an army life; she was in poor health during her husband's short term in office. Taylor despised politics and said he was not qualified to be president. No man ever entered the office knowing less about what he was supposed to do. He was days late in officially accepting his presidential nomination because he refused to pay the postage due on his formal letter of notification. Taylor was expected to favor slavery, but instead he tried to prevent its extension westward. He might have vetoed the Compromise of 1850--had he lived.

On July 13, 1850, more than 100,000 people lined the funeral route in the nation's capital. The catafalque was drawn by eight white horses accompanied by grooms dressed in white. The hearse was followed by dignitaries, military units, and the president's beloved horse, "Old Whitey," which had grazed on the White House lawn. The procession stretched for two miles.

The military hero turned president was committed to national service and to the preservation of the Union. With only one year and 127 days in the White House, he had little impact on the highest office of the land. It has been said that, "Old soldiers never die, they just fade away." This was certainly true of Taylor, who is one of the least remembered presidents today.

My 2 cents

What would you nickname this president?

_____

The Author's Idea: Postage Due

ULYSSES S. GRANT

18th President of the United States

POLITICAL PARTY: Republican

ELECTION OPPONENTS:

  1868: Horatio Seymour, Democrat

  1872: Horace Greeley, Liberal Republican/Democratic

TERM OF OFFICE: March 4, 1869 to March 5, 1877

VICE PRESIDENTS:

  1868: Schuyler Colfax

  1872: Henry Wilson (died 1875, not replaced)

The birthplace of Ulysses Grant, Point Pleasant, Ohio

WIKI, Greg Hume

Fun Assignment!

Where is Grant's Tomb?

Grant's Tomb is in New York City, overlooking the Hudson River. New York City was one of three burial sites considered by Grant himself.

Personal Profile

BORN: April 27, 1822; Point Pleasant, Ohio

SIBLINGS: Eldest of six children

RELIGION: Methodist

EDUCATION: U.S. Military Academy, West Point; graduated 1843

CAREER: Farmer, real estate agent, clerk at leather store

MILITARY: Commissioned 2nd lieutenant; rose to lieutenant general (1864)

MARRIAGE: Julia Boggs Dent, August 22, 1848, St. Louis, Missouri

OFFSPRING: Three sons, one daughter

DIED: July 23, 1885 Mount McGregor, New York

Julia Boggs Dent Grant

1869
Previous president:
Andrew Johnson

1869
Louisa May Alcott publishes
Little Women

1869
Leo Tolstoy completes
War and Peace

Visiting the President

BIRTHPLACE: Grant Birthplace
1551 State Route 232, Point Pleasant, Ohio
BOYHOOD HOME: The Grant Boyhood Home
219 East Grant Avenue, Georgetown, Ohio
HOMESTEAD: Ulysses S. Grant National Historic Site
7400 Grant Road, St. Louis, Missouri
GRAVESITE: General Grant National Memorial
Riverside Drive and 122nd Street
New York City, New York

Grant is one of the few presidents to be portrayed on a U.S. postage stamp more than twice—he was so honored three times.

Tell me more!

What decision saved Grant's life?

President Abraham Lincoln invited General and Mrs. Grant to accompany him to the theater on the night of April 14, 1865. Grant declined the invitation, thereby avoiding certain assassination.

Grant's boyhood home in Georgetown, Ohio.

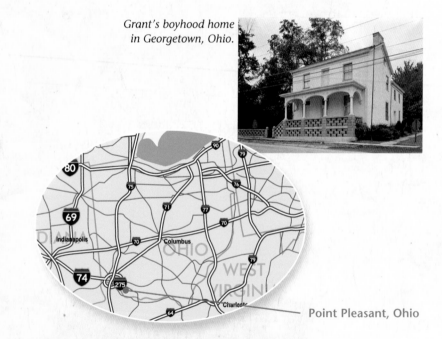

Point Pleasant, Ohio

Political Profile

- President of the United States

1869	1869	1870
The first American all-professional baseball team, the Cincinnati Red Socks, is formed	The Transcontinental Railroad is completed	Construction on the Brooklyn Bridge is begun

The Grant Administration Highlights

- Wyoming Territory grants women the right to vote (1869)
- The Department of Justice is created (1870)
- The Fifteen Amendment to the Constitution (right to vote) is ratified (1870)
- Act to establish the first national park, Yellowstone, is signed (1872)
- Colorado becomes a state (1876)

An 1885 engraving titled "Grant from West Point to Appomattox." Depictions include the Battle of Shiloh; the Siege of Vicksburg; the Battle of Chattanooga; appointment as Lieutenant General by Abraham Lincoln; and the Surrender of General Robert E. Lee at Appomattox Court House.

A year after Hiram Ulysses Grant was born, his father moved the family to Georgetown, Ohio, to operate a tannery and farm. "Lyss," as Grant was called, preferred farming to working in the tannery and he did most of the plowing. He also had a reputation for being a good horseback rider and horse trainer. In 1839, Grant's father arranged an appointment for his son at West Point. When Grant arrived at the academy, he found that he had been registered as Ulysses Simpson Grant. He preferred the name because the initials of his given name lent themselves to the nickname "HUG." Instead his classmates called him "Uncle Sam." Upon graduation, Grant, who loved horses, hoped for cavalry duty, but instead was posted to the infantry. Although assigned quartermaster during the Mexican-American War, Grant fought under such popular military generals as Zachary Taylor and Winfield Scott.

In 1848, Grant married Julia Boggs Dent, despite the reluctance of her father who did not want his daughter

1870
The United States Weather Bureau is established

1870
The U.S. census shows a population of 19.8 million people

1871
The Great Chicago Fire nearly destroys Chicago

to marry a poor soldier. Grant's abolitionist parents refused to attend the wedding because the bride's father was a slaveholder. After the war, Grant was stationed as far away as California. Unable to bring his family to him, and being lonely and bored, he turned to alcohol. In 1854, he resigned his commission at the request of his commanding officer. Over the next thirteen years Grant was dogged with failure. He tried farming, real estate, and clerking, finally working at his father's leather business. When President Abraham Lincoln called for volunteers to defend the Union, the 39-year-old Grant saw an opportunity. Initially appointed a colonel, he rose through the ranks to lieutenant general and commander of the Union forces. Grant's troops took heavy losses and some called him a butcher, but Grant was an outstanding tactician and a relentless fighter. Lincoln defended Grant saying: "I can't spare this man—he fights."

Ulysses Grant and his wife Julia gave each other life-long loyalty. Julia rejoiced in her husband's fame as a victorious general and enthusiastically supported his run for president. She described her time in Washington as "the happiest period" of her life. She extravagantly and expensively remodeled the White House, entertained lavishly, and dressed in the best finery. When Grant left office in 1877, Julia followed reluctantly. Grant, Julia, and their son Jesse made a triumphant world tour for two years. On his return, Grant realized he had to find a way to make a living. He had no profession other than military and no experience in business.

Grant invested all his money in a brokerage firm in which one of his sons was a partner. By 1884, the firm, overdrawn and unable to meet its obligations, went bankrupt. One day Grant had an estimated one and a half million dollars, the next he was destitute. To earn money, Grant wrote articles on his military battles for a popular magazine. Although he had no writing experience, his articles were well received. Samuel Clemens, who wrote under the pen name of Mark Twain, was a publisher and a great admirer of the general and his writing style. Clemens negotiated an agreement with Grant to publish his memoir. That same year Grant was diagnosed with throat cancer. Foremost in Grant's mind was the financial security of his wife and family.

Ulysses S. Grant and his family at their cottage at Long Branch, New Jersey, 1870.

The completion of his memoir became paramount. The old soldier showed the tenacity and courage of the past. He fought a battle against pain and a race against time. He managed to complete his memoir within a year and only weeks before his death. Samuel Clemens turned the book's profits over to Julia, a sum exceeding half a million dollars. In death, Ulysses S. Grant provided Julia's financial security and his memoir remains to this day one of the classics of military literature.

1872
Lewis Clark publishes *Through the Looking Glass*

1874
The Women's Christian Temperance Union is founded

1875
The first Kentucky Derby is run

Yellowstone National Park was signed into law in 1872 by President Grant.

At the end of the war, Grant was a national and international hero. His hometown of Galena built him a house, Philadelphia presented him with a mansion, and New York gave him a cash gift, raised by popular subscription, of $105,000. Although never interested in politics, Grant accepted the Republican presidential nomination and won the presidency convincingly under the campaign slogan: "Let us have peace." With no political savvy, Grant's party treated him like a puppet and Grant surrounded himself with untried, dishonest, and/or opportunistic family and former military associates. Both of Grant's presidential terms were racked with corruption, scandal, illegal dealings, fraud, and financial panic. Investigations led to resignations, censorships, and court cases. However, Grant himself was honest. Despite the turmoil and disgrace in his administration, when his second term ended, he was still a very popular man.

The General Grant National Memorial, also known as "Grant's Tomb," in New York City.

My 2 cents

What would you nickname this president?

_____

The Author's Idea: Lincoln's General

1876
Mark Twain publishes
The Adventures of Tom Sawyer

1876
Alexander Graham Bell
patents the telephone

1877
Successor president:
Rutherford B. Hayes

115

The United States Military Academy at West Point is located in New York's Hudson River Valley. Former members of the Corps include Ulysses S. Grant and Dwight D. Eisenhoower.

116

RUTHERFORD B. HAYES
19th President of the United States

POLITCAL PARTY: Republican
ELECTION OPPONENT: Samuel Tilden, Democrat
TERM OF OFFICE: March 4, 1877 to March 3, 1881
VICE PRESIDENT: William Wheeler

*The Rutherford B. Hayes
birthplace in Delaware, Ohio.*

Fun Assignment!

Of the five future presidents who served in the Civil War, Hayes
was the only one wounded. Can you name the other four future
presidents?

Ulysses S. Grant, James Garfield, Benjamin Harrison and William McKinley

Personal Profile

BORN: October 4, 1822, Delaware, Ohio
SIBLINGS: Youngest of five children
RELIGION: Unaffiliated, attended
   Methodist Church
EDUCATION:
   Kenyon College, graduated 1842
   Harvard Law School, graduated 1845
CAREER: Lawyer

MILITARY: Brevet major;
   rose in rank to brigadier general
MARRIAGE: Lucy Ware Webb
   December 30, 1852; Cincinnati, Ohio
OFFSPRING: Seven sons, one daughter
DIED: January 17, 1893
   Spiegel Grove, Fremont, Ohio

*Lucy Ware
Webb Hayes*

1877
Previous president:
Ulysses S. Grant

1877
The first Westminster Dog
Show is held

117

Visiting the President

BIRTHPLACE: East William St., Delaware, Ohio; marker at site
RESIDENCE/LIBRARY/MUSEUM/GRAVESITE:
The Rutherford B. Hayes Presidential Center
Spiegel Grove, Hayes and Buckland Avenues
Fremont, Ohio

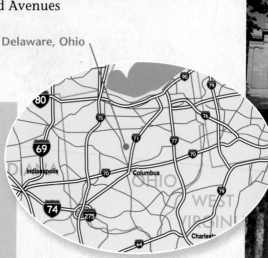

Delaware, Ohio

Tell me more!

When was the first time the Secret Service was used to protect a president?

After being declared president by committee, Hayes received death threats. It was suggested he go to Washington in secret. Instead, Hayes rode into town in an open carriage, surrounded by six special government agents--it was the first time the "Secret Service" was assigned to protect a president.

The Rutherford B. Hayes Presidential Center in Fremont, Ohio. On the same property is the Hayes home (below).

Political Profile

- Member, United States House of Representatives
- Governor of Ohio
- President of the United States

1878	1878	1878
Thomas Edison patents a "talking machine," a phonograph	Gilbert and Sullivan premiere *H.M.S. Pinafore*	The American Bar Association is founded

The Hayes Administration Highlights

- Frederick Douglass is appointed marshal of Washington, D.C. (1877)
- An 1877 Executive Order forbids federal employees from political involvement in an effort to end civil service corruption
- The Nez Perce tribe battles U.S. army forces in northwestern U.S. territory (1877)
- Railroad workers strike and clash with federal troops (1877)
- The Timber and Stone Act of 1878 provides for the sale of western land deemed unfit for farming, but fit for timbering and mining in 160-acre parcels at $2.50 per acre

Official White House portrait of President Hayes.

Rutherford B. Hayes was born to his widowed mother in Delaware, Ohio. His father left a large enough estate to provide for the family. Hayes's uncle became his guardian and surrogate father. Hayes, called "Rud" as a boy, was sickly and over-protected by his mother. In 1842, Hayes graduated from Kenyon College in Ohio as the class valedictorian. He began to read law, but his uncle thought he should acquire a formal education in law. Therefore, Rutherford attended Harvard University and graduated in 1845. He began a law practice, eventually in Cincinnati, earning a solid reputation for himself. He also served as a volunteer attorney for the Underground Railroad.

When Hayes was thirty, he married 21-year-old Lucy Ware Webb, the daughter of a physician. Hayes entered politics in 1858 as city solicitor and helped found the Republican Party in Ohio. With the outbreak of the Civil War, Hayes joined the Ohio Volunteer Infantry as a major and distinguished himself repeatedly. He was wounded five times and had his horse shot out from under him four times. He was promoted to brigadier general.

While still in the Army, Hayes was nominated for the United States House of Representatives. He replied tersely: "Thanks, I have other business just now," and refused to campaign. He was elected anyway. Hayes resigned from Congress to run for governor of Ohio. He served two terms only to return for an interrupted third term in 1875. Hayes espoused hospital, prison, school, and civil service reform. Republican Party organizers viewed him as a presidential candidate for 1876, as he was untainted by the corrupt Grant administration. Hayes was elected on the seventh ballot to head the Republican's presidential ticket. His Democratic opponent was Samuel Tilden, who won the popular vote but only 184 of the required 185 electoral votes. The Republicans disputed twenty of the casted electoral votes. The

1878	1879	1879
The artificial sweetener Saccharin is discovered	Frank Woolworth opens his first 5 and 10 cent store	Gilbert and Sullivan premiere *The Priates of Penzance*

country was without a president-elect for months. The Democrats agreed to allow an electoral commission to determine the election outcome if the Republicans would agree to withdraw federal troops from the South. A fifteen-member commission finally determined Hayes the winner by a margin of only one vote. This was just fifty-six hours before the inauguration was to take place. As a result, Hayes served under a cloud, was called "His Fraudulency," and suffered a Congressional motion to investigate the 1876 election. Despite his efforts, Hayes was unable to overcome the stigma of the political bargain that brought him to the White House. He did honor that bargain, though, and withdrew troops from the South, ending Reconstruction.

With a Democratic-controlled House of Representatives and Senate the last two years of his term, Hayes had little chance to obtain passage of any legislation he favored. The Hayes Administration was above patronage, partisanship, and political self-interest — a direct contrast to that of his predecessor. Hayes declined to run for a second term. He was at the height of his limited popularity just as he was leaving office. Hayes had shown the American people that he was a man of integrity, character, and honesty.

The red-headed, blue-eyed **Rutherford B. Hayes** was regarded by his acquaintances as a rather stuffy fellow. As a Civil War warrior, he brought forth qualities he never knew he had, leading charges and joining in hand-to-hand combat. As a governor, he ran such a strict government that some unhappy politicians called him "Old Granny." In the White House, he put forward legislation he knew had little likelihood to move forward. In retirement, he was involved in numerous educational and humanitarian projects and charitable enterprises. Few men in the nation had been involved in as many civic and reform movements as the nineteenth president of the United States.

Rutherford B. Hayes was the first president to graduate from a formal law school. His wife, Lucy, was the first wife of a president to have a college degree. Lucy shared many of her husband's interests: visiting hospitals, mental institutions, and orphanages. She was a popular, cheery, and intelligent hostess. Although she was given the nickname "Lemonade Lucy," it was actually her husband who would not allow alcohol to be served in the White House -- after an invited guest, a congressman, became intoxicated. The first family spent evenings singing hymns, and on their twenty-fifth wedding anniversary, the couple happily renewed their wedding vows. Lucy died in 1889 and was deeply missed by her husband. Hayes said when Lucy died: "The charm of my life left me." In 1893, just prior to his death, he said: "I know I'm going where Lucy is."

My 2 cents
What would you nickname this president?

_____

The Author's Idea: Lemonade Lucy's Man

1880
The 1880 census shows the U.S. population as 50 million

1881
Successor president: James A. Garfield

JAMES A. GARFIELD

20th President of the United States

POLITICAL PARTY: Republican
ELECTION OPPONENT: Winfield Hancock, Democrat
TERM OF OFFICE: March 4, 1881 to September 19, 1881
VICE PRESIDENT: Chester A. Arthur

Fun Assignment!

The music at Garfield's inauguration and inaugural ball was played by what famous director and band?

John Phillip Sousa and the Marine Corps Band

A replica log cabin sits on the site of the James A. Garfield birthplace in Cuyahoga County, Ohio.

Personal Profile

BORN: November 19, 1831
   Orange Township, Cuyahoga County, Ohio
SIBLINGS: Youngest of five children
RELIGION: Disciples of Christ
EDUCATION: Williams College; graduated 1856
CAREER: Teacher, ordained minister, college president, lawyer

MILITARY: Lieutenant
   rose in rank to major general
MARRIAGE: Lucretia Rudolph
   November 11, 1858, Hiram, Ohio
OFFSPRING: Five sons, two daughters
DIED: September 19, 1881
   Elberon, New Jersey

Lucretia Rudolph Garfield

Visiting the President

BIRTHPLACE: Route 91
Moreland Hills, Ohio (marker at site)
RESIDENCE/LIBRARY/MUSEUM:
James A. Garfield National Historic Site
8095 Mentor Avenue, Mentor, Ohio
GRAVESITE: Lake View Cemetery
12316 Euclid Avenue, Cleveland, Ohio

Moreland Hills, Ohio

CONNECTIONS

Clara Barton founded the American Red Cross in May 1881. The American Red Cross is a volunteer-led humanitarian organization providing emergency assistance, disaster relief, and aide inside the United States. Millions of volunteers have provided services during more than 67,000 disasters. One of the first major relief efforts was the Johnston Flood of 1889.

Lawnfield, the Garfield home at the James A. Garfield National Historic Site in Mentor, Ohio.

WIKI, Andrew DeFratis

Political Profile

- Member, Ohio State Senate
- Member, United States House of Representatives
- Member, United States Senate
- President of the United States

1881
Clara Barton founds the
American Red Cross

The Garfield Administration Highlights

- Frederick Douglass is appointed recorder of deeds (1881)
- Chief Sitting Bull surrenders to federal troops (1881)

James Garfield was born in a log cabin in Orange County, Ohio. Both his parents could trace their heritage back to seventeenth century settlers in America. Before Garfield was two years old, his father died. Though poor, Garfield's mother kept her family together. They worked the farm, barely eking out a living. Garfield, recognizably intelligent, attended local schools and developed a great love of reading. At seventeen, Garfield worked as a sailor and then as a tow boy, driving mules along the Ohio Canal. Disenchanted, he turned to education, briefly attending Geauga Seminary and the Hiram Institute. During this time, Garfield converted to the Disciples of Christ and was a volunteer preacher for the sect. He then left for Massachusetts to attend Williams College and graduated second in his class. After graduating, Garfield returned to Ohio to teach Latin and Greek at Hiram Institute; by 1857, at the age of twenty-five, he had become president of the school.

During this period, he studied law and was admitted to the Ohio bar in 1861. In 1858, Garfield married Lucretia Rudolph, a farmer's daughter and former classmate. He was elected to the Ohio state legislature in 1859 where he spoke out against slavery and secession and campaigned for Abraham Lincoln. During the Civil War, Garfield distinguished himself in the Union militia, demonstrating bravery under fire; he rose in military rank rapidly. While on active duty, Garfield was elected to the United States Congress. He resigned from the Army in December 1863 to serve in the House of Representatives. Thus began an unbroken period of twenty-two years in Congress. Garfield served on the Military Affairs, the Bank and Currency, and the Appropriations Committees, and he was a member of the electoral commission that decided the controversial 1876 presidential election.

Garfield also was an opponent of President Andrew Johnson, voting for his impeachment, as well as being a supporter of Ulysses S. Grant for president in 1868 and 1872. At the 1880 Republican National Convention, two factions emerged: the first was the Stalwarts, headed by powerful New York senator Roscoe Conkling, who wanted Ulysses

The Garfield monument, Washington, D.C.

1881
Tuskegee Normal and Industrial Institute
is founded by Booker T. Washington

1881
The first U.S. men's single
tennis championships are held

123

S. Grant as the presidential candidate; the second was the Half-Breeds who opposed the idea of a third term for Grant. After five days and thirty-three ballots, there was a stalemate. On the thirty-sixth ballot, Garfield, the dark horse, was chosen as the presidential candidate for the Party. To reconcile the Stalwarts, Chester A. Arthur was chosen to be the vice presidential candidate. Garfield narrowly won the popular vote over his Democratic opponent, but received 214 of the 369 electoral votes. After being sworn in on the Capital steps in March 1881, the 49-year-old Garfield's first act as president was to turn and kiss his aged mother. Garfield soon was embroiled in a power struggle over cabinet and civil service appointments, leading to a Democratic filibuster.

On the morning of July 2, 1881, Garfield was at Washington's Baltimore and Potomac railroad station where he was to board a train to attend the twenty-fifth reunion of his class at Williams College. A mentally disturbed and disaffected office seeker named Charles J. Guiteau fired two shots, hitting Garfield in the arm and back.

In direct contrast to **James A. Garfield**'s purposeful and successful short life, Charles Guiteau was a misfit and a failure at everything he tried to do. Prior to the assassination, he had stalked the president several times. On one occasion he followed Garfield and Lucretia with the intent to harm, but she looked so frail and dependent that he could not bring himself to commit the act. Finally, the "appropriate" time came for Guiteau. He shot Garfield, but did not kill him outright -- the president lingered for eighty days. Doctors gave what medical care was available in the day. White House reports on the President's condition were initially optimistic. The nation responded with affection and prayers. Lucretia, who was in New Jersey convalescing from an illness when her husband was shot, was firm and quiet, filled with purpose to help save her husband's

An 1881 engraving showing Garfield just after being shot.

life. Her grief, devotion, and fortitude won the respect and sympathy of the country. Garfield longed to be near the ocean breeze and cooler temperatures, so, on September 6, 1881, he was moved to Elberon on the New Jersey coast by train. Over the next thirteen days, his condition worsened. On September 19, 1881, the twentieth President of the United States died. Guiteau, his assassin, met his fate when he was hanged nine months later. Lucretia Garfield survived her husband by thirty-six years, during which she was active in preserving the records of her husband's career. She passed away on March 14, 1918.

My 2 cents

What would you nickname this president?

_____

The Author's Idea: Mule Driver

BENJAMIN HARRISON
23rd President of the United States

POLITICAL PARTY: Republican
ELECTION OPPONENTS:
  Grover Cleveland, Democrat; Clinton Fisk, Prohibition;
  Alson Streeter, Union Labor
TERM OF OFFICE: March 4, 1889 to March 4, 1893
VICE PRESIDENT: Levi Morton

Historical marker at Benjamin Harrison's birthplace, North Bend, Ohio.

Fun Assignment!

Harrison is the only president to be preceded and succeeded by the same man. Who was he?

Grover Cleveland

Personal Profile

BORN: August 20, 1833, North Bend, Ohio
SIBLINGS: Second of ten children
RELIGION: Presbyterian
EDUCATION: Miami University, Oxford, Ohio; graduated 1852
CAREER: Lawyer
MILITARY: Second lieutenant; rose in rank to brigadier general

MARRIAGES:
  • Caroline Lavinia Scott
  October 20, 1853, Oxford, Ohio

  • Mary Scott Lord Dimmick
  April 6, 1896, New York City, New York
OFFSPRING:
  • With Caroline: a son and daughter
  • With Mary: a daughter
Died: March 13, 1901, Indianapolis, Indiana

Caroline Lavinia Scott Harrison

1889
Previous president:
Grover Clevelalnd

1889
The Johnstown Flood in Johnstown, PA
leaves more than 2,000 dead

 125

Visiting the President

BIRTHPLACE: Benjamin Harrison Home
  Symmes and Washington Avenues
  North Bend, Ohio (marker at site, privately owned)
RESIDENCE/MUSEUM/LIBRARY:
  President Benjamin Harrison Museum
  1230 North Delaware Street, Indianapolis, Indiana
GRAVESITE: Crown Hill Cemetery
  700 West 38th Street, Indianapolis, Indiana

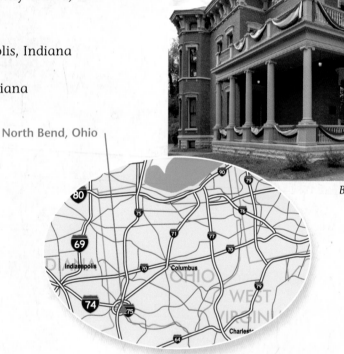

North Bend, Ohio

*Benjamin Harrison's home
Indianapolis, Indiana.*

CONNECTIONS

*An early form of the jukebox used phonograph
cylinders and was mass-produced in 1889.
The original musical coin-operated device
required the listener to crank a handle after
depositing the coin. Jukeboxes were popular
during the 1940s through the mid 1960s.
They have been superceded by new digital
technology.*

Political Profile

- Member, United States Senate
- President of the United States

1889
The first *Wall Street Journal*
is published

1890
The United Mine Workers
Union is founded

The Harrison Administration Highlights

- Theodore Roosevelt is appointed U.S. Civil Service Commissioner (1889)
- The first Pan-American Conference is convened (1889)
- North Dakota, South Dakota, Montana, and Washington become states (1889)
- Idaho and Wyoming become states (1890)
- The U.S. Army massacres Sioux Indians at Wounded Knee, South Dakota (1890)
- Nine circuit courts of appeal are created (1891)

Surviving members of the Big Foot band of Indians following the Battle at Wounded Knee (also called the Wounded Knee Massacre) in South Dakota. An estimated 150 men, women, and children of the Lakota Sioux were killed.

Benjamin Harrison was named for his great-grandfather, who was a signer of the Declaration of Independence. He lived five miles down the Ohio River from his grandfather, William Henry, the future ninth president of the United States. His father, John, a successful farmer, was a member of the United States House of Representatives when Harrison was twenty years old. Harrison was tutored at home and then attended a preparatory school before entering Miami University in Oxford, Ohio, graduating fourth in his class in 1852. As a young man, Harrison was reserved and serious. In 1853, the nineteen-year-old Harrison married twenty-year-old Caroline Scott, the daughter of a Presbyterian minister. Harrison read law and moved his family to Indianapolis to begin his law practice. To earn money while building his practice, Harrison worked as a court crier. He joined the Republican Party and was elected city attorney and state reporter for the Indiana Supreme Court. When the Civil War broke out, Harrison joined the infantry as a 2nd lieutenant. He saw

A Harrison-Morton campaign poster shows their platform and images of Presidents Washington, Lincoln, and Grant.

heavy fighting and led charges against Confederate positions. He was rewarded with promotions. His troops called the five-foot, six-inch Harrison "Little Ben." At the end of the war, Harrison returned to his law practice, but he harbored political ambitions and hoped to be nominated for the governor's post in 1872. He was not nominated. In 1876, he declined the nomination, but accepted after the chosen candidate withdrew. After all this, Harrison lost. However, he was elected to the United States Senate in 1881, supporting a high tariff, a strong navy, and civil service reform. He played an unobtrusive role, siding with party leaders. At the 1888 Republican National Convention, the deadlocked party nominated Harrison as their presidential candidate; he was considered "safe" and easy to control. He conducted his campaign from his home state, giving speeches to those who called upon him. Harrison lost the popular vote, but the distribution of electoral votes—particularly from New York—won him the election. Harrison was inaugurated one hundred years after the inauguration of George Washington and was called the "Centennial President." With a Republican controlled House and Senate, the Harrison Administration passed a number of domestic bills, causing the Democrats to dub it the "Billion-Dollar Congress." The country grew

Harrison is portrayed as wasting the Cleveland-administration surplus in his so-called "billion-dollar congress."

Benjamin Harrison was a five-foot, six-inch, prematurely gray man with a large head and loud voice. He was perceived as cold and austere. His hands were so badly afflicted with dermatitis that he often wore gloves. Harrison was upright, honest, and patriotic. He was a magnetic speaker, able to sway large audiences, yet he often offended people when he encountered them personally. He was not a charismatic president and at no time was he popular. After the presidency, Harrison did not enjoy living alone in his large, empty house. At the age of sixty-two, he married 37-year-old Mary Lord Dimmick, a widow and a niece of the first Mrs. Harrison. The wedding was simple. Harrison's two children -- Russell, age forty-one, and Mary, age thirty-six -- did not think it appropriate that their father marry again. As a result, they did not attend the wedding. In 1897, a baby girl was born to the new couple when Harrison was sixty-four years old. A new social life opened for the Harrisons and the couple lived happily together for almost five years. Benjamin Harrison died in 1901 at the age of sixty-seven. Just as Benjamin Harrison had followed three consecutive generations into public service, so did a number of Harrison's descendants continue that tradition.

Mary Dimmick Harrison, Benjamin's second wife.

1891
Thomas Hardy publishes
Tess of the d'Urbervilles

1892
Ellis Island opens for the reception of
immigrants to the United States

with six new states admitted to the Union, bringing the total to forty-four. At the same time, the population increased by more than twenty-five percent; the western frontier no longer existed and the country was

The grave of Benjamin Harrison and his two wives in Crown Hill Cemetery, Indianapolis, Indiana.

settled coast to coast. Harrison's wife, Caroline, refurbished the White House. Electric lights were installed. She started the tradition of the White House Christmas tree, established the White House's collection of china, raised money for the John Hopkins Medical School, and was one of the founders of the national chapter of the Daughters of the American Revolution. Harrison won re-nomination on the first ballot in 1892. Grover Cleveland was his Democratic opponent. It was the only time in history that an incumbent president ran against a former president. During most of the campaign, Caroline was ill, and just weeks before the election, she died. Harrison lost the election and said: "For me, there is no sting to it." Depression colored every aspect of his last months in office. Harrison followed the customs of a presidential departure from office. He left Washington a 59-year-old widower.

Tell me more!

The first White House Christmas tree

First Lady Caroline Harrison is credited with having the first White House Christmas tree. She helped decorate the tree in what is today's second-floor Yellow Oval Room.

My 2 cents

What would you nickname this president?

_____

The Author's Idea: Tippy's Grandson

1892
The University of Chicago
begins classes

1893
Successor president:
Grover Cleveland

129

John Phillip Sousa leading the Marine Corps Band, about 1893.
Inset: sheet-music cover for "Star and Stripes Forever."

WILLIAM McKINLEY
25th President of the United States

POLITICAL PARTY: Republican
ELECTION OPPONENTS:
   1896: William Jennings Bryan, Democrat
         John Palmer, National Democrat
         Joshua Levering, Prohibition
         Charles Matchett, Socialist Labor
   1900: William Jennings Bryan, Democrat
         John Woolley, Prohibition
         Eugene Debs, Socialist
         Wharton Barker, Populist
         Joseph Maloney, Socialist Labor
TERM OF OFFICE: March 4, 1897 to September 14, 1901
VICE PRESIDENTS:
   1897: Garret Hobart (died in office)
   1901: Theodore Roosevelt

*The William McKinley home,
Canton, Ohio.*

Personal Profile

BORN: January 29, 1843, Niles, Ohio
SIBLINGS: Seventh of nine children
RELIGION: Methodist
EDUCATION: Allegheny College (left because
   of illness); Albany Law School (one term)
CAREER: Lawyer

MILITARY: Enlisted as private;
   rose to brevet major
MARRIAGE: Ida Saxton
   January 25, 1871, Canton, Ohio
OFFSPRING: two daughters
   (one died at age four; the other, at 5 mos.)
DIED: September 14, 1901,
   Buffalo, New York

*Ida Saxton
McKinley*

1897	1897	1897	
Previous president: Grover Cleveland	Grant's Tomb is dedicated	John Philip Sousa's "Stars and Stripes Forever" is first performed	131

Visiting the President

BIRTHPLACE: 36 South Main Street
Niles, Ohio (marker at site)
RESIDENCE: The Saxton McKinley House/
The National First Ladies Library
331 South Market Avenue, Canton, Ohio
MUSEUM/LIBRARY/GRAVESITE:
William McKinley Presidential Library and Museum
800 McKinley Monument Drive, NW Canton, Ohio
MONUMENT: The McKinley Monument
Intersection of Delaware, Niagara,
Genesee and Court Streets, Buffalo, New York

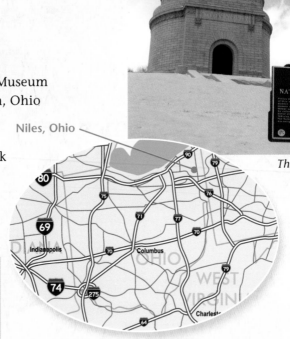

Niles, Ohio

The McKinley National Memorial, Canton, Ohio.

Fun Assignment!

McKinley often wore a red carnation in his lapel. What state made the red carnation its official state flower?

Ohio

Political Profile

- Member, United States House of Representatives
- Governor of Ohio
- President of the United States

1897
The first section of Boston's subway system is opened

1897
The first issue of *McCall's* Magazine is published

1897
The New York Sun answers a little girl's question, replying, "Yes, Virginia, there is a Santa Claus"

The McKinley Administration Highlights

- The U.S. battleship Maine is blown up by a mine and sunk in Havana Harbor (1898)
- The United States annexes Hawaii (1898)
- The Gold Standard Act establishes gold as the only medium of exchange (1900)

McKinley campaigns using the gold standard in an effort to restore prosperity.

William McKinley was born in Niles, Ohio. His ancestors were Scottish-Irish immigrants who settled in Pennsylvania before moving to Ohio. He attended local schools and took an early interest in oratory, becoming president of the local debating society. McKinley attended Allegheny College in Pennsylvania, but dropped out due to illness.

When the Civil War began, McKinley, then eighteen, followed in the tradition of his great-grandfather who fought in the Revolutionary War and his grandfather who fought in the War of 1812. He enlisted as a private, distinguished himself, and rose to major. When the war was over, McKinley, now twenty-two, had changed from a pale, sickly boy into a healthy, robust young man. He read law and then entered law school in Albany, New York; he was admitted to the Ohio bar in 1867. McKinley settled in Canton, Ohio, and began to take part in Republican Party politics. In 1871, he married Ida Saxton, the daughter of a banker. Five years later, McKinley was elected to Congress, serving almost continuously for fifteen years. In 1891, he ran for governor of Ohio and won.

In 1896, McKinley actively pursued the Republican Party's nomination for president. He won on the first ballot with the help of an industrialist friend, millionaire Mark Hanna.

The USS Maine in Havana Harbor in January 1898, where the ship exploded the next month. The event sparked the phrase "Remember the Maine, to hell with Spain," and was a factor leading to the Spanish American War.

1898	1899	1900
H. C. Wells publishes *The War of the Worlds*	The trademarked name "Aspirin" is first used by the Bayer Company	The American League of Professional Baseball Clubs is organized

Tell me more!

Thomas Edison didn't invent just the light bulb

McKinley's first inauguration was recorded by the gramophone and the motion picture camera. Following the shooting of McKinley, doctors were reluctant to use the x-ray machine exhibited at the Pan American Exposition. All three technologies were invented by Thomas Edison.

McKinley ran a "front porch" campaign, speaking to supporters from the porch of his Canton home. He won both the popular and electoral vote. While his aged mother and invalid wife looked on, McKinley took the oath of office. The most important event of the McKinley presidency was the Spanish-American War. Cubans were seeking independence from Spain. Popular sympathy, rumors of cruelties fueled by powerful newspapers, and the mysterious sinking of the United States battleship Maine in Havana Harbor put pressure on McKinley. He advocated "neutral intervention," but Congress passed resolutions that led to a declaration of war against Spain on April 11, 1898. One hundred days later, Cuba was declared independent from Spain and the United States took control of the Philippines, Guam, and Puerto Rico.

On the domestic front, the Gold Standard Act was passed, recognizing gold as the standard for United States currency. In 1900, McKinley was unanimously nominated for a second term, running against the same Democratic

William McKinley loved everyone and wanted everyone to love him back. He was easy-going and gregarious and at the same time dignified and smart. McKinley said: "I have never been in doubt…that I would someday be made president." McKinley was at times compared to Napoleon because of his short stature and his habit of putting one hand inside his coat while speaking. He often wore a red carnation in his lapel.

As a young couple, McKinley and his wife Ida were full of life and great promise. All that changed. Ida's mother and two daughters died in close succession. She was distraught and inconsolable and soon suffered from depression and seizures. She became an invalid, totally dependent on her husband. At this time, the McKinleys had a suite at a hotel across the street from his gubernatorial office in Ohio. Each morning, after leaving the

hotel, the president would pause outside, remove his hat, and bow to her window before proceeding to his office and then, at exactly 3 p.m., McKinley would interrupt business, step to the window of his office, and wave his handkerchief to his wife, who waited for the greeting from the hotel.

In the White House, McKinley broke protocol, having his wife seated at his side during state dinners. If a seizure began, McKinley would cover Ida's face with his handkerchief until it passed. The sincere affection he showered on Ida won him sympathy; on the other hand, many thought his devotion bordered on the absurd. On that fateful day in September 1901, the wounded McKinley gasped: "My wife, be careful how you tell her—oh, be careful." Ida McKinley managed to live five more years without her caretaker.

1900
L. Frank Baum publishes *The Wonderful Wizard of Oz*

1900
The 1900 census shows a U.S. population of 76.2 million people

1900
The first Davis Cup tennis match is held

McKinley's final speech on September 5, 1901 at the Pan-American Exposition in Buffalo, New York.

opponent as in 1896. McKinley spent most of the campaign at his home in Canton, confident of victory. In September 1901, the re-elected McKinley traveled to Buffalo, New York, to make a planned address at the Pan-American Exposition. He visited Niagara Falls, rode the trolley along the scenic gorge route, lunched by the falls, and visited the exhibits.

The public had been promised that the president would greet people at the Music Temple. McKinley's secretary was concerned about his safety and asked McKinley to omit the handshaking. He replied: "Why should I? No one would wish to hurt me." At approximately 4:10 p.m., two shots were heard. McKinley stood stock still for a moment, a red stain growing over his abdomen. Eight days later, President William McKinley died. Swift justice followed. The anarchist assassin, Leo Czolgosz, was indicted on September 16th, brought to trial September 23rd, and executed October 29th.

CONNECTIONS

L. Frank Baum published The Wonderful Wizard of Oz in 1900. Under the name The Wizard of Oz, it was made into a stage play in 1902 and a highly successful movie in 1939. The Wonderful Wizard of Oz is one of the best-known stories in American pop culture and has been reprinted countless times and widely translated.

Mugshots of Leon Czolgosz after his arrest for the assassination of President McKinley in 1901.

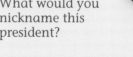

My 2 cents
What would you nickname this president?

_____

The Author's Idea: Faithful Caregiver

1901
Rudyard Kipling
publishes Kim

1901
Successor president:
Theodore Roosevelt

135

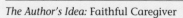

The U.S. Supreme Court
William Howard Taft is the only president to serve on the Supreme Court. He was Chief Justice from 1921 until before his death in 1930.

WILLIAM HOWARD TAFT

27th President of the United States

POLITICAL PARTY: Republican
ELECTION OPPONENT:
   William Jennings Bryan, Democrat
TERM OF OFFICE: March 4, 1909 to March 4, 1913
VICE PRESIDENT: James Sherman

Fun Assignment!

What was built in the center of the West Wing of the
White House during Taft's presidential term?

The Oval Office

*The Taft house at the William Howard Taft National
Historic Site in Cincinnati, Ohio.*

Personal Profile

BORN: September 15, 1857, Cincinnati, Ohio
SIBLINGS: Second of five children
RELIGION: Unitarian
EDUCATION: Yale University;
   graduated 1878
   University of Cincinnati Law School;
   graduated 1880

CAREER: Lawyer, reporter, college professor,
   dean of law school
MILITARY: None
MARRIAGE: Helen Herron
   June 19, 1886, Cincinnati, Ohio
OFFSPRING: Two sons, one daughter
DIED: March 8, 1930, Washington, D.C.

*Helen Herron
Taft*

1909
Previous president:
Theodore Roosevelt

1909
U.S. explorer Robert Perry
reaches the North Pole

137

Visiting the President

BIRTHPLACE/HOMESTEAD/MUSEUM:
William Howard Taft National Historic Site
2038 Auburn Avenue, Cincinnati, Ohio
GRAVESITE: Arlington National Cemetery
Memorial Drive, Arlington, Virginia

Tell me more!

Taft throws the first presidential pitch...ever

Taft started the presidential tradition of throwing the first pitch of the major league baseball season. The game was between the Washington Senators and the Philadelphia Athletics in April, 1910.

Cincinnati, Ohio

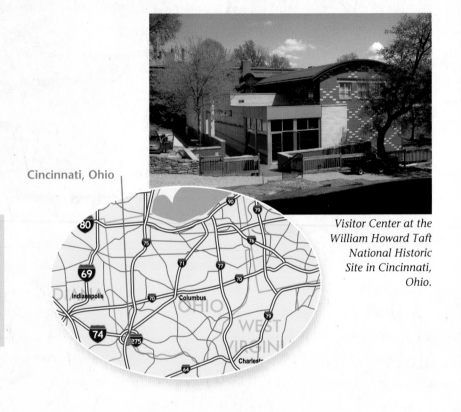

Visitor Center at the William Howard Taft National Historic Site in Cincinnati, Ohio.

Political Profile

- Judge, Ohio Supreme Court
- United States Solicitor General
- United States Circuit Court Judge
- Governor-General of the Philippines
- Secretary of War
- President of the United States
- Chief Justice of the United States Supreme Court

138

1909
Astronomer H. Knox Shaw
photographs Halley's Comet

1910
William D. Boyce launches the
Boy Scouts of America

1910
The 1910 census shows a U.S.
population of 92.2 million people

The Taft Administration Highlights

- Congress passes the 16th Amendment to the Constitution, allowing the levy for a personal income tax, 1909; the Amendment is ratified in 1913
- Congress passes a law that sets the number of members of the House of Representatives at 435 in 1911; the law takes effect in 1913
- New Mexico and Arizona become states (1912)
- Congress passes the 17th Amendment to the Constitution, providing for the direct election of U.S. Senators in 1912; the Amendment is ratified in 1913
- Bill establishes the Children's Bureau, charged with studying and reporting on the welfare of children (1912)

Taft with Secretary of War Elihu Root. Taft would later assume this position in February 1904 under president Theodore Roosevelt.

William Howard Taft was the son of Louisa and Alphonso Taft. Alphonso was a lawyer, civic leader, judge, secretary of war, and United States Ambassador. Louisa was an independent woman, organizing book clubs, an art association,

President Taft in 1907.

and a kindergarten. The couple had high expectations of all their children. Taft, called "Willie," reached full height and a powerful physique by the time he entered high school. In 1874, he enrolled at Yale University and graduated second in his class at the age of twenty. Taft received his law degree and was admitted to the Ohio bar in 1889. His father's connections won him an appointment as assistant prosecutor and then assistant county solicitor.

In 1886, Taft married Helen (Nellie) Herron, a schoolteacher and the daughter of a law partner of Rutherford B. Hayes. Taft was appointed a judge of the Ohio Supreme Court in 1887. At the age of thirty, Taft was made United States solicitor general when he befriended Theodore Roosevelt, then serving on the Civil Service Commission. Soon Taft became a federal circuit court judge. In 1900, President McKinley named Taft president of the Philippine Commission to establish a civil government there. After he drafted a constitution for the island, Taft became their governor general. In 1904, President

1910	1911	1912
E. M. Forster publishes *Howard's End*	The first Indianapolis 500 race is held	Juliette Gordon Low establishes the Girl Scouts

Theodore Roosevelt appointed Taft secretary of war and provisional governor of Cuba. Taft became the most widely traveled American of his time, making trips to Panama, Japan, and Cuba. He became Roosevelt's confidant and the two men were close friends.

From 1906 on, it became clear that Roosevelt had chosen Taft as his successor, but Taft was not sure he wanted the presidency. Roosevelt and Mrs. Taft convinced him otherwise. At the 1908 Republican National Convention, Taft won the presidential nomination by acclamation on the first ballot. Taft won the White House by more than one million popular

Taft and Roosevelt, once friends when Roosevelt gladly handed the presidency to Taft in 1909, became bitter political enemies in the 1912 election.

William Howard Taft was friendly, approachable, and unassuming. He had a Herculean frame. The six- foot, two-inch man with the walrus mustache was huge and slow-moving. As a graduate from Yale, he weighed 230 pounds; when he entered the oval office he was 340. This caused Taft to get stuck in the White House bathtub, requiring several aides to pull him out. Taft was prodded into the presidency by his wife Nellie. She had dreamed of becoming First Lady since she was sixteen years old, after attending a White House reception. Nellie lobbied hard for her husband's nomination and campaigned more fervently than the candidate. As First Lady, she was outspoken and forceful. Her lasting memorial is Washington, D.C.'s famous Japanese cherry trees, planted at her request along the Tidal Basin.

Of all the United States presidents, none had held as many high positions as Taft, but his principle desire was to serve on the United States Supreme Court. When Taft's term in office ended, the 55-year-old private citizen accepted an appointment as law professor at Yale University, a position he held for eight years. Finally, in 1921, President Warren G. Harding appointed Taft to the Supreme Court, not as a justice, but as the Chief Justice. Taft felt that his work as Chief Justice was the most important service of his life and the happiest. As president, Taft described the White House as the "loneliest place in the world." As Chief Justice, he declared: "I don't remember that I ever was president."

Cherry trees in Washington, D.C.

1912
The ship Titanic sinks
in the North Sea

1912
Fenway Park in
Boston opens

Supreme Court Chief Justice Taft with President Warren G. Harding and former Secretary of War Robert Todd Lincoln in 1922.

votes and by 159 electoral votes. Nellie Taft joined her husband on the reviewing stand as Taft took the oath of office -- the first First Lady to do so. As president, Taft unexpectedly departed from the Roosevelt legacy. His cabinet was more conservative and he was less interested in conservation matters. Taft suffered a major defeat by the Republican Congress when they passed an act that kept tariff rates high. He disliked the measure, but he did not veto it. As a consequence, he, more than Congress, was blamed for continuing high prices. Taft's foreign policy, dubbed "Dollar Diplomacy," strove to expand United States trade by making investments in countries and, in some instances, providing financial aid.

At the 1912 Republican National Convention, Taft found himself opposed by his friend Theodore Roosevelt, who was upset with the direction Taft's administration had taken.

President Taft's grave site at Arlington National Cemetery.

Roosevelt and his supporters organized the Progressive Party with Roosevelt its candidate. Roosevelt purposely wrecked the Republican Party to prevent Taft from having a second term. Taft was bewildered, dismayed, and then angry. Taft campaigned, but knew he could not win the interesting three-cornered race: himself, the sitting president; Roosevelt, the former president; and Woodrow Wilson, the Democratic candidate and future president. Taft said: "If I cannot win, I hope Wilson will." In the end, Taft suffered the worst defeat by any incumbent president in election history up to that point.

CONNECTIONS

The Boy Scouts of America was launched February 8, 1910. Two years later the Girl Scouts was established. Gerald Ford was an Eagle Scout and Bill Clinton was a scout. Lou Hoover was elected the national president of the Girl Scouts in 1922 and maintained her own local troop the entire time she lived in Washington.

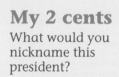

My 2 cents
What would you nickname this president?

_____

The Author's Idea: The Big Judge

The National Cathedral
Woodrow Wilson is the only United States president buried in the National Cathedral and the only president buried within the District of Columbia.

WOODROW WILSON

28th President of the United States

POLITICAL PARTY: Democrat
ELECTION OPPONENTS:

  1912: William Howard Taft, Republican
  Theodore Roosevelt, Progressive
  Eugene Debs, Socialist
  1916: Charles Hughes, Republican
  Allan Benson, Socialist
TERM OF OFFICE: March 4, 1913 to March 4, 1921
VICE PRESIDENT: Thomas Marshall

The Woodrow Wilson birthplace in Staunton, Virginia.

Personal Profile

BORN: December 28, 1856, Staunton, Virginia
SIBLINGS: Third of four children
RELIGION: Presbyterian
Education: College of New Jersey
  (Princeton University); graduated 1879
  Johns Hopkins University; graduated 1886
Career: Lawyer, history instructor,
  professor of jurisprudence and political
  economy, university president

MILITARY: None
MARRIAGES:
  • Ellen Axson
  June 24, 1885, Savannah, Georgia
  • Edith Bolling Galt
  December 18, 1915, Washington, D.C.
OFFSPRING: Three daughters
DIED: February 3, 1924, Washington, D.C.

Edith Bolling Galt Wilson

Ellen Axson Wilson

1913
Previous president:
William Taft

1913
George Bernard Shaw
publishes *Pygmalion*

143

Visiting the President

BIRTHPLACE/MUSEUM/LIBRARY:
The Woodrow Wilson Birthplace
24 North Coalter Street, Staunton, Virginia
RESIDENCE: Woodrow Wilson House
2340 S Street N.W., Washington, D.C.
GRAVESITE: Washington National Cathedral
Massachusetts and Wisconsin Avenues N.W.
Washington, D.C.

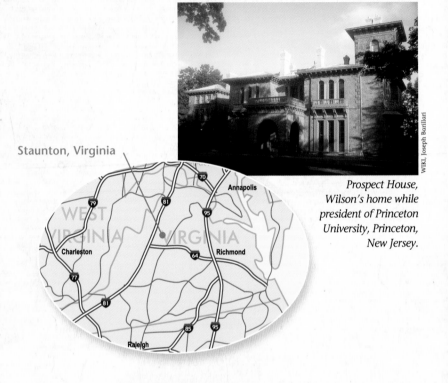

Staunton, Virginia

Prospect House, Wilson's home while president of Princeton University, Princeton, New Jersey.

WIKI, Joseph Barillari

Tell me more!

White House Sheep
During World War I, Wilson gave permission to sheep owners to graze their sheep on the White House lawn. The wool was used by the American Red Cross in the war effort.

Political Profile
- Governor of New Jersey
- President of the United States

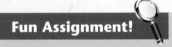

Fun Assignment!
Wilson signed the orders to make what day a national holiday?

Mother's Day

1913
Edgar Rice Burroughs
publishes *Tarzan of the Apes*

1914
The Panama Canal opens for traffic, first
ship through is a U.S. ship, the Ancon

The Wilson Administration Highlights

- First form 1040 appears (1913)
- The 17th Amendment to the Constitution (direct election of U.S. senators) is ratified (1913)
- The Federal Trade Commission is created (1914)
- Mother's Day becomes a national holiday (1914)
- "Act to Create the Coast Guard" is signed (1915)
- National Park Service is established (1916)
- The U.S. purchases the Danish West Indies which becomes the U.S. Virgin Islands (1917)
- Daylight savings time is established (1918)
- The 18th Amendment to the Constitution (prohibits consumption of alcohol) is passed (1917) and ratified (1919)
- The 19th Amendment to the Constitution (women's right to vote) is passed (1919) and ratified (1920)
- Wilson wins the Nobel Peace prize (1920)

President Wilson asks Congress to declare war on Germany April 2, 1917, causing the United States to enter World War I.

Woodrow Wilson was born in Staunton, Virginia, the son of a Presbyterian minister. His family moved further south and identified with the Confederacy. Because southern schools were disrupted by the Civil War, Wilson was taught at home. In 1875, Wilson enrolled at the College of New Jersey (now Princeton University). In 1879, Wilson entered the University of Virginia, only to find the study of law monotonous. Illness forced him to drop out in 1880, so once again, he studied at home. He received his law degree in absentia. Wilson practiced law for a time, but then left the profession to enter graduate school at Johns Hopkins; he was granted his Ph.D. in history and political science. In 1885, Wilson married Ellen Axson, the daughter of a Presbyterian minister. Wilson accepted academic appointments at Bryn Mawr College

1915
D.W.Griffith's *Birth of a Nation* premieres

1916
The lithograph of Uncle Sam proclaiming "I want you!" is published on the cover of *Leslie's Weekly*

Born **Thomas Woodrow Wilson**, the twenty-eighth President of the United States was called "Tommie" in his boyhood. He was ten before he learned how to read and as a teenager he used shorthand to compensate for his reading disability. Wilson was determined and self-disciplined. He could be warm and witty, but also cold and austere. He was a progressive who brought his ideology to Princeton, to the capitol of New Jersey, and to Washington. He was steadfast and stubborn in his convictions. In 1914, his wife Ellen died in the White House. The next year, he married Edith Galt, the widow of a successful Washington jeweler. Following Wilson's stroke, Edith was his link to the political world. She decided what matters were important and when to present them to the President. She also screened his visitors, both political and personal. Questions about Wilson's ability to perform his duties were met with anger from his physician, his secretary, and his wife. No other First Lady had more influence on the presidency than Edith did. One senator exclaimed: "We have a petticoat government; Mrs. Wilson is president!"

A young Woodrow Wilson.

Woodrow Wilson's first posed photograph after suffering a stroke in 1919, paralyzing his left side.

The great tragedy in Wilson's administration was his handling of the Treaty of Versailles, including his concept of a League of Nations. He made the tactical error of not including a representative of the United States Senate or the Republican Party in his peace delegation to France. Unwilling to compromise with the Republican-held Senate to obtain ratification, Wilson chose to take his cause to the American people. His failure to bring the treaty to fruition is considered one of the greatest errors on the part of an American president. Wilson contributed to his own defeat, holding sole ownership of his "sacred mission." Wilson may have stumbled as a politician, but his vision of a world organization for peace was vindicated in the form of the United Nations a quarter of a century after his death.

1920
The 1920 U.S. census shows a population of 106 million people

1920
The National Football League is founded with Jim Thorpe as its first president

The Harding Administration Highlights

- Dedication of the Tomb of the Unknown Soldier (1921)
- Budget and Accounting Act of 1921 provides for an annual budget to be submitted to Congress by the president
- William Howard Taft is appointed Chief Justice of the Supreme Court (1921)
- The Lincoln Memorial is dedicated (1922)
- The Federal Narcotics Control Board is established (1922)
- The White House Police Force is established (1922)

W arren G. Harding was born on a farm in Morrow County in north-central Ohio. His father, George, was a homeopathic physician and his mother, Phoebe, a midwife. George was part owner of a local newspaper where Harding learned to set type and run the press. Harding attended Ohio Central College; after graduation in 1882, he tried teaching, studying law, and selling insurance. In the end, he preferred shooting pool and playing poker. Almost nineteen, Harding became a reporter for a weekly newspaper. His political leanings did not sit well with the Democratic owner and he was fired. After attempting to rescue a bankrupt newspaper, he started his own, The *Weekly Star*. There he was free to express his political views in editorials.

In 1891, Harding married Florence Mable Kling DeWolf, the daughter of a wealthy banker and a divorced mother of a son. By the end of the 1890s, Harding was financially successful, a prominent citizen, and an influential voice in the Republican Party. He was elected to the Ohio Senate in 1898 where he became known for his party loyalty. Harding sought and won personal popularity with his fellow lawmakers, always willing to have a drink and play poker. In 1903, he was elected lieutenant governor of Ohio and, in 1910, ran unsuccessfully for governor. However, Harding was elected to the United States Senate in 1914. Once again, he sought popularity among his peers, stuck to party lines, displayed few convictions, and never sponsored legislation.

Harding gave keynote talks at both the 1912 and 1916 Republican National Conventions. His noble appearance and eloquent words impressed the delegates. At the 1920 Republican

The official White House portrait of Warren G. Harding, 1922.

1922
James Joyce's *Ulysses*
is published

1922
The first *Reader's Digest*
is published

Convention, with the delegates at a stalemate, Warren G. Harding was nominated the compromise presidential candidate with Massachusetts Governor Calvin Coolidge as his running mate. Harding conducted a "front porch" campaign, using the slogan "Back to Normalcy" to appeal to the war-weary public.

Testimony before the Senate Committee investigating the Teapot Dome oil leases in 1924, above. Below, Senator Albert B. Fall, a key figure in the scandal, was the first former U.S. cabinet official sentenced to prison.

The Republican ticket won sixty percent of the popular vote, and Harding selected close political allies for his cabinet. He brought in many of his old Ohio pals, soon dubbed the "Ohio Gang." Many of these men had talent, but most were of dubious character. Meanwhile, in 1921, the Harding Administration hosted an International Conference for the Limitation of Armament.

On the domestic stage, Harding established a system of preparing a national budget, appealed to the steel industry to abolish the twelve-hour workday, and supported quotas for immigration, but soon

Warren G. Harding was handsome and congenial. He was also a tobacco-chewing, poker-playing, womanizing man who suffered from depression and ill health. Because he recognized his own limitations, he was not enthusiastic about running for president. Nonetheless, Mrs. Harding believed they were destined for the White House. The domineering "Duchess," as Harding called her, became a bold and forceful First Lady. There were many "firsts" in Harding's brief, scandal-ridden administration: he was the first sitting senator to be elected president; his election was the first in which women had the right to vote; his was the first election in which results were announced on the radio; he was the first president to be heard on the radio; and he was the first president to travel to his inauguration by automobile.

Senator Warren G. Harding.

Despite all of these firsts, he apparently was the last to know the crooked underpinnings of his own administration. The perpetrators were forced to resign, were sentenced to prison or committed suicide. Few believe today that Harding was personally or deliberately involved in these acts of corruption.

At the dedication of the Harding Tomb in 1931, President Herbert Hoover said: " Warren Harding had a dim realization that he had been betrayed by a few of the men who he had believed were his devoted friends." Yet Warren G. Harding himself said it all: "I am not fit for this office and should never have been here."

CONNECTIONS

Secretary of Commerce Herbert Hoover listens to a radio. Hoover regulated the radio industry in the early 1920s and was later elected the 31st President of the United States in 1928.

irregularities in the Harding administration began to appear. The Navy Department transferred oil-rich fields, one in Teapot, Wyoming, intended for future naval needs, to the Department of the Interior. That agency then leased the land to oil businesses.

The resulting scandal was referred to as the "Teapot Dome" affair. The failure of the Attorney General to investigate and prosecute individuals was questioned. Harding's "friends" were in the process of destroying his administration. To improve public relations, Harding undertook a vigorous cross-country trip called "Voyage of Understanding" on June 20, 1923. During the trip, Harding became increasingly fatigued and on July 29th complained of abdominal pain. Harding left Washington State for San Francisco where he was taken to the Palace Hotel to recuperate. He was feeling better when Mrs. Harding joined him to read a magazine article flattering to the president. After she left, the nurse entered the room and saw Harding slump to the side. The president was gone.

CONNECTIONS

On March 3, 1923, Henry Luce introduced Time *magazine. Luce, an influential publisher, developed a media empire that included Fortune magazine (1929), Life magazine (1936) and Sports Illustrated (1954). Luce purchased the famous Zapruder film of the assassination of John F. Kennedy and negotiated with Marina Oswald for the exclusive rights for her story.*

The Harding Tomb in Marion, Ohio, is the final resting place of both the president and his wife.

My 2 cents
What would you nickname this president?

_____

The Author's Idea: The Roving Reporter

The Treasury Department building in Washington, D.C.
The building is a National Historic Landmark.

ANDREW JACKSON
7th President of the United States

POLITICAL PARTY: Democratic
ELECTION OPPONENTS:

1828	John Quincy Adams, National Republican
1832	Henry Clay, National Republican
	William Wirt, Anti-Masonic
	John Floyd, Republican

TERM OF OFFICE: March 4, 1829 to March 4, 1837
VICE PRESIDENT:

1829	John C. Calhoun
1832	Martin Van Buren

Andrew Jackson birthplace marker at Charlotte Highway (U.S. 521) and Andrew Jackson State Park Road in Lancaster County, South Carolina.

Fun Assignment!

Andrew Jackson was the first president to use the "pocket veto." What is the "pocket veto"?

An indirect veto of a bill as a result of the president's failure to sign it within ten days of the adjournment of Congress. This expression dates from the 1830s and alludes to putting the unsigned bill inside one's pocket.

Personal Profile

BORN: March 15, 1767, Waxhaw, South Carolina
• Actual place is unknown; near the border of North and South Carolina
SIBLINGS: Third of three sons
RELIGION: Presbyterian
EDUCATION: Minimal schooling
CAREER: Lawyer

MILITARY: Joined Continental Army at age 13; rose to rank of major general
MARRIAGE: Rachel Donelson Robards August 1791 and again January 17, 1794
OFFSPRING: Had no biological children, but adopted a son (nephew)
DIED: June 8, 1845
The Hermitage, Nashville, Tennessee

Rachel Donelson Robards Jackson

Visiting the President

BIRTHPLACE: Actual site unknown, there are two markers:
one at U.S. Highway 521 and Old Church Road; the other at U.S. Highway 521 at
the entrance to Andrew Jackson State Park, Lancaster, South Carolina

BOYHOOD HOME/MUSEUM: Andrew Jackson State Park
196 Andrew Jackson Park Road, Lancaster, South Carolina

HOMESTEAD/GRAVESITE: The Hermitage
4580 Rachel's Lane, Hermitage, Tennessee

The Hermitage, home of Andrew Jackson, Nashville, Tennessee.

Lancaster, South Carolina

Tell me more!

Scarred for Life

Thirteen-year-old Jackson was captured by the British during the Revolutionary War. He received a sword cut across his forehead (which would later leave a scar) when he refused to clean a British officer's boots.

Political Profile

- Member, United States House of Representatives
- United States Senator
- Justice, Tennessee Supreme Court
- Governor, Florida Territory
- President of the United States

1829
The *Encyclopedia Americana*
is published

1829
James Smithson dies, leaves his fortune
to create a museum (the Smithsonian)

The Jackson Administration Highlights

- The Indian Removal Act is passed authorizing forcible removal of various tribes to lands west of the Mississippi (1830)
- Force Bill of 1833 authorizes the use of arms, if needed, to collect tariff revenues in the states (1833)
- The Battle of the Alamo ends in the defeat of the Americans (1836)
- Arkansas becomes a state (1836)
- Michigan becomes a state (1837)

A daguerreotype of Jackson.

Andrew Jackson was the third son of Scotch-Irish immigrant parents. His father died before he was born; his mother earned her family's keep caring for her invalid sister and her family. Jackson received little education, but was able to read by the age of five. He was an active and mean-tempered boy when, at the age of thirteen, he and his brother joined the militia during the Revolutionary War. His brothers and mother died by 1781, and, as a result, Jackson became an orphan by the age of fourteen.

Bust of Jackson where he was sworn in as military governor of Florida at Plaza Ferdinand VII in Pensacola, Florida.

The future president took up the study of law, spending his spare time drinking, fighting, and racing horses. He was admitted to the bar in 1787, moved to Nashville, and gained a reputation as a fearless attorney. He collected his fees in land, the currency of the frontier. In 1791, Jackson married Rachel Donelson Robards, believing her former husband had obtained a divorce. They lived together two years before discovering that the divorce was not finalized. The couple remarried in 1794. Between 1791 and 1804, Jackson held a number of judicial positions and served as the first member of the House of Representatives from the new state of Tennessee and in the United States Senate. In 1802, he was elected major general of the Tennessee militia. During the

War of 1812 ,Jackson led his militia against the Creek Indians, forcing the Creeks to give up millions of acres of land. Jackson was given military command of the entire southwestern part of the country. In New Orleans, the British had amassed a huge fleet and army. Neither side realized that the war had officially ended. The British attacked in force-- only to suffer one of the worst defeats in British military history. Jackson was hailed as the hero of the war. After Spain sold Florida to the United States, Jackson was appointed territorial governor. Within months, he resigned his army commission and his governorship and returned to the Hermitage, his property in Tennessee.

Jackson made a run for the presidency in 1824. Since no candidate in the three-way race received a majority of votes, the selection of the next president fell to the House of Representatives. Supporters of Andrew Jackson were accused of corrupt political bargaining, but despite their efforts to elect Jackson, the House chose John Quincy Adams. Jackson

Andrew Jackson was a smart but poorly educated orphan, a boy-militiaman, a wild teenager, a self-taught frontier lawyer, a victorious Indian fighter, a war hero, and a president who believed that the entire executive power was vested in him as the president of the United States. Jackson was reckless, hot-tempered, and obstinate--and he bore the wounds to prove it in the form of a permanent facial scar from a British officer due to his refusal to shine the officer's boots and a life-long bullet lodged near his heart as a result of a duel over a horse-racing bet. Jackson's tenacious loyalty toward his friends was matched by an equally unquenchable enmity for anyone who insulted or betrayed him. In particular, he protected Rachel. He fought four duels, killing several people over innuendos and accusations cast at her over their marriage. Political enemies talked about the adulterous couple who were going to pollute the White House. In the White House, he was referred to as "King Andrew," the "Chieftain" or the "Dictator." In Jackson's eyes, he knew what was best, and anyone who opposed him was either stupid or a traitor. When Jackson left the presidency, he had $90 in his pocket and faced a mountain of debt, largely caused by his adopted son. Despite this and ill health, Jackson constantly gave political matters his personal attention. In the twilight of life, old and ill as he was, "Old Hickory" continued to exert considerable influence, proud to be an American and proud to represent the cause of the common people.

THE BRAVE BOY OF THE WAXHAWS.

Andrew Jackson, the Seventh President of the United States, in 1780 when a boy of 13 enlisted in the cause of his country, and was taken prisoner by the British. Being ordered by an officer to clean his boots, he indignantly refused, and received a sword cut for his temerity.

An 1876 lithograph shows a young Jackson refusing to clean Major Coffin's boots.

1834
Cyrus McCormick patents
his mechanical reaper

1835
Hans Christian Andersen publishes
his first volume of fairy tales

Statue of Andrew Jackson in front of the St. Louis Cathedral in Jackson Square, French Quarter, New Orleans, Louisiana.

felt cheated and resolved to avenge himself. He formed political ties with the new party, the Democrats, and over the next four years devoted his attention to winning the election of 1828, which he did with a clear majority, but, in his moment of vengeful glory, his wife Rachel died.

During Jackson's two terms, passions flared. Protective tariffs, thought to protect northern manufacturing interests, were opposed by the south. In 1832, Jackson issued the Nullification Proclamation, reaffirming the principle that states could not nullify federal laws. South Carolina responded with the Ordinance of Nullification in an attempt to nullify federal tariff laws. Jackson threatened military force to collect tariff revenues. Vice President Calhoun resigned in protest.

History would note that Jackson did not honor the terms of treaties that he himself had drawn up with the Indians. Jackson forced most of the eastern Indian tribes to give up their land to white settlers and move west of the Mississippi, including the infamous "Trail of Tears" expulsion of Creeks and Cherokees.

Sick and tired, Jackson gladly turned the White House over to his handpicked successor, Martin Van Buren. He quipped that there were two things left undone: he had not had the opportunity to shoot Henry Clay or to hang John C. Calhoun--the two senators who had often vigorously opposed him.

My 2 cents
What would you nickname this president?

_____

The Author's Idea: The Dueler

Westward Ho!
The phrase "Manifest Destiny" is associated with James K. Polk's administration.
During his one term in office, the country expanded to the Pacific Ocean.

JAMES KNOX POLK

11th President of the United States

POLITICAL PARTY: Democratic
ELECTION OPPONENT: Henry Clay, Whig
TERM OF OFFICE: March 4, 1845 to March 5, 1849
VICE PRESIDENT: George Dallas

Fun Assignment!

One of Polk's nicknames comes from his strong support of Andrew Jackson. What is the nickname?

Andrew Jackson was called "Old Hickory". James Polk was called "Young Hickory."

The Polk home in Columbia, Tennessee.

WIKI, TarHippo

Personal Profile

BORN: November 2, 1795
   Mecklenburg, North Carolina
SIBLINGS: Eldest of ten children
RELIGION: Presbyterian; baptized Methodist
   on his deathbed
EDUCATION: University of North Carolina;
   graduated 1818
CAREER: Lawyer

MILITARY: None
MARRIAGE: Sarah Childress
   January 1, 1824, Murfreesboro,
   Tennessee
OFFSPRING: None
DIED: June 15, 1849,
   Nashville, Tennessee

Sarah Childress Polk

Visiting the President

BIRTHPLACE: President James K. Polk State Historic Site
12031 Lancaster Highway, Pineville, North Carolina
HOMESTEAD/MUSEUM: James K. Polk Ancestral Home
301 West 7th Street, Columbia, Tennessee
GRAVESITE: Tennessee State Capital
Charlotte Avenue and 7th Avenue,
North Nashville, Tennessee

1844 Polk/Dallas campaign banner, produced by Nathaniel Currier.

Tell me more!

Goals: Four Great Measures

Polk's inaugural address outlined what he hoped to achieve during his presidency, his "four great measures:" a reduction of the tariff on exported goods, a reestablishment of the independent treasury, a settlement of the Oregon border dispute and the acquisition of California. Four years later, he achieved his goals.

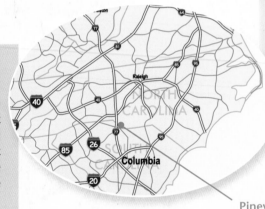

Pineville, North Carolina

Political Profile

- Member, United States House of Representatives
- United States Senator
- Justice, Tennessee Supreme Court
- Governor, Florida Territory
- President of the United States

1845
Alexander Dumas publishes
The Count of Monte Cristo

1845
Edgar Allan Poe publishes
The Raven and Other Poems

1846
The planet Neptune
is discovered

The Polk Administration Highlights

- Texas becomes a state (1845)
- The United States Naval Academy is founded (1845)
- The Oregon Treaty settles the border of the Oregon territory between the United States and Great Britain at the 49th parallel (1846)
- Act of Congress establishes the Smithsonian Institute, eight years after the United States received James Smithson's bequest (1846)
- Iowa becomes a state (1846)
- Gold is discovered at Sutter's Mill in California (1848)
- The first two U.S. postage stamps are issued (1847)
- Congress establishes a uniform election day, the first Tuesday following the first Monday of November (1845)
- Wisconsin becomes a state (1848)
- The cornerstone of the Washington Monument is laid (1848)
- The Home Department, later known as the Department of the Interior, is formed (1849)

CONNECTIONS

Nathaniel Currier, who printed an 1844 Polk campaign poster (see opposite page), is the same Currier of the iconic Currier & Ives Americana prints.

James Knox Polk, born in North Carolina and raised in Tennessee, was the son of one of the largest landholders in the region. During his youth he suffered from poor health. He attended local schools, was tutored at home, and then graduated first in his class from the University of North Carolina. Polk read law while serving as chief clerk for the Tennessee legislature. He was admitted to the bar in 1820 and, at the age of twenty-four, established a law practice.

In 1823, Polk entered politics as a successful candidate for the Tennessee Legislature and, because of his small stature, earned the nickname "Napoleon of the Stump." In 1824, Polk married Sarah Childress, the daughter of a merchant and planter. Polk entered the United States Legislature in 1825 as one of the many Andrew Jackson supporters determined to see Jackson elected president in 1828. He rose to prominence swiftly, serving President Jackson faithfully as chairman of the Ways and Means Committee, majority leader for the Democratic Party, and Speaker of the House -- he was the only speaker to become president.

In 1839, the 43-year-old Polk left Congress to run for, and win, the governorship of Tennessee. Polk's political star waned when he twice lost bids for re-election. He attended the 1844 Democratic National Convention hoping to be

1846
The final ringing of the Liberty Bell on the fiftieth anniversary of Washington's death

1846
Elias Howe invents a lock-stitch sewing machine

1848
The first women's rights convention is held in Seneca Falls, New York

nominated vice president on the ticket with the presumed presidential candidate, Martin Van Buren. The delegates were deadlocked. Polk supporters began spreading the word that Polk was former president Andrew Jackson's choice and, on the ninth ballot, Polk was unanimously chosen -- the first "dark horse" presidential candidate of a major party. Polk's nomination was flashed from Baltimore to Washington by Samuel F. B. Morse's telegraph, the first official use of the new communication system.

The 49-year-old Polk took office on a rainy March day with a four-point plan. The Democratically-controlled congress quickly passed one of the lowest tariffs in United States history and reestablished an independent treasury. The remainder of Polk's plan was territorial expansion, glamorized as the "Manifest Destiny" of the United States to stretch from coast to coast. The Oregon Treaty, signed in 1846, settled the border of the Oregon Territory between the United States and Great Britain, not at the campaign cry of "54-40 or Fight," a reference to the proposed latitude for the border, but at the 49th parallel. The treaty was reached with diplomacy rather than violence.

The acquisition of New Mexico, California, and Texas proved more difficult. The Mexican government protested the annexation of Texas, calling it "an act of aggression." Polk sent a diplomatic mission to Mexico

James Knox Polk was an astute, austere, arrogant protégé of Andrew Jackson. His supporters called him, "Young Hickory." He knew what the people wanted and he gave it to them, including more land to settle than Jefferson had given the country with the Louisiana Purchase.

Polk's wife Sarah was bright, outspoken, opinionated, and ambitious; the marriage was a partnership of equals, both devoting their energies to the advancement of James' career. So committed were they to the presidency that they did not take a single vacation during his four-year term. Polk, a strait-laced Methodist, and Sarah, a strict Presbyterian, banned dancing, drinking, and card playing from the White House. Socializing did not cease, but work always came first.

James and Sarah Polk.

When Polk left the chief executive's office, he said: "I feel exceedingly relieved that I am now free from all public cares." His weeks-long road home to Tennessee was exhausting and arduous. Polk arrived in Nashville a gravely ill man, probably from cholera. He suspected he would not recover. On June 15, 1849, only fifty-three years old and only 103 days out of office, Polk died, very quietly and with no struggle. He was laid to rest in a common cemetery, and then was moved to a vault at Polk Place, the home he never occupied. His body was finally moved to the grounds of the Tennessee State Capital in Nashville. Polk is the only president buried on the grounds of a state capital and the only president to have had three burial sites.

1849
Elizabeth Blackwell becomes the first
woman physician in the United States

The tomb of James Knox Polk and his wife Sarah in Nashville, Tennessee.

to reach a settlement for Texas, along with an offer to purchase territories corresponding to New Mexico and California. A dispute over the military breaching of the boundary between Texas and Mexico brought on hostilities. Polk called for a Declaration of War on May 9, 1846. Within two years and, after a string of hard-fought battles, the United States acquired not only Texas and California, but the entire southwestern portion of the country.

By the end of Polk's term, the dark horse turned workhorse was extraordinarily weary. James Buchanan, his Secretary of State, said that Polk, in a brief period of four years, had assumed the appearance of an old man. Polk made no effort to run for a second term. In 1849, inauguration day fell on a Sunday. Polk's term ended, but the President-elect, Zachary Taylor, was not sworn in until the next day, Monday. For one day, the country was without a leader.

Tell me more!

What were the first U.S. postage stamps?

The first two U.S. postage stamps were issued in 1847; one for five cents featured Benjamin Franklin's picture and the other for ten cents featured George Washington's picture.

My 2 cents
What would you nickname this president?

_____

The Author's Idea: Mr. Manifest Destiny

"Four score and seven years ago our fathers brought forth on this continent, a new nation, conceived in Liberty, and dedicated to the proposition that all men are created equal. Now we are engaged in a great civil war, testing whether that nation, or any nation so conceived and so dedicated, can long endure. We are met on a great battlefield of that war. We have come to dedicate a portion of that field, as a final resting place for those who here gave their lives that that nation might live. It is altogether fitting and proper that we should do this. But, in a larger sense, we can not dedicate--we can not consecrate--we can not hallow--this ground. The brave men, living and dead, who struggled here, have consecrated it, far above our poor power to add or detract. The world will little note, nor long remember what we say here, but it can never forget what they did here. It is for us the living, rather, to be dedicated here to the unfinished work which they who fought here have thus far so nobly advanced. It is rather for us to be here dedicated to the great task remaining before us- that from these honored dead we take increased devotion to that cause for which they gave the last full measure of devotion--that we here highly resolve that these dead shall not have died in vain- that this nation, under God, shall have a new birth of freedom--and that government of the people, by the people, for the people, shall not perish from the earth."

Abraham Lincoln
The Gettysburg Address
November 19, 1863

ABRAHAM LINCOLN
16th President of the United States

POLITICAL PARTY: Republican
ELECTION OPPONENTS:
  1860: Stephen Douglas, Democrat
          John Breckinridge, Democrat
          John Bell, Constitutional Union
  1864: George McClellan, Democrat
TERM OF OFFICE: March 4, 1861 to April 15, 1865
VICE PRESIDENTS:
  1860: Hannibal Hamlin
  1864: Andrew Johnson

Fun Assignment!

The U.S. minister to Great Britain under Lincoln was Charles Francis Adams. Who was his father?

John Quincy Adams; his grandfather was John Adams.

A reproduction of Abraham Lincoln's log-home birthplace at the Abraham Lincoln Birthplace National Historical Park in Hodgenville, Kentucky.

Personal Profile

BORN: February 12, 1809, Sinking Spring Farm Hardin County, Kentucky
SIBLINGS: Second of three children
RELIGION: Unaffiliated
EDUCATION: Limited
CAREER: Rail-splitter, postmaster, storekeeper, surveyor, lawyer

MILITARY: Captain, Illinois Militia, Black Hawk War (did not see action)
MARRIAGE: Mary Ann Todd November 4, 1842, Springfield, Illinois
OFFSPRING: Four sons
DIED: April 15, 1865, at boarding house across from Ford's Theatre, Washington, D.C.

Mary Ann Todd Lincoln

Visiting the President

BIRTHPLACE: Abraham Lincoln Birthplace National Historic Park
2995 Lincoln Farm Road, Hodgenville, Kentucky

BOYHOOD HOME: Knob Creek Farm
Route 31E, Hodgenville, Kentucky

HOMESTEAD: Lincoln Home National Historic Site
413 South Eighth Street, Springfield, Illinois

LIBRARY/MUSEUM:
The Abraham Lincoln Presidential Library and Museum
212 North Sixth Street, Springfield, Illinois

LINCOLN LAW OFFICE:
Lincoln-Herndon Law Offices, State Historic Site
6th and Adams Streets, Springfield, Illinois

GRAVESITE: Lincoln Tomb
Old Ridge Cemetery
1441 Monument Avenue, Springfield,
Illinois

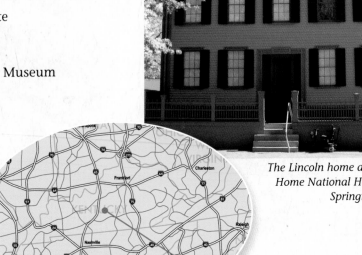

WIKI, Ian Manka

The Lincoln home at the Lincoln Home National Historic Site in Springfield, Illinois.

Hodgenville, Kentucky

Political Profile

- Member, Illinois legislature
- Member, United States House of Representatives
- President of the United States

1861
Julia Ward Howe writes the
Battle Hymn of the Republic

1861
Photographer Mathew Brady begins his historic photographic coverage of the Civil War

1861
Charles Dickens publishes
Great Expectations

The Lincoln Administration Highlights

- Congress creates the territories of Nevada and Colorado (1861)
- Slavery is abolished in the District of Columbia (1862)
- Congress establishes the Bureau of Internal Revenue (1862)
- The Arizona Territory is formed (1863)
- The Idaho Territory is formed (1863)
- West Virginia becomes a state (1863)
- Nevada becomes a state (1864)
- Salmon Chase becomes Chief Justice of the Supreme Court (1864)
- Congress passes the Thirteenth Amendment to the Constitution freeing all slaves (1865)

Lincoln's 1860 candidacy depicted as held up by the slavery issue, with a slave on the left and party organization on the right.

braham Lincoln's parents, uneducated and nearly illiterate, were typical of thousands of American frontier families in the nineteenth century who spent their lives in an endless struggle against poverty and the wilderness. Lincoln was born in a crude log cabin in Kentucky and raised in a three-sided lean-to in Indiana. His mother died when he was ten. A year later, his father married Sarah Johnston, who brought Lincoln affection and instilled in him a desire to learn. Lincoln developed a love for books and would walk miles to borrow one from a neighbor. In 1830, the Lincolns moved to Illinois.

During these frontier years, Lincoln worked the land, but also did countless odd jobs. At the age of twenty-one, Lincoln left home, settling in New Salem, Illinois, where he became a store clerk, popular for his wrestling, funny stories, and dependability. He continued his restless pursuit of self-education, concentrating on the study of law. Lincoln's political career started in 1834 with a successful run for the state legislature, where he remained for four terms. Lincoln passed the bar in 1836. In 1839, Lincoln embarked on his law career in Springfield. He met Mary Todd, the pretty, popular, and well-educated daughter of a banker. They planned to marry in 1840, but Lincoln broke off the engagement; they reconciled and wed in 1842. At the age of thirty-eight, Lincoln was elected to the United States House of Representatives, where he opposed the Mexican War and supported attempts to prohibit slavery in territories

1861
George Eliot publishes
Silas Marner

1861
Richard Jordan Gatling takes out
a patent for the first machine gun

1862
Louis Pasteur and Claude Bernard
complete the first trial of pasteurization

169

acquired as a result of the war. He returned to his law practice in 1849 and lost most of his political influence.

Lincoln was roused back into politics by the passage of the Kansas-Nebraska Act, which allowed territories to decide the slavery question by popular sovereignty. He then abandoned the dissolving Whig Party and joined the new anti-slavery Republican Party, becoming its candidate for senator from Illinois. His Democratic opponent was Stephen Douglas, sponsor of the Kansas-Nebraska Act. Lincoln kicked off his campaign with "A house divided against itself cannot stand" and challenged Douglas to a series of debates. Lincoln gained national attention, but lost the race. The master orator threw his energies into supporting Republican candidates throughout the North and enhancing his public image. At the 1860 National Republican Convention, Lincoln won on the third ballot. With the Democratic Party splintered, Lincoln won the presidency with less

Painting of Lincoln meeting with military leaders to discuss plans for the final months of the Civil War.

Abraham Lincoln was a six-foot, four-inch, thin, awkward, and homely looking man with coarse black hair and a high-pitched voice. He was a self-deprecating man of quick wit and oratory eloquence. His sorrowing, bearded face and gaunt black garb became a symbol of the weight he carried to preserve the Union. Lincoln's innate wisdom and humanity, his lack of pretension, and his commitment that "the Union of these States is perpetual" were suited to the critical period in which he served his country.

Abraham and Mary Todd Lincoln were of opposite

President Abraham Lincoln reading a book with his youngest son, Tad.

temperaments and backgrounds, but had a close, devoted marriage and were doting parents to four boys. Tragically, their son Eddie died in 1850 at the age of four and Willie died at the age of twelve during the wartime gloom in the White House. The war weighed heavily on the couple. They remained supportive and affectionate, but Abraham became moody and Mary mentally fragile.

Shortly after Lincoln's reelection, he had a dream that there was a catafalque with a body on it in the East Room. In his dream, he asked one of the soldiers on guard who it was that had died. The soldier replied: "The president was killed by an assassin." Lincoln, happier than anyone could remember, now was more troubled than he cared to admit -- even though he did not believe that dreams predicted the future. On Good Friday, April 14, 1865, Lincoln went to Ford's Theater when he would have preferred to stay at home. In Lincoln's case, it appears that dreams do come true; or, perhaps, it was Lincoln's time to leave the Union.

1863	1863	1864
The Red Cross is formed	The U.S. National Academy of Science is founded	Rebecca Lee Crumpler is the first U.S. African-American woman to earn a medical degree

than forty percent of the popular vote, but with the majority of the electoral votes.

When Lincoln took office, seven southern states had left the Union -- and others were preparing to do so too. Most federal ports in the South had been taken over by the secessionists. Fort Sumter, located in the harbor of Charleston, South Carolina, remained in federal hands. Lincoln made it a symbol of his determination and ordered much needed supplies be sent to the fort. On April 12, 1861, the Confederates bombarded the fort; Lincoln took this as a signal that only force could preserve the Union. He then called for volunteers to enlist in the army, while four more states seceded. Although the North had three times the population, better manufacturing capabilities and food supplies, and had two-thirds of the nation's railroads, the South had better military leadership. Lincoln searched in vain for a commanding general who could seize the initiative and crush the South. Between July 1861 and February 1864, four commanders failed to push the offensive progression of the war.

Finally, Lincoln appointed Ulysses S. Grant commander of all Union armies; it soon became only a matter of time until the war would be ended. In the midst of the war, Lincoln ran for a second term, urging voters not to "change horses in midstream." He won a resounding victory. In Lincoln's first inaugural address, he appealed to the "better angels" of the national character. At the dedication of the Soldiers' National Cemetery on the grounds of the Gettysburg Battlefield, he called for a "new birth of freedom." In his second inaugural address, Lincoln expressed a wish for "lasting peace among ourselves, with malice toward none, with charity for all."

The Civil War came to an end a month after the beginning of Lincoln's second term, but death came to Lincoln five days later at the hands of a brooding Southern sympathizer, John Wilkes Booth, who shot Lincoln in the head crying, "The South is avenged."

Lincoln's Tomb, Oak Ridge Cemetery, Springfield, Illinois.

Tell me more!

Assassination Plots

Lincoln was the target of two assassination plots. The first incident occurred during his train trip from Illinois to Washington after winning the election. When he was informed of a plot afoot in Baltimore, Lincoln secretly left his hotel in Harrisburg, Pennsylvania, and traveled by night train through Baltimore.

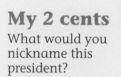

My 2 cents
What would you nickname this president?

_____

The Author's Idea: The Wood Splitter

The Textile Museum on S Street, NW in Washington, D.C.
Andrew Johnson had humble beginnings in textiles as a tailor in Greeneville, Tennessee.

ANDREW JOHNSON

17th President of the United States

POLITICAL PARTY: Democrat
ELECTION OPPONENTS: None
TERM OF OFFICE: April 15, 1865 to March 4, 1869
VICE PRESIDENT: None

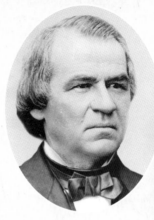

Fun Assignment!

More than a century separates the impeachment trials of Andrew Johnson and what other president?

Bill Clinton

Reconstruction of Andrew Johnson's birthplace, Raleigh, North Carolina.

WIKI, Mikehelms

Personal Profile

BORN: December 29, 1808
    Raleigh, North Carolina
SIBLINGS: Youngest of three children
RELIGION: Unaffiliated
EDUCATION: No formal education
CAREER: Master tailor

MILITARY: Military Governor of Tennessee
    with rank of Brigadier General
MARRIAGE: Eliza McCardle
    May 17, 1827, Warrensburg, Tennessee
OFFSPRING: Two daughters, three sons
DIED: July 31, 1875; Carter's Station,
    Tennessee

Eliza McCardle Johnson

1865
Previous president:
Abraham Lincoln

1865
Lewis Carroll publishes
Alice's Adventures in Wonderland

Visiting the President

BIRTHPLACE: Wake Forest Road, Raleigh, North Carolina
  • Birthplace structure (kitchen) and marker at site,
  located one mile from where it originally stood
BOYHOOD HOME/HOMESTEAD/GRAVESITE:
  Andrew Johnson National Historic Site
  121 Monument Avenue, Greeneville, Tennessee

WIKI, Brian Stansberry

The Andrew Johnson House in Greeneville, Tennessee.

Raleigh, North Carolina

Tell me more!

Play Ball!

Did you know that Andrew Johnson was a baseball fan? He was the first president to watch a Washington inter-city baseball game, the first to invite an entire baseball team to the White House and Johnson was the guest of honor at the opening of the new ballpark for the National Base Ball Club of Washington.

Political Profile

• Alderman, Greeneville, Tennessee
• Mayor, Greeneville, Tennessee
• Member, Tennessee Legislature
• Member, Tennessee State Senate
• Member, United States House of Representatives

• Governor of Tennessee
• Member, United States Senate
• Vice President of the United States
• President of the United States
• Member, United States Senate

1866
The Massachusetts Institute
of Technology opens

1866
The Ku Klux Klan
is formed

The Johnson Administration Highlights

- Proclamation grants amnesty to southerners who take an oath of loyalty to the Union (1865)
- The U.S. Secret Service is established (1865)
- Congress passes the Fourteenth Amendment to the Constitution, establishing citizenship of African-Americans, including their right to vote (1866)
- Tennessee is readmitted to the Union (1866)
- Nebraska becomes a state (1867)
- The United States purchases Alaska from Russia for $7.2 million (1867)
- The United States takes possession of the Midway Islands (1867)

A ndrew Johnson was born in poverty in Raleigh, North Carolina. His father, a laborer, died when Andrew was three. His mother was a seamstress and washerwoman. Both parents were illiterate. When he was fourteen, Johnson was apprenticed to a local tailor, but within a year, he ran away. He became a wandering tailor, honing his skill. In 1826, Johnson settled in Greeneville, Tennessee, and opened his own tailor shop. In 1827, the eighteen-year-old Johnson married sixteen-year-old Eliza McCardle, the daughter of a shoemaker, who taught him writing and simple arithmetic. A naturally gifted public speaker, Johnson served as alderman and then mayor of his town. Elected to both the state legislature and senate, Johnson became known as a friend of the common man and an enemy of the state's slave-holding aristocracy.

The fast-rising political star was elected to the United States House of Representatives for four terms, was governor of Tennessee for two terms, and then United States Senator

THE 'RAIL SPLITTER' AT WORK REPAIRING THE UNION.

1865 cartoon illustrating Lincoln and Johnson trying to reconstruct the United States after the Civil War.

1866
Howard University
is founded

1866
The American Society for the Prevention
of Cruelty to Animals is chartered

in 1857. In 1860, after Abraham Lincoln was elected president, Johnson spoke in the Senate, denouncing the secessionist movement. He became the only southern member of Congress to remain with the Union, despite his home state joining the Confederacy. Lincoln appointed Johnson military governor of Tennessee. During Johnson's tenure, Tennessee amended their constitution to abolish slavery, the only seceding state to end slavery by its own action. In 1864, at the National Union Convention, Johnson was chosen the vice presidential running mate of President Lincoln. The presence of a Democrat on the ticket helped to run up a large majority over the Democratic opponent. At the inauguration, Johnson gave

Illustration of Johnson's impeachment trial in the United States Senate, published in Harper's Weekly, *April 11, 1868.*

Andrew Johnson was a man of integrity, courage, and honesty. He also was proud, rude, vindictive, and combative in nature. The former tailor who had never been to school a day in his life, Johnson, an accidental president, was thrust into the White House by an assassin's bullet. No other president before or since have had a term of office filled with more malevolence, turmoil, and violent politics.

Johnson's wife, Eliza ,was a gentle, unpretentious woman who once said she and Andrew were "two souls and minds merged into one." Eliza was an invalid and rarely left her room in the White House; she willingly handed over all social duties to her daughter Martha.

Johnson left Washington by train. One of his stops was at Lynchburg, Virginia, where he had earlier been threatened and burned in effigy. Now, however, the city welcomed him. In his hometown of Greeneville, Tennessee, a banner across the Main Street read: "Welcome Home, Andrew Johnson, Patriot." In 1861, a banner in the same spot had read, "Andrew Johnson, Traitor." Johnson had a burning desire for political vindication. With no power base, little help, and several attempts, Johnson succeeded, winning a United States senate seat in 1874, ironically by a single vote. He is the only former president to be elected as a senator. Only five months into his senatorial term, Johnson died of a stroke. In accord with his wishes, his body was wrapped in a United States flag and his own copy of the Constitution was placed under his head. His wife, Eliza, whose support was vital to him, followed him in death five months later.

a rambling, incoherent speech, appearing drunk. Lincoln responded, "I've known Andy a great many years, and he ain't no drunkard."

On the night Lincoln was shot, the conspirators also intended to kill Johnson, but plans went awry. After an

1867
Johann Strauss, Jr. publishes
the *Blue Danube*

1867
Alfred Nobel obtains
a patent on dynamite

WIKI, Brian Stansberry

Statue of President Andrew Johnson in Greeneville, Tennessee, at the Andrew Johnson National Historic Site.

agonizing night-long deathwatch at Lincoln's bedside, Johnson was sworn in as President of the United States. The new president quickly became embroiled in a bitter inter-governmental conflict over the reconstruction of the South. He advanced policies that were viewed as lenient toward the South. Radical Republicans were outraged, believing that the South should be punished and the rights of the black freedmen protected. Johnson relentlessly vetoed Radical Republican legislation. In all cases, Congress overrode his vetoes. Johnson challenged the Tenure of Office Act, which forbade the president to remove any federal office holder who had been appointed by and with the advice and consent of the Senate by removing his Secretary of War from office. The Supreme Court refused to rule on the dispute, and this led to a resolution in the House of Representatives for Johnson's impeachment. The trial in the Senate lasted three months, but Johnson was acquitted on May 26, 1868, by a single vote. After the trial, the deadlock between Johnson and Congress continued. The president entertained some hope of receiving a presidential nomination from the Democrats in 1868, but it was not forthcoming. Johnson did not accompany the incoming president, Ulysses S. Grant, to the Capital for his inauguration.

CONNECTIONS

On April 10, 1866, the American Society for the Prevention of Cruelty to Animals (SPCA) was chartered in New York. The first SPCA had been organized in England in 1824, primarily to prevent the abuse of carriage horses in the days before the automobile. The SPCA now has locations worldwide.

My 2 cents
What would you nickname this president?

_____

The Author's Idea: Lincoln's Tailor

The Hoover Dam

Completed in 1936, the dam stands above the Colorado River between Arizona and Nevada, and controls water flow to agricultural areas and provides hydroelectric energy. It also creates a gigantic reservoir, Lake Mead.

HERBERT CLARK HOOVER

31st President of the United States

POLITICAL PARTY: Republican
ELECTION OPPONENTS:
 Alfred Smith, Democrat
 Norman Thomas, Socialist
TERM OF OFFICE: March 4, 1929 to March 4, 1933
VICE PRESIDENT: Charles Curtis

Fun Assignment!

Herbert Hoover's length of retirement after leaving the White House, thirty-one years, is the longest to date. Can you name the presidents with the second and third longest retirements?

Gerald Ford, twenty-nine years and John Adams, twenty-five years.

Birthplace of Herbert Hoover, West Branch, Iowa.

WIKI, Billwhittaker

Personal Profile

BORN: August 10, 1874, West Branch, Iowa
SIBLINGS: Second of three children
RELIGION: Quaker
EDUCATION: Stanford University;
 graduated 1895
CAREER: Mining Engineer

MILITARY: None
MARRIAGE: Lou Henry
 February 10, 1899, Monterey, California
OFFSPRING: Two sons
DIED: October 20, 1964, New York,
 New York

*Lou Henry
Hoover*

1929
Previous president:
Calvin Coolidge

1929
The first Academy Awards
is held

1929
Erich Maria Remarque publishes
All Quiet on the Western Front

Visiting the President

BIRTHPLACE/LIBRARY/MUSEUM/GRAVESITE:
Herbert Hoover National Historic Site
110 Parkside Drive, West Branch, Iowa
HOMESTEAD:
Lou Henry and Herbert Hoover House
Stanford University Campus, Palo Alto, California

Stanford Graduates

Herbert Hoover was a member of the first graduating class from Stanford University; his wife, Lou, was the first woman to major in geology at the same university.

The Lou Henry and Herbert Hoover House at Stanford University in Palo Alto, California. The house was designed by Lou Henry Hoover.

West Branch, Iowa

Political Profile

- Head, Commission for Relief in Belgium
- United States Food Administrator
- Director, American Relief Administration

- Secretary of Commerce
- Chairman, Street and Highway Safety Commission
- President of the United States

1930	1930	1930
The planet Pluto is discovered	Construction of the Hoover Dam begins	The 1930 census shows a U.S. population of 123.2 million

The Hoover Administration Highlights

- "Black Thursday" occurs, the overly inflated stock market crashes (1929)
- The Veterans Administration is established (1930)
- "The Star-Spangled Banner" is officially adopted as the national anthem (1931)
- The Twentieth Amendment to the Constitution is passed, changing swearing-in dates of elected officials from March to January (1932)
- The Twenty-First Amendment to the Constitution is passed, repealing prohibition of alcohol (1933)

Herbert Hoover was born in the middle of the horse and buggy age of the nineteenth century. By the time he was nine, both his parents had died. Hoover was sent to live with his uncle, a doctor and farmer, in Oregon. During his adolescent years, Bert, as he was called, did chores on the farm. His uncle established a real estate office and Bert clerked for him while attending school at night.

After meeting several mining engineers, Hoover decided to major in geology at Stanford University in California, graduating in 1895. Hoover initially worked as a typist in an engineering office, but was quickly sent to work in the gold mining fields in Australia. In 1899, Hoover married Lou Henry, a fellow student at Stanford, and together they went to China where Hoover was appointed as China's leading engineer. In 1909, Hoover set up his own international engineering and financial consulting firm. While in London, World War I abruptly ended Hoover's career as an engineer by opening a new one as a public servant. Merging his organizational and humanitarian instincts, Hoover fed and clothed millions in German-occupied Belgium. In

Herbert Hoover at about 4 years old.

The Statue of Isis was given to Herbert Hoover by the people of Belgium in 1922. It resides at the Herbert Hoover National Historic Site in West Branch, Iowa.

1930
Uruguay wins the first World Cup for soccer

1931
The state of Nevada legalizes gambling and shortens the residency requirement for divorce

1931
The Empire State Building opens in New York City

A "Hooverville" shanty town, this one along the Willamette River in Portland, Oregon. These "towns" were named after President Herbert Hoover because many people thought he knowingly let the nation slide into the Great Depression of 1929. During this time, Bennett buggies, or "Hoover wagons," were cars pulled by horses because farmers were too poor to purchase gasoline.

Tall and sturdy with broad shoulders, hazel eyes, and a round face, **Herbert Hoover** was soft-spoken, very private, and predictably proper and reserved. A penniless orphan, he was a self-made millionaire before the age of forty. Hoover opposed direct federal aid to those in need because it contradicted his philosophy of helping people to help themselves. He believed the federal government should be the last resort, not the first, and regarded the "dole" as contrary to the ideals of the American people. Nonetheless, during his term, Hoover donated his presidential salary to charity and personally paid for all White House entertainment.

The country was impatient that it had to wait four months before Hoover's successor could take office. This impatience helped bring about the Twentieth Amendment to the Constitution, which advanced the president-elect's inauguration from March 4th to January 20th.

Hoover and his wife Lou shared an appetite for adventure and a love of geology. In the early years of their marriage, they produced the first Latin to English translation of the sixteenth-century classic work Agricola's De Re Metallica. Their language facility also allowed them to speak in Chinese if they wanted to avoid being understood by the White House staff. Lou said Hoover's faith in God helped him through the dark days of the Depression. She was a great source of comfort to her husband, not seeking the limelight or publicity, but being constantly at his side. Following Lou's death in 1944, Hoover, distraught and feeling he could not live in the California home Lou had planned, lived the remainder of his life in Suite 31-A at the Waldorf Tower in New York City. Hoover remained an active public servant, receiving ninety honorary degrees. He lived long enough to see the public's perception of him change dramatically. Becoming president, in retrospect, would turn out to be the least of Herbert Hoover's many accomplishments.

The Waldorf-Astoria Hotel in New York City where Hoover lived out his final days.

1932	1932	1932
Amelia Earhart becomes the first woman to fly solo across the Atlantic	The atom is split, producing a nuclear reaction	CBS becomes the first television network to air coverage of a presidential election

1917, as the United States Food Administrator, Hoover advocated "Meatless Mondays," "Wheatless Wednesdays," and "War Gardens" since food producers needed to feed not only the country's citizens, but also the United States' troops and their allies. After the war, as director of the American Relief Administration, Hoover continued to help feed millions in more than twenty countries.

CONNECTIONS
In both the 1932 summer Olympics in Los Angeles, California, and the 1932 winter Olympics at Lake Placid, New York, the U.S. won the most medals.

Hoover served as Secretary of Commerce under Presidents Harding and Coolidge. He was urged to seek the Republican presidential nomination in 1928. When he asked President Coolidge if it was alright, Coolidge replied, "Why not?" Hoover was nominated on the

first ballot and became president of the United States in his first attempt to win an elected office. Hoover entered the White House optimistic. He intended his administration to be a progressive, reform regime. Totally unforeseen was the stock market crash of October 1929, just seven months after his inauguration. The ensuing depression turned his dream into a nightmare. Millions were unemployed, and bread lines appeared everywhere. Businesses were going bankrupt by the thousands. Desperate World War I veterans marched on Washington as a "Bonus Army," seeking immediate cash for military bonus certificates not payable until 1945. They camped in ramshackle huts on the outskirts of the city in what was called "Hooverville."

The president's attempts to stop the financial bleeding were a matter of "too little, too late" in the public's eyes and his opposition to direct federal aid to the unemployed was seen as callous and uncaring. Hoover was reluctant to take aggressive measures to right the economy. However,

This iconic 1936 photo by Dorothea Lange represented the desperation born of both the Great Depression and the Dust Bowl.

he did launch new public works initiatives, some of which were continued by the next administration. In 1932, the Republicans re-nominated Hoover with little enthusiasm; Hoover lost re-election by a landslide to his Democratic opponent, Franklin D. Roosevelt. Photographs of Hoover during the closing days of his administration show a very harried and distressed man. He left the White House frustrated and saddened.

My 2 cents
What would you nickname this president?

_____

The Author's Idea: Mr. Humanitarian

WIKI, AgnosticPreachersKid

The Blair House, Washington, D.C.
During Harry S. Truman's full term as president, the Blair House served as his interim home while the White House underwent major renovations. After twenty-seven months, the Trumans moved back into the White House on March 27, 1952.

HARRY S. TRUMAN

33rd President of the United States

POLITICAL PARTY: Democratic
ELECTION OPPONENTS:
  1948: Thomas Dewey, Republican
           Strom Thurmond, Dixiecrat
TERM OF OFFICE: April 12, 1945 to January 20, 1953
Vice President: 1945, none; 1949, Alben Barkley

The Harry S. Truman birthplace,
Lamar, Missouri.

Fun Assignment!

Harry Truman had poor vision. At the age of six, he acquired his first pair of eyeglasses. How did Truman manage to pass the eye test for entrance to the Army?

Truman memorized the eye chart.

Personal Profile

BORN: May 8, 1884, Lamar, Missouri
SIBLINGS: Second-born, but eldest of four
  surviving children
RELIGION: Baptist
EDUCATION: University of Kansas City Law
  School; did not graduate
CAREER: Railroad timekeeper, bank clerk,
  farmer, investor in an oil company,
  and haberdasher.

MILITARY: First lieutenant, discharged as
  a major, retired as a colonel
MARRIAGE: Elizabeth Virginia Wallace
  June 28, 1919, Independence, Missouri
OFFSPRING: one daughter
DIED: December 26, 1972, Kansas City,
  Missouri

Elizabeth
Virginia Wallace
Truman

1945	1945	1945
Previous president: Franklin Delano Roosevelt	The Nuremberg trials begin	George Orwell publishes *Animal House*

Visiting the President

BIRTHPLACE: Harry S. Truman Birthplace State Historic Site
1009 Truman Street, Lamar, Missouri

FARM: Truman Farm
12302 Blue Ridge Boulevard, Grandview, Missouri

HOMESTEAD: Truman House
219 North Delaware Street, Independence, Missouri

SUMMER HOME: The Little White House
111 Front Street, Key West, Florida

LIBRARY/MUSEUM/GRAVESITE:
Harry S. Truman Library and Museum
500 West U.S. Highway 24
Independence, Missouri

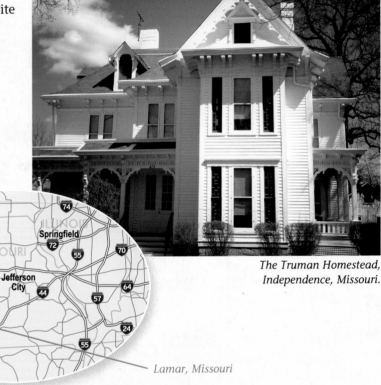

The Truman Homestead,
Independence, Missouri.

WIKI, Nationalparks

Lamar, Missouri

Political Profile

- Judge, Presiding Judge, Jackson County, Missouri

- Member, United States Senate
- Vice President of the United States
- President of the United States

1946
The United Nations Children's
Fund (UNICEF) is founded

1946
Tupperware
is introduced

1946
Eugene O'Neill publishes
The Iceman Cometh

The Truman Administration Highlights

- Charter for the United Nations is signed (1945)
- President's Committee on Civil Rights is instituted (1946)
- The 22nd Amendment to the Constitution is passed, limiting presidents to two terms in office (1947)
- Presidential Succession Act is signed (1947)
- The National Security Act is signed which establishes the National Security Council, the Central Intelligence Agency, the Department of Defense and the Department of the Air Force (1947)
- The North Atlantic Treaty Organization (NATO) is created (1949)
- The first hydrogen bomb is detonated by the United States (1952)

Truman's famous "The Buck Stops Here" sign sat on his oval-office desk.

The son of a mule trader, Harry S. Truman was born in a small house in Lamar, Missouri. Over the next six years, the Truman family moved three times before settling in Independence, Missouri. Because of his need for eyeglasses and months of illness with diphtheria, he was excluded from play with friends. Therefore, he spent a great deal of time reading and practicing piano. After graduating from high school, Truman moved from job to job, until, at the age of twenty-two, he moved back home, now his grandfather's farm. He was a dirt farmer for the next ten unhappy years.

With World War I looming, Truman enlisted in the army and received special artillery training. He proved to be a tough captain, earning the respect of his men. Truman saw heavy action in the Vosges Mountains and the Argonnes, both in France. He was discharged May 1919 and, at the age of thirty-five, married his long-time sweetheart, Elizabeth Wallace. That same year, Truman opened a haberdashery in Kansas City; however, the business failed three years later.

Unsuccessful in a number of career endeavors, Truman turned to politics. With the endorsement of the local Democratic kingpin, he served as judge and presiding judge of his county, overseeing property and finances for ten years. In 1934, Truman ran for the United States Senate and won. With astounding

Tell me more!

The First Medicare Recipients

On July 30, 1965, in a ceremony at the Truman Library, President Lyndon Johnson signed the bill that created Medicare. Harry and Bess Truman received the first two Medicare registration cards.

1947	1947	1947
Dr. Edwin Land demonstrates the Polaroid instant "Land" Camera	Jackie Robinson is the first African-American major league baseball player	Air Force pilot Chuck Yeager is the first to fly faster than the speed of sound

suddenness, the fifty-year-old Truman was launched into big-time politics. He won a second term against great odds, proving to be a skillful and indefatigable campaigner. During his second term, Truman became nationally prominent as head of a Special Senate Committee investigating defense spending. At the 1944 Democratic National Convention, Truman was seen as having mainstream voter appeal and was nominated to be Franklin Roosevelt's running mate, despite his assertions that he did not want the nomination.

After Roosevelt's fourth-term victory, the sixty-year-old Truman was sworn in as Vice President. Eighty-two days later, on April 12, 1945, Truman was called to the White House at 5:25 p.m., where Mrs. Roosevelt greeted him with the words: "Harry, the president is dead." Truman became the nation's seventh accidental president. Twenty-five days later, on Truman's sixty-first birthday, Germany

Harry S. Truman's middle initial was chosen by his parents to represent both his paternal and maternal grandfathers. Though he was a self-admitted "sissy" who would run rather than get into a fistfight, he later enlisted in the army. In fact, he was so determined to enlist that he memorized the eye chart, fearing that his poor eyesight might disqualify him. Later, he served meritoriously in France during World War I. After he left the army, and following the near bankruptcy of his clothing store business, he decided to make politics his career, since it suited his personality well.

In his personal life, Truman's relationship with his wife Bess was always central to him. Harry had met Bess in Sunday school when he was six and she five, setting off a devotion that would last his lifetime. Truman wrote countless love letters and upon his third marriage proposal, she accepted. Bess detested her years in the White House, but was always an advisor and confidante to her husband. She rarely participated in the social life of the Capitol. She did not like the public role and resented the public scrutiny into her family's privacy. Consequently, Bess was considerably more pleased about leaving Washington than Harry. She was packed and ready to move out on January 20, 1953. Truman called Bess "The Boss," and she was.

The Trumans' wedding photo.

Harry Truman was a confident, earnest and incorruptible man who thrived on the rough and tumble of politics. During his term in office, Truman personified three of his favorite expressions: "The buck stops here," "If you can't take the heat, get out of the kitchen," and "Give 'em hell, Harry."

The city of Independence donated a large part of a city park to Truman for his library and museum. The location was close to his home at 219 North Delaware Street, near enough for the aging former president to walk to his office at the library. The ground-breaking ceremony was held on Truman's seventy-first birthday. To celebrate the opening of the library and museum, all 150 guests attended an old-fashioned country dinner at the Truman home, just the way Harry and Bess liked it. Harry S. Truman is buried in the library courtyard because, as he quipped, "I can get up and walk into my office if I want to."

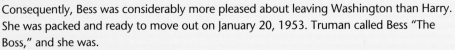

1947
Meet the Press has its television premiere

1947
The Howdy Doody Show debuts on television

1948
The national political conventions are televised for the first time

surrendered. Over the next year, Truman spoke at the United Nations founding conference meeting, attended the Potsdam Conference, authorized the use of the atomic bomb against Japan, and moved the nation toward a peacetime economy. He sent Congress a twenty-one point message outlining his Fair Deal program, his vision for a post-war America.

In the foreign policy arena, Truman feared the expansion of Communism. In a speech to Congress in March 1947, he announced the Truman Doctrine, which was meant to support free people who were resisting attempted subjugation. An outgrowth of the Doctrine was the Marshall Plan, providing U.S. resources to stimulate European post-war recovery. In 1948, despite inter-party conflicts, Truman was nominated to run for a full presidential term. The race pitted Truman, a blue-collar Midwesterner, against a sophisticated New York politician. Truman waged an exhaustive "whistle stop" campaign across the country. Despite the odds, he ended up pulling off an astonishing upset.

The atomic bombing of Nagasaki, August 9, 1945. Hiroshima had been bombed first, three days earlier.

Replica of the Truman Oval Office at the Harry S. Truman Presidential Library and Museum, Independence, Missouri.

Not long into his term, another military conflict would test Truman's acumen for leadership. In June 1950, North Korea invaded South Korea. The United Nations called on members to provide military assistance to South Korea. To avoid asking Congress for a declaration of war, Truman called the United States military involvement a "police action." With the American public growing more and more discontented with him and his administration, and with party support ebbing, Truman announced he would not seek reelection and instead campaigned for the Democratic presidential candidate, attacking his Republican opponent, Dwight (Ike) Eisenhower. The transition of authority to the incoming Eisenhower Administration was neither warm nor friendly. Harry was furious and Ike was icy as the two men rode side-by-side to the president-elect's inauguration.

My 2 cents
What would you nickname this president?

_____

The Author's Idea: The Piano Man

1949
George Orwell
publishes *1984*

1951
J.D. Salinger publishes
Catcher in the Rye

1953
Successor president:
Dwight D. Eisenhower

189

National World War II Memorial
The War Memorial was dedicated May 29, 2004. It is flanked by the Washington Monument and the Lincoln Memorial. The World War II Memorial honors the 16 million who served in the United States armed forces and the more than 400,000 who died in the war.

DWIGHT DAVID EISENHOWER

34th President of the United States

POLITICAL PARTY: Republican
ELECTION OPPONENTS:
  1952 and 1956, Adlai Stevenson, Democrat
TERM OF OFFICE: January 20, 1953 to January 20, 1961
VICE PRESIDENT: Richard Nixon

Fun Assignment!

Eisenhower renamed the presidential retreat in Maryland to Camp David, in honor of his grandson. What was its original name?

Franklin Roosevelt called it Shangri-la.

Eisenhower's birthplace,
Denison, Texas.

Personal Profile

BORN: October 14, 1890, Denison, Texas
SIBLINGS: Third of seven sons
RELIGION: Presbyterian
EDUCATION: United States Military
  Academy at West Point; graduated 1915
CAREER: President of Columbia University,
  New York, New York

MILITARY: Commissioned 2nd lieutenant;
  rose to five-star general
MARRIAGE: Mamie Geneva Doud
  July 1, 1916, Denver, Colorado
OFFSPRING: Two sons
  (Firstborn "Icky" died before the age of 4)
DIED: March 28, 1969, Washington, D.C.

Mamie
Geneva Doud
Eisenhower

1953
Previous president:
Harry S. Truman

1953
Maureen Connolly becomes the first
woman to win the Grand Slam of tennis

191

Visiting the President

BIRTHPLACE: 208 East Day Street, Denison, Texas
HOMESTEAD: Eisenhower Farm, Gettysburg, Pennsylvania
• Tours available through the Gettysburg Battlefield
Visitors Center
LIBRARY/MUSEUM/GRAVESITE:
Dwight D. Eisenhower Library and Museum
200 Southeast 4th Street, Abilene, Kansas

Eisenhower's office in his Gettysburg, Pennsylvania farmhouse.

Denison, Texas

Tell me more!

50th Anniversary

The Eisenhowers celebrated their 50th wedding anniversary in 1966 after his presidency. They were the first presidential couple to celebrate a 50th wedding anniversary since Louisa and John Quincy Adams in 1847.

Political Profile

• President of the United States

The Eisenhower Center grounds, Abilene, Kansas.

1954	1954	1955
British physician Roger Bannister becomes the first person to run a mile in less than 4 minutes	The first issue of *Sports Illustrated* is published	Physicist Albert Einstein dies

The Eisenhower Administration Highlights

- Department of Health, Education and Welfare (HEW) created (1953)
- United States and North Korea sign armistice (1953)
- Earl Warren appointed Chief Justice of the Supreme Court (1953)
- First nuclear submarine, The USS Nautilus is launched (1954)
- United States Air Force Academy is created (1954)
- In Brown v the Board of Education of Topeka, Kansas, the Supreme Court rules segregated schools unconstitutional (1954)
- The Presidential Libraries Act allows construction of presidential libraries through private funds but their maintenance by the federal government (1955)
- Bill signed adding "under God" to the Pledge of Allegiance (1956)
- A joint resolution of Congress authorizes "In God We Trust" as the national motto of the United States (1956)
- The Federal Aid Highway Act standardizes the interstate highway system of the United States (1956)
- U.S. Surgeon General reports link between cigarette smoking and lung cancer (1957)
- The National Aeronautics and Space Agency (NASA) is created (1958)
- Alaska and Hawaii become states (1959)
- Diplomatic relations with Cuba are severed (1961)

CONNECTIONS
In 1957, Leroy Edgar Burney was the first Surgeon General to warn of a link between smoking and lung cancer. Eisenhower's four-pack-a-day habit took a huge toll on his health.

Mamie and Dwight D. Eisenhower in 1916.

Following the failure of his general store in Hope, Kansas, David Jacob Eisenhower moved his family to Denison, Texas, where his third son, Dwight David, was born. A year later the family returned to their roots in Abilene, Kansas. With six boys, the Eisenhowers struggled to make ends meet. The family was religious, resourceful, hardworking, and close knit. As a young boy, Dwight's classmates had difficulty pronouncing his last name and a shortened version surfaced: "Ike." He enjoyed football and reading history, particularly about military heroes.

Following his high school graduation, Eisenhower was denied admittance to the United States Naval Academy because of his age; he then applied to the Military Academy at West Point. Eisenhower entered

West Point on June 14, 1911 at the age of twenty. He was honest, open, and likable; he also showed skills in interpersonal relationships. These characteristics would bode him well in his future military career. His graduating class would later be known as "The class that the stars fell upon," as many from the Class of 1915 would go on to become generals. Eisenhower was posted to San Antonio, Texas, as a second lieutenant. He was introduced to eighteen-year-old Mamie Doud from Denver, Colorado; they married within ten months. It is said that Eisenhower told Mamie that his country came first and she came second.

Over the next twenty-five years, Eisenhower was assigned posts in Panama, Europe, and the Philippines. Five days after the Japanese attack on Pearl Harbor, Eisenhower was appointed chief of the

The **Eisenhower** brothers were close-knit and were raised in an environment that emphasized fairness, hard work, thrift, and community service. Their parents were devout members of a pacifist Protestant sect called the River Brethren. His mother Ida, mindful of the River Brethren pacifism, cried when her son Dwight left for West Point. However, she did live to see him become a five-star general. All her other sons were successful as well. At a ceremony honoring the General, Ida was asked by the press if she was proud of her son. She replied, "Which one?"

Eisenhower left the Oval Office extremely popular with the American people, but he was not a well man. In 1955, he suffered his first heart attack followed by a mild stroke in 1957. His four-pack-a-day smoking habit in combination with occupational stress over a long period of time had taken its toll on his health.

Eisenhower and Mamie retired to their farm near Gettysburg, Pennsylvania, on the edge of the famous battlefield. He was familiar with the terrain, having been stationed at nearby Camp Colt during World War I. Eisenhower suffered a series of debilitating heart attacks and was gradually forced to curtail his activities. Finally, on May 14, 1968, he was admitted to Walter Reed Hospital in Washington, D.C., where he remained for the last eleven months of his life. On March 28, 1969, surrounded by the family he loved, the old soldier gave his last command: "I want to go. God take me." He was seventy-nine years old.

The Eisenhower home in Gettysburg, Pennsylvania.

War Plans Division and then general of the European Theater of Operations. In 1943, he was appointed Supreme Commander of all Allied forces in Europe. Eisenhower directed the greatest amphibian invasion in history on June 6, 1944 -- "D-Day" -- the beginning of the end of the European conflict. In late 1945, he was appointed Chief of Staff of the Army. Eisenhower retired from active service in 1948 as a five-star general and accepted a position as president of Columbia University. In 1950, Eisenhower returned to active duty to serve as Supreme Allied Commander of the North Atlantic Treaty Organization (NATO). As the presidential election of 1952 neared, politicians from both the major political parties made overtures to Eisenhower. Declaring himself a Republican, he sought and won that party's nomination and ultimately the presidency.

1957
Dr. Seuss publishes
The Cat in the Hat

1959
The Guggenheim Museum, designed by
Frank Lloyd Wright, opens in New York

Eisenhower Statue at West Point, New York.

During Eisenhower's eight years in the White House, he was faced with major foreign and domestic issues. His first action was to secure an armistice with North Korea. He crafted the Southeast Asian Treaty Organization (SETO) in response to the threat of Communism in that region. He also proposed United States support, both military and economic, for countries in the Middle East threatened by Communism. He attempted to reach accord and ease Cold War tensions with the Soviet Union. He urged nuclear disarmament and the peaceful development of atomic power.

Communism in the United States also was considered a threat. In 1954, Joseph McCarthy chaired hearings during which he claimed that there was Communist infiltration in the United States Army and Communist sympathizers in the government. Eisenhower insisted the hearings be televised. The public became disenchanted with McCarthy when he was unable to substantiate his claims. The domestic revolution for the civil rights of African-Americans also began during the Eisenhower Administration. In 1954, the Supreme Court ruled that segregation in public schools was unconstitutional. A year later, segregation on interstate buses and trains was banned. That same year Rosa Parks was arrested for refusing to give her seat on a bus to a white man, triggering a bus boycott in Montgomery, Alabama. In 1957, Eisenhower sent federal troops to Little Rock, Arkansas, to quell attempts to block black students from entering previously all white public schools. Eisenhower signed the Civil Rights Act of 1957, ensuring blacks the right to vote.

A lasting legacy for Eisenhower was the improvement in the interstate highway system. More than 40,000 miles of road were built. Conversely, a major disappointment for him was the disintegration of U.S.-Soviet Union relations. In May 1960, a United States reconnaissance plane (U-2) was shot down over the Soviet Union; the pilot was captured and convicted of espionage. The Soviet leader demanded an apology from Eisenhower; the president refused and future proposed talks were cancelled by the Soviets, ending hopes for progress toward nuclear disarmament.

In 1961, Eisenhower returned to private life after forty-six years of military and public service. He was 72 -- the oldest president to leave the White House at the time. He was disappointed that the Republican ticket lost, but welcomed his successor, John F. Kennedy, the youngest president ever elected to the office.

My 2 cents
What would you nickname this president?

_____

The Author's Idea: 5 Stars

1959
Barbie is introduced at the
New York City Toy Fair

1961
Successor president:
John F. Kennedy

195

Vietnam Veterans Memorial
The Vietnam Veterans Memorial Wall listed 58,175 servicemen and women killed in the conflict when it was completed in 1993.

LYNDON BAINES JOHNSON

36th President of the United States

POLITICAL PARTY: Democratic
ELECTION OPPONENT: 1964 Barry Goldwater, Republican
TERM OF OFFICE: November 22, 1963 to January 20, 1969
VICE PRESIDENT:
  1963: None
  1965: Hubert Humphrey

Fun Assignment!

In Johnson's 1965 State of the Union address he outlined his domestic political agenda and domestic policies. What was this program called?

It was referred to as the "Great Society."

Johnson's birthplace in Johnson City, Texas. Below, a young Lyndon at home in 1915.

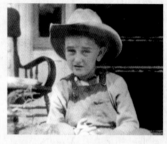

Personal Profile

BORN: August 27, 1908, Johnson City, Texas
SIBLINGS: Eldest of five children
RELIGION: Disciples of Christ
EDUCATION: Southwest Texas State Teachers
    College; graduated 1930
    Georgetown Law School (1934)
CAREER: Public School Teacher

MILITARY: Lieutenant Commander,
  United States Naval Reserve
MARRIAGE: Claudia Alta Taylor
  November 17, 1934, San Antonio, Texas
OFFSPRING: Two daughters
DIED: January 22, 1973, Stonewall, Texas

Claudia "Lady Bird" Alta Taylor Johnson

1963
Previous president:
John F. Kennedy

1963
The Pro Football Hall of Fame
opens in Canton, Ohio

197

Visiting the President

BOYHOOD HOME/NATIONAL PARK VISITOR CENTER:
Lyndon B. Johnson National Historic Park
Johnson City, Texas
BIRTHPLACE/RANCH/GRAVESITE:
Lyndon B. Johnson National Historic Park
14 miles west of Johnson City, Texas
LIBRARY/MUSEUM:
Lyndon Baines Johnson Library and Museum
2313 River Street, Austin, Texas

Tell me more!

Oath of office

Johnson is the only president sworn into office
by a woman. He took the oath from Judge Sarah
T. Hughes of Texas aboard Air Force One. The
ceremony took place at Love Field in Dallas.

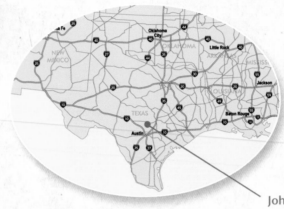

Johnson City, Texas

*President Nixon and
former President Johnson
at the Lyndon Baines
Johnson Library and
Museum dedication
in 1971.*

Political Profile

- Legislative Secretary
- Director, National Youth
  Administration

- Member, United States House of
  Representatives
- Member, United States Senate
- Vice President of the United States
- President of the United States

1963	1964	1964
John Le Carre publishes *The Spy Who Came in from the Cold*	The U.S. Surgeon General links cigarette smoking to lung disease	Dr. Martin Luther King Jr. is awarded the Nobel Prize for Peace

The Johnson Administration Highlights

- The 24th Amendment to the Constitution is passed, eliminating the poll tax (1962)
- The Civil Rights Act is signed (1964)
- The Economic Opportunity Act is signed (1964)
- The Social Security Act of 1965 is passed, establishing the Medicare and Medicaid programs (1965)
- The Department of Housing and Urban Development is established (1965)
- Executive Order 11246 enforces affirmative action (1965)
- The Immigration Bill is signed, abolishing national-origin quotas (1965)
- The Supreme Court rules in Miranda v Arizona that statements made by prisoners under interrogation cannot be used as evidence unless minimum legal safeguards are in place (1966)
- The Freedom of Information Act is signed; mandates that the government must provide information to citizens on request (1966)
- The Transportation Act is signed, creating the Department of Transportation (1966)
- The 25th Amendment to the Constitution is passed, specifies the presidential line of succession in the event of presidential disability (1965)
- Thurgood Marshall is sworn in as the first black U.S. Supreme Court justice (1967)
- The Air Quality Act is signed; federal air quality standards are set (1967)
- Formal peace talks begin in Paris between the United States and North Vietnam (1968)

Johnson signs the Medicare bill in 1965.

Lyndon Johnson grew up hearing the inside story of politics; his father and both of his grandfathers had been members of the Texas legislature. Like most families in their small town, the Johnsons struggled economically. As a result, Lyndon took odd jobs for spending money. After graduating from high school, he moved to California and lived the life of a hobo. Returning home, the future president enrolled in a local college, again working odd jobs to earn his way. One of these jobs involved teaching poor Mexican children, which shaped his view of the effects of

Lyndon Baines Johnson takes the oath of office aboard Air Force One in November 1963.

1964	1964	1965
General Douglas MacArthur publishes *Reminiscences*	*Hello Dolly!* and *Fiddler on the Roof* debut on Broadway	Edward H. White II becomes the first astronaut to walk in space

poverty on the nation's minorities. Johnson found his way to Washington as a legislative secretary to a Texas congressman, and over the next three years, he learned how Congress worked.

In 1934, after a two-month whirlwind courtship, Johnson married Claudia Taylor. Three years later, Johnson won a seat in the House of Representatives in a special election; he would then stand unopposed for reelection three times. Johnson was the first member of Congress to go on active military duty in World War ll, receiving a Silver Star for gallantry under enemy fire. In 1941, he ran unsuccessfully for the United States Senate. Not easily discouraged, he ran again in 1948. He won the Democratic primary by eighty-seven votes, but the senate seat by a two-to-one ratio. He quickly rose in the Senate hierarchy; first as party whip in 1951, then as Senate minority leader in 1953, and, finally, as

Lyndon Baines Johnson was a six foot, three inch, thin, restless youth. He grew up to be a man who relished power. Being fiercely competitive and a master of manipulation, his political methods were famously described as "The Johnson Treatment." He knew what he wanted and went after it. A case in point was his determination to marry Claudia Taylor the day he met her. Claudia, known as Lady Bird since the age of two, was an intelligent, refined woman, a sharp contrast to her husband, who could be crass and ruthless. By 1941, Johnson was known on the Hill as LBJ; his wife, two daughters and even their dog had the same initials. In 1967, Johnson had a secret actuarial study done to determine how long he was likely to live. The prediction was made that he probably would not see his sixty-fifth birthday, and he did not. In December, 1972, there were two living former presidents, Truman and Johnson. Truman died December 26, 1972 less than a month before Johnson. For the fifth time in American history, there were no living former presidents.

President Lyndon B. Johnson signs the 1964 Civil Rights Act.

Senate majority leader in 1954. At the age of forty-six, he was the youngest man ever elected Senate floor leader by either Democrats or Republicans. At the 1960 Democratic National Convention, Johnson hoped for the presidential spot on the ticket, but was nominated by acclamation to be the running mate for John Kennedy.

Although President Kennedy gave Johnson greater responsibility than ever before given to a vice president, his role was incompatible with his ambition and ego and far from the center of real power. That changed November

1965
Ralph Nader publishes
Unsafe at Any Speed

1966
The National Organization for
Women (NOW) is founded

1968
Martin Luther King, Jr. and Robert
F. Kennedy are shot and killed

Black civil rights leaders including Dr. Martin Luther King were welcomed to the White House by President Johnson in 1966.

CONNECTIONS

Beatlemania arrived in the United States when the English rock band, the Beatles appeared on the Ed Sullivan Show on February 9, 1964, drawing approximately 74 million viewers.

22, 1963 -- less than two hours after the assassination of John F. Kennedy, Johnson became the nation's eighth accidental president, sworn-in aboard Air Force One. Five days later, Johnson addressed a special joint session of Congress, calling for the continuation of the fallen president's New Frontier program.

In 1964, Johnson won a full presidential term by one of the greatest landslides in American history. He successfully pushed his Great Society initiatives: federally funded education programs, Medicare, expansion of anti-poverty programs, and civil rights. However, as Johnson escalated United States' involvement in Viet Nam by increasing troop numbers and air strikes, anti-war protestors swarmed the Capitol. As Johnson sought a better life for minorities, racial tensions flared into riots in major American cities. Johnson was a defeated man, unable to bring the military conflict to an acceptable conclusion, facing domestic violence in the streets, and enduring national discontent. These issues and events would turn out to be Johnson's undoing. On March 31, 1968, in a surprising and memorable television address to the American people, he said, "I shall not seek, and I will not accept, the nomination of my party for another term as your president." In so doing, Johnson followed the historic precedent that no "accidental" president ever had been elected twice to the presidency.

At this point, Johnson was tired and aged. He flew home to Texas on Air Force One, the same plane which five years earlier had flown him to Washington as the newly sworn-in president. Ironically, four years later, Air Force One would carry Lyndon Baines Johnson for the last time. It would carry his body back to his political home, the town he loved—Washington, D.C.—to lie in state in the Capital.

The Johnson grave, Johnson City, Texas

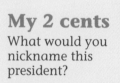

My 2 cents

What would you nickname this president?

_____

The Author's Idea: The Beltway Rancher

1968
Apollo 8 successfully
orbits the moon

1969
Successor president:
Richard Milhous Nixon

201

A majority of our presidents had pets in the White House or on its grounds. Famous among them were Lyndon Johnson's beagles, named Him and Her, and Richard Nixon's cocker spaniel, Checkers. Gerald Ford had his not-so-famous golden retriever, Liberty.

RICHARD MILHOUS NIXON

37th President of the United States

POLITICAL PARTY: Republican
ELECTION OPPONENTS:
   1968: Hubert Humphrey, Democrat
           George Wallace, American Independent
   1972: George McGovern, Democrat
           John Hospers, Libertarian
TERM OF OFFICE: January 20, 1969 to August 9, 1974
VICE PRESIDENT:
   1969, Spiro Agnew; 1973, Gerald Ford

The Richard Nixon birthplace,
Yorba Linda, California

Fun Assignment!

How many times was Richard Nixon on the Republican presidential ticket?

Five times: first two as vice president, one in his loss to John Kennedy and twice for president.

Personal Profile

BORN: January 9, 1913, Yorba Linda, California
SIBLINGS: Second of five brothers
RELIGION: Quaker
EDUCATION: Whittier College, graduated 1934;
   Duke University Law School, graduated 1937
CAREER: Lawyer

MILITARY: United States Navy lieutenant
   junior grade, retired lieutenant commander
MARRIAGE: Thelma Catherine Ryan
   June 21, 1940, Riverside, California
OFFSPRING: Two daughters
DIED: April 22, 1994, New York, New York

WIKI, http://www.nixonlibraryfoundation.org

*Thelma
Catherine "Pat"
Ryan Nixon*

1969
Previous president:
Lyndon Baines Johnson

1969
The Anglo-French Concorde aircraft
makes its maiden flight

203

Visiting the President

BIRTHPLACE/MUSEUM/LIBRARY/GRAVESITE:

Richard Nixon Presidential Library and Museum
18001 Yorba Linda Boulevard, Yorba Linda, California

*The Nixon Library Museum,
Yorba Linda, California*

Tell me more!

Threat of Impeachment

Nixon became the third president against whom articles of impeachment were drawn up, the others being Andrew Johnson and John Tyler. Of the three, Johnson was the only president to have been impeached, and subsequently tried by the Senate.

Yorba Linda, California

Political Profile

- Member, United States House of Representatives
- Member, United States Senate
- Vice President of the United States
- President of the United States

1969
James Earl Ray is sentenced for the murder of Dr. Martin Luther King, Jr.

1969
Neil Armstrong becomes the first human to set foot on the lunar surface

1969
The Woodstock Festival takes place

The Nixon Administration Highlights

- The Nuclear Weapons Non-Proliferation Treaty is signed (1969)
- The Environmental Protection Agency is established (1970)
- The Clean Air Act is signed (1970)
- Columbus Day is established as a federal holiday (1971)
- The 21-year-old trade embargo on China ends (1971)
- Louis Powell and William Rehnquist are confirmed as Supreme Court associate justices (1971)
- The Equal Opportunity Act is signed (1972)
- The Paris Peace Accords are signed, formally ending American military involvement in Vietnam (1973)

Richard Nixon was born into a family of meager means in Yorba Linda, California, and grew up in Whittier. His father ran a gas station and general store. During his early years, Nixon described his life as "family, church, and school." After graduating from Whittier College, Nixon won a scholarship to Duke University Law School, where he was known as "Gloomy Gus." He graduated in 1937. After passing the California bar, he settled on a position in his hometown. In June 1940, he married Thelma Ryan, a high school teacher, whom he met through a local amateur theater group. Despite his Quaker background, Nixon decided to enlist in the Navy after the United States entered World War II.

Richard Nixon gives his trademark double "victory" sign in his 1968 campaign for president in Philadelphia.

In 1945, Nixon entered politics when he responded to an ad looking for a Congressional candidate with no previous experience. He won handily, portraying the five-term incumbent as a Communist sympathizer. Nixon gained national attention as a member of the House Un-American Activities Committee. He took center stage in the prosecution of a former State Department official, Alger Hiss, who was charged with Communist affiliations. In 1950, riding on his fame as a Communist hunter, Nixon ran for the United States Senate, accusing his opponent of being a supporter of Communist policies. Again, Nixon won. It was this campaign where he earned the nickname "Tricky Dick." At the 1952 Republican National Convention, Nixon was nominated for vice president. His home state had a large electoral vote and his youth offset the presidential candidate's age. Shortly thereafter,

1971	1972	1972
Congress passes the 26th Amendment, lowering the voting age from 21 to 18	Governor George Wallace is shot while campaigning for president	The Supreme Court declares the death penalty unconstitutional

Nixon was accused of financial wrongdoing, which threatened his spot on the ticket. He challenged those allegations in a nationally televised "Checkers" speech, referring to their family dog. The Republicans went on to win both the 1952 and 1956 elections.

In 1960, Nixon ran for president. The campaign included the first televised presidential debates, which would turn out to be a factor in his loss in the election. Nixon, weary, with the shadow of a heavy beard, seemed uneasy in front of the camera, whereas his opponent, John Kennedy, looked young and energetic. In 1962, defeat came again when he ran for governor of California. Frustrated, he blamed the press for his setbacks and poor public image, telling reporters, "You won't have Nixon to kick around anymore." His political career seemed over. However, following his own creed, "I am not a quitter," Nixon launched a political comeback, culminating in his victory in the 1968 presidential election.

Nixon visits the Apollo 11 astronauts in quarantine following their moon landing in July 1969. This was one of three manned missions to the moon that year.

Richard Milhouse Nixon was industrious and serious with a reserved, sober demeanor. He was determined to make up for the loss of his younger brother by becoming a success and making his parents proud of him. He graduated first in his high school class, second in his college class, and third in law school. He overcame handicaps that he believed life imposed with a combination of quick wit and dogged hard work.

Nixon in the Oval Office.

In the White House, Nixon was secretive, trusting no one. A mood of resentment and suspicion pervaded the Nixon Administration from its earliest days. He was convinced that he faced enemies in Congress, the media, and the Democratic Party.

In such a hostile environment, he apparently thought he had to be ready for political warfare.

Nixon had an inscrutable core that few penetrated. He himself said, "A major public figure is a lonely man. You cannot enjoy the luxury of intimate personal friendships." He proclaimed himself "an introvert in an extrovert's profession." Nixon has been described as lonely and narcissistic, a man torn by inner conflict.

Richard Nixon made one of the greatest recoveries in American political history, but oversaw one of the worst presidential scandals in the history of our country. During his post-presidential years, he sought to rehabilitate his historical image and establish himself as an elder statesman. To this day, historians and the American people grapple with -- and likely will continue to in the future -- how to judge his political skill against a Watergate backdrop.

1972
Palestinian terrorists kill eleven Israeli athletes at the Munich Olympics

1973
Roe v. Wade ruling gives women the right to have an abortion

In his first term, Nixon enhanced the federal role in welfare and the environment, but foreign policy was Nixon's passionate interest. He pursued diplomatic negotiations in Vietnam, cooled tensions with Russia, and ended a two-decade-long embargo with China. In his 1972 bid for reelection, Nixon defeated his Democratic opponent by one of the widest margins recorded. His second term was riddled with scandal; one that was significant involved his Vice President, Spiro Agnew. Agnew was caught in bribery and tax-evasion schemes, forcing him to resign in 1973. However, the next scandal would make that one pale by comparison. It was the historic "Watergate Affair," an umbrella term for a number of events that eventually would force Nixon out of office. In 1971, covert operators burglarized the office of a psychiatrist whose patient had leaked the "Pentagon Papers," a detailed study of the Vietnam War. Their intent was to find privileged information to discredit the individual, and then, in June 1972, in an effort to prevent any politically damaging "leaks" prior to the presidential election, "plumbers" were hired to break into the Democratic National Committee's headquarters at the Watergate complex in Washington, D.C. The goal was to install "bugging" devices. This skullduggery was under the auspices of CREEP, the Committee to Reelect the President. The saga escalated into criminal conduct, political espionage, cover-ups, obstruction of justice, senate investigations, claims of executive privilege, subpoenas, expulsion of Justice Department officials, and, finally, cries for impeachment.

Nixon gives his resignation to the White House staff on his final day in office, August 9, 1974. From left to right are David Eisenhower, Julie Nixon Eisenhower, the president, First Lady Pat Nixon, Tricia Nixon Cox, and Ed Cox.

Denying any personal involvement, yet seeing his hold on the presidency untenable and facing what seemed almost certain impeachment, Nixon resigned on August 9, 1974. The one who had vowed never to quit saw no alternative.

WIKI, Happyme22

The gravestones of Richard Nixon and First Lady Pat Nixon at the The Nixon Library and Museum, Yorba Linda, California.

My 2 cents
What would you nickname this president?

_____

The Author's Idea: The Shakespearean Tragedy

1973
Pablo Picasso dies
at the age of 91

1974
Successor president:
Gerald R. Ford

PRESIDENTIAL SUCCESSION
ACT OF 1947 (AMENDED)

The United States presidential line of succession defines who may become or act as President of the United States upon the incapacity, death, resignation, or removal from office (by impeachment and subsequent conviction) of a sitting president or a president-elect.

VICE PRESIDENT
PRESIDENT PRO TEMPORE OF THE SENATE
SECRETARY OF STATE
SECRETARY OF THE TREASURY
SECRETARY OF DEFENCE
ATTORNEY GENERAL
SECRETARY OF THE INTERIOR
SECRETARY OF AGRICULTURE
SECRETARY OF COMMERCE
SECRETARY OF LABOR
SECRETARY OF HEALTH AND HUMAN SERVICES
SECRETARY OF HOUSING AND DEVELOPMENT
SECRETARY OF TRANSPORTATION
SECRETARY OF ENERGY
SECRETARY OF EDUCATION
SECRETARY OF VETERANS AFFAIRS

Cabinet members have been in the line of succession since 1886. The current law preserves the tradition of ranking the cabinet departments by the year they were created.

GERALD R. FORD

38th President of the United States

POLITICAL PARTY: Republican
ELECTION OPPONENTS: Not applicable
TERM OF OFFICE: August 8, 1974 to January 20, 1977
VICE PRESIDENT: None

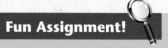

Fun Assignment!

In the 1940s, Ford briefly worked as a fashion model for what two popular magazines?

Cosmopolitan and Look

The Gerald R. Ford Birthplace & Gardens in Omaha, Nebraska.

Personal Profile

BORN: July 14, 1913, Omaha, Nebraska
SIBLINGS: 4 half-brothers and 2 half-sisters
RELIGION: Episcopalian
EDUCATION:
   University of Michigan; graduated 1935
   Yale University Law School; graduated 1941
CAREER: Lawyer

MILITARY: U.S. Naval Reserve, gunnery officer, discharged lieutenant commander
MARRIAGE: Elizabeth Ann Bloomer Warren October 15, 1948, Grand Rapids, Michigan
OFFSPRING: Three sons, one daughter
DIED: December 26, 2006 Rancho Mirage, California

Elizabeth "Betty" Ann Bloomer Warren Ford

Visiting the President

BIRTHPLACE:

Gerald R. Ford Birth Site and Gardens

1326 South 32nd Street, Omaha, Nebraska

LIBRARY:

1000 Beal Avenue, Ann Arbor, Michigan

MUSEUM/GRAVESITE:

303 Pearl Street, NW, Grand Rapids, Michigan

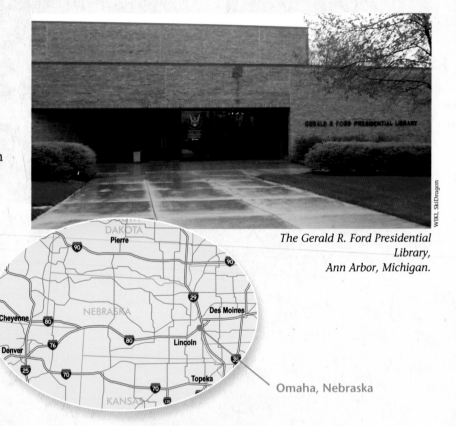

The Gerald R. Ford Presidential Library, Ann Arbor, Michigan.

Omaha, Nebraska

Tell me more!

Medical Records

Ford was the first president to publicly disclose the results of his annual medical checkup. He was given a clean bill of health.

Political Profile

- Member, United States House of Representatives
- Member, Warren Commission
- Vice President of the United States
- President of the United States

1974	1974	1975
Woodward and Bernstein publish *All the President's Men*	Stephen King publishes *Carrie* and James Michener publishes *Centennial*	Popular Mechanics features the Altair 8800, the first personal computer

The Ford Administration Highlights

- Limited clemency is granted to Vietnam-era draft evaders and deserters in exchange for some other public service (1974)
- Privacy Act of 1974, stipulating that the government will not have secret recordkeeping systems (1974)
- U.S. President's Commission on CIA Activities within the United States is established to investigate illegal surveillance activity and abuses of power by the CIA (1975)
- The Helsinki Accords are signed, an agreement to respect human rights (1975)
- Law passed mandating free public education for handicapped children (1975)

Leslie Lynch King, Jr. in 1916, the same year he was given his adoptive name of Gerald R. Ford. However, his name was not legally changed until 1935.

Gerald Ford was born Leslie Lynch King, Jr. in Omaha, Nebraska. After his parents divorced, his mother moved to Michigan, remarried, and renamed Ford after his adoptive stepfather. Ford was a spirited, industrious, and athletic youth. He attended the University of Michigan on a partial athletic scholarship. In 1935, he was hired as an assistant football coach at Yale University. Because of his full-time duties as a coach, he was initially denied admission to Yale's law school, but, after his persistent efforts, he was admitted in 1939 and graduated in 1941. After forty-seven months of active duty during World War II, he began to practice law.

Ford playing football for the University of Michigan in 1933.

That same year, the 35-year-old Ford married thirty-year-old divorcee Elizabeth Ann Bloomer Warren, a former model and dancer. Encouraged by his politically active stepfather and others, he entered politics, winning a seat in the House of Representatives. Over the next two decades, Ford won reelection to the House handily. He was easygoing, diligent, and honest; his power in Congress grew over the years. From 1964 to 1973, he was the House Minority Leader. His ambition was to be Speaker of the House. However, by his thirteenth

1975	1975	1975
U.S. Apollo and Soviet Soyuz spacecrafts dock with each other in orbit	Microsoft is founded by Bill Gates and Paul Allen	*A Chorus Line* debuts on Broadway

211

term in 1972, the Republicans remained the minority party. Ford decided he would make one more run for the House in 1974 and then retire from politics. Following the forced resignation of Spiro Agnew for charges of federal income tax evasion, Ford was nominated and confirmed the new vice president under the provisions of the 25th Amendment. He was sworn in on December 6, 1973, becoming an accidental vice president.

President Nixon was embattled in a scandal linking a break-in at the Watergate complex in Washington, D.C. to illegal activities conducted on

Cabinet members Dick Cheney and Donald Rumsfeld with President Ford in 1975. Both Cheney and Rumsfeld later held powerful positions in the George W. Bush Administration in 2001.

Raised in the conservative Midwest, **Gerald Ford**'s parents instilled in him the values of honesty, integrity, and hard work. Ford assumed his stepfather was his biological father until he was told otherwise at the age of twelve. As a teenager, he met his biological father for the first time. The encounter left him shaken and in tears. Ford did not let his family history hold him back though; later he became a popular and athletic student in his high school and college years. Ford excelled in football and received offers to play professional football for the Green Bay Packers and the Chicago Bears, both of which he declined.

Ford was not a comfortable public speaker, but as president, he granted news correspondents a great deal of access and gave numerous one-on-one interviews. He was an athletic and physically fit president, but gained the reputation of being a clumsy oaf after several unfortunate falls.

Ford emerged unscathed after two assassination attempts in California within weeks of each other. Two women on the fringe of society, Lynette ("Squeaky") Fromme and Sara Jane Moore, each fired shots at Ford, but failed to hit him.

Ford's wife, Betty, became a media star. After undergoing a mastectomy for breast cancer, her courage and candor alerted women to the importance of early detection. She spoke out for women's rights, abortion rights, and the appointment of women to the Supreme Court. After the White House years, Betty revealed her addiction to alcohol and drugs and established the Betty Ford Clinic.

Gerald Ford became the thirty-eighth president of the United States as a result of extraordinary constitutional circumstances following the Watergate debacle. Unlike any previous chief executive, he had never been elected as part of a national ticket. Betty Ford said of her husband, "He was an accidental vice president and an accidental president, and in both jobs, he replaced disgraced leaders." Ford's ascension to the vice-presidency and presidency were historic and, though the Nixon pardon will always engender debate, Ford weathered the storm of controversy with grace and dignity.

Gerald Ford is sworn in by Supreme Court Chief Justice Warren Burger following Richard Nixon's resignation on August 9, 1974.

1976
Summer Olympics are held
in Montreal, Canada in July

1976
The United States celebrates
its Bicentennial

1976
Construction of the first space
shuttle, Enterprise, is completed

President Ford appears at the House Judiciary Subcommittee hearing on pardoning former President Richard Nixon in October 1974.

behalf of his reelection campaign. To avoid possible impeachment, Nixon resigned. Eight months after being sworn-in as vice president, Gerald Ford, now an accidental president, took the oath of office. In his first address to the nation, Ford spoke the now famous words that described the mood of the country, "My fellow Americans, our long national nightmare is over." Just one month later, Ford shocked the country by granting Richard Nixon "a full, free, and absolute pardon for all offences."

From that point on, Ford and his Administration were unable to counteract the fallout from the pardon. However, Ford faced a difficult political environment in Washington from the outset. He was plagued by the remnants of the Vietnam War, inflation, high unemployment, and government over-spending. In 1976, with the advantage of incumbency, Ford ran for a full presidential term in his own right. Overcoming a serious challenge from future president Ronald Reagan, Ford secured his party's nomination. He came very close to winning the presidency, but ultimately was disappointed.

CONNECTIONS
On November 20, 1974, the United States Department of Justice filed an antitrust suit against communications giant AT&T; the suit led to the breakup of the conglomerate, "Ma Bell," in the early 1980s.

In the last known public photo of President Ford, he and his wife Betty appear with President George W. Bush on April 23, 2006 in Rancho Mirage, California.

The grave site of both Gerald and Betty Ford, Grand Rapids, Michigan.

My 2 cents
What would you nickname this president?

_____

The Author's Idea: House Bound

1976
Alex Haley publishes *Roots*

1977
Shortages of electrical power and natural gas cause factories, offices and schools to close temporarily

1977
Successor president: James Earl Carter

213

USS Jimmy Carter
The third and last Seawolf-class nuclear submarine, it was christened June 5, 2004, by former First Lady Rosalyn
Carter. Jimmy Carter is the only United States president to graduate from the United States Naval Academy.

JAMES EARL CARTER
39th President of the United States

POLITICAL PARTY: Democrat
ELECTION OPPONENT: Gerald Ford, Republican
TERM OF OFFICE: January 20, 1977 to January 20, 1981
VICE PRESIDENT: Walter Mondale

Carter's campaign headquarters was the train depot in his hometown of Plains, Georgia.

Fun Assignment!

While at the Naval Academy, Carter was paddled and hazed for defiantly refusing to sing what song?

General Sherman's Civil War battle hymn, Marching Through Georgia.

Personal Profile

BORN: October 1, 1924, Plains, Georgia
SIBLINGS: Eldest of four children
RELIGION: Southern Baptist
EDUCATION:
   Georgia Southwestern College, 1941
   Georgia Institute of Technology, 1942-1943
   U.S. Naval Academy, graduated 1946
   Union College, 1952-1953

CAREER: Farmer, warehouseman, university professor
MILITARY: Commissioned ensign, promoted to lieutenant senior grade
MARRIAGE: Eleanor Rosalynn Smith July 7, 1946, Plains, Georgia
OFFSPRING: Three boys, one girl
DIED: Still living

Eleanor Rosalynn Smith Carter

1977
Previous president:
Gerald R. Ford

1977
Silent film star
Charlie Chaplin dies

215

Visiting the President

BIRTHPLACE/RESIDENCE:
Jimmy Carter National Historic Site
300 North Bond Street, Plains, Georgia
LIBRARY/MUSEUM:
Jimmy Carter Library and Museum
441 Freedom Parkway, Atlanta, Georgia

The Jimmy Carter Presidential Library at the Carter Center, Atlanta, Georgia.

Plains, Georgia

WIKI, Bubba73

Tell me more!

A Diplomatic First

Carter was the first president to send his mother on a diplomatic mission. He appointed Lillian Gordy Carter, who previously served as a Peace Corps nurse in India, to head the U.S. delegation to New Delhi to attend the funeral of the Indian president.

President Carter with his mother Lillian following her trip to India in 1977.

Political Profile

- Member, Georgia State Legislature
- Governor of Georgia
- President of the United States

1977
Colleen McCullough publishes
The Thorn Birds

1978
John Irving publishes
The World According to Garp

The Carter Administration Highlights

- The Department of Energy established (1977)
- Panama and the United States reach agreement turning over control of the U.S.-run Panama Canal, effective 1999 (1977)
- The Presidential Records Act enacted, establishes that presidential papers are public property (1978)
- Diplomatic relations with the People's Republic of China are established (1979)
- Peace Treaty between Israel and Egypt is signed (1979)
- The Department of Education established (1979)
- The Moscow Summer Olympics begin without United States participation (1980)

A young Jimmy Carter with his dog Bozo in 1937.

Jimmy Carter grew up working the fields of his family's farm and selling roasted peanuts in his hometown of Plains, Georgia. Although the Carters were well off by community standards, they had no electricity or running water. In 1941, Carter graduated from high school as valedictorian. He was determined to join the Navy and attended Georgia Institute of Technology for one year to improve his chances in the competitive admission process. He secured admission to the United States Naval Academy, graduating in June 1946. One month later he married Rosalynn Smith, a friend of his sister's. Carter had obtained a choice naval assignment to help develop the first atomic submarine, taking courses in reactor technology and nuclear physics at New York's Union College. He was appointed chief engineer of the "Seawolf," a prototype of a nuclear submarine. When his father died in 1953, and despite his wife's misgivings, Carter resigned from the navy to manage the family farm. He turned it into a successful business within five years.

Carter's home town, Plains, Georgia.

Carter became involved in politics in his community. His first elected office was a seat on the county's Board of Education. From there he went on to serve two terms in the state senate and then, on his second attempt, he won the governorship of Georgia in 1970. In October 1974, despite being a "dark horse candidate" who was not even listed in the public opinion polls, Carter declared his candidacy for the Democratic presidential nomination. He was such an obscure political figure that he appeared as a guest on the television show, "What's My Line," and nearly stumped the panel! However, Carter campaigned at his political best and won both the nomination and the presidency -- the first man from the Deep South to be elected since Zachary Taylor in 1848.

President Carter and Soviet General Secretary Leonid Brezhnev sign the Strategic Arms Limitation Talks (SALT II) treaty in 1979 in Vienna, Austria.

Jimmy Carter is a complex man. Carter, the private person, is unpretentious, introspective, self-disciplined, and able to confront his shortcomings. Carter, the political persona, reveals a partisan, conflicted, self-righteous, stubborn, uncompromising, and arrogant man. Anyone who balked at his ideas was regarded as selfish. His administration behaved as though it did not need to court Washington or the nation's political establishment and his staff was inept at handling Capitol Hill. Congressional relations seemed to matter little to Carter in deciding how issues were to be managed and he had little sense of how Republicans and Democrats interacted in Washington.

The heavy presence of Georgians in his administration limited the outside advice that Carter received and used. He came into office without a mandate and his administration was never able to establish momentum. He appeared ineffective and indecisive. His acceptance speech at the Democratic National Convention in 1980 was described as failing to communicate "a vision of his goals that would lead and inspire the nation." In the final analysis, Carter did not fulfill the country's expectations and the America people abandoned him.

It could be said that Jimmy Carter's post-presidency career has been more effective than his term as president. He travels as an official representative of international organizations and his work with Habitat for Humanity is well known and admired. In 1999, Carter and his wife were presented with the Presidential Medal of Freedom, and in 2002 he was awarded the Nobel Peace Prize. James Earl Carter's presidential legacy stands as one of noble intent destroyed by poor leadership and of great hope turned into profound disappointment.

WIKI: Bubbo73

Former President Jimmy Carter remains active, here bicycling in 2008. He also volunteers for Habitat for Humanity.

1980
At least nine people are killed when Mount St. Helens erupts in Washington state

1980
1980 census estimates a U.S. population of 226.5 million

His first act as president was the unconditional pardon of all Vietnam draft resisters and the withdrawal of American weapons in South Korea, but he failed to adequately consult with Congress and the military on both these matters. As a result, he was seen on Capitol Hill as self-righteous and arrogant, acting hastily and weakening America's defenses in Asia. His complex energy conservation plan was highly criticized and, once again, he failed to consult with Congressional leaders. Carter did succeed, though, in negotiating the Camp David accords with Israel and Egypt, and he did obtain enactment of his watered down energy plan. Also, he appeared to waffle in giving his approval to use the weapons given to Iran to crush the rebels and the finalization of the SALT II treaty with Russia. His foibles included the handling of the drawn-out Iran hostage crisis, the attempted hostage rescue resulting in the deaths of eight soldiers, and his speech on the nation's ongoing energy issues. Some dubbed that talk as the "crisis of confidence" speech and others as the "malaise speech."

When the Soviet Union invaded Afghanistan in December 1979, Carter withdrew American participation in the 1980 Summer Olympics being held in Moscow. He announced his boycott at an inopportune time -- during the White House reception for the Olympic gold winning United States hockey team. Despite an approval rating of twenty-one percent, Carter secured his party's nomination for a second term. The Republican candidate, Ronald Reagan, soundly defeated him in the 1980 election. In a particularly stinging gesture, Iran waited until just after Reagan's inauguration to release the American hostages after 444 days in captivity, depriving Carter of that accomplishment.

CONNECTIONS

Under Carter's supervision, President Anwar Sadat and Israeli Prime Minister Menachem Begin signed the Camp David Accords in September 1978. Later that year, Sadat and Begin were jointly awarded the Nobel Peace Prize for their efforts to build a lasting peace in the Middle East. In 2002, former president Jimmy Carter received the Nobel Peace Prize for his decades of untiring effort to find peaceful solutions to international conflicts.

The largest gathering of living presidents occurred in January 2009 when President George W. Bush hosted a meeting and lunch at The White House. Left to right: G.H.W. Bush; Barack Obama; George W. Bush; Bill Clinton; and Jimmy Carter.

My 2 cents

What would you nickname this president?

_____

The Author's Idea: Peanuts & Peace

The Berlin Wall
Twenty-four years after John F. Kennedy pronounced "Ich bin ein Berliner," Ronald Reagan stood before the Brandenburg Gate at the Berlin Wall and challenged the Soviet Union to "Tear down this wall."

RONALD REAGAN

40th President of the United States

POLITICAL PARTY: Republican
Election Opponents:
   1980   Jimmy Carter, Democrat
          John Anderson, Independent
   1984   Walter Mondale, Democrat
TERM OF OFFICE: January 20, 1981 to January 20, 1989
VICE PRESIDENT: George H. W. Bush

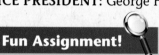

Fun Assignment!

Ronald Reagan never won an Academy Award, but he did receive a Golden Globe Award for his performance in what movie?

Hollywood Citizenship in 1957

Ronald Reagan was born in a second-floor apartment above the First National Bank on South Main Street in Tampico, Illinois.

Personal Profile

BORN: February 6, 1911, Tampico, Illinois
SIBLINGS: One brother
RELIGION: Presbyterian
EDUCATION: Eureka College; graduated
      1932
CAREER: Radio announcer, screen actor,
      president of the Screen Actors Guild,
      and company spokesperson
MILITARY: Enlisted as private, Army Reserve;
      discharged captain, Army Air Forces

MARRIAGES:
   • Jane Wyman
   January 24, 1940, Glendale, California
   • Nancy Davis
   March 4, 1952, Los Angeles, California
OFFSPRING: With Jane, 1 daughter and 1
      adopted son;
      With Nancy, a son and daughter
DIED: June 5, 2004, Bel-Air, California

Jane Wyman Reagan

Nancy Davis Reagan

1981
Previous president:
James Earl Carter

1981
Charles, Prince of Wales, and Lady Diana
Spencer exchange wedding vows

Visiting the President

BIRTHPLACE: 119 South Main Street, Tampico, Illinois
(open by appointment)
BOYHOOD HOME: 816 Hennepin Avenue, Dixon, Illinois
VACATION HOME: Rancho del Cielo
Santa Ynez Mountain Range, northwest of Santa Barbara, California
(owned by the Young America's Foundation, closed to the public,
visits by appointment only)
LIBRARY/MUSEUM/GRAVESITE: The Ronald Reagan
Presidential Library and Museum
40 Presidential Drive, Simi Valley, California

Ronald Reagan's boyhood home,
Dixon, Illinois.

Tell me more!

Jelly Beans

Reagan was such a fan of jelly bean candies that the
Jelly Belly company created a blueberry flavor in honor
of his 1981 inauguration. The president ordered three
tons of the jelly beans for the occasion.

Tampico, Illinois

Ronald Reagan in Dixon,
Illinois, in 1922.

Political Profile

• Governor of California

• President of the United States

1981
Martin Cruz Smith
publishes *Gorky Park*

1982
Princess Grace of Monaco,
(former Hollywood star Grace Kelly) dies

The Reagan Administration Highlights

- Sandra Day O'Connor becomes the first woman to be sworn in as a Supreme Court Associate Judge (1981)
- Reagan dismisses 11,000 striking air traffic controllers (1981)
- Congress amends the Social Security Act to keep the retirement program solvent through 2050 (1989)
- The birthday of Martin Luther King, Jr. is established as a national holiday (1983)
- The Space Shuttle Challenger explodes seconds after liftoff (1986)
- Chief Justice William Rehnquist is sworn in (1986)
- On "Black Monday," the stock market crashes 508 points (1987)

Ronald Reagan was the son of a shoe salesman. His father nicknamed him "Dutch" because Ronald looked like "a little fat Dutchman." The Reagan family lived in several homes before settling in Dixon, Illinois. Despite the poverty of his youth and the anguish of his father's alcoholism, Reagan recalled his childhood as the happiest time of his life.

As a teenager, Reagan spent his summers as a lifeguard, rescuing seventy-seven people. In 1928, he entered Eureka College on a partial football scholarship. Following

Ronald Reagan as the host of General Electric Theater.

Ronald and Nancy Reagan in the Inaugural Parade in Washington, D.C. on January 20, 1981.

graduation, Reagan went on to become the most popular radio sportscaster in Iowa. His baseball commentary was taken from wire service reports, and sometimes combined with details he fabricated because the radio station could not afford to send him to the actual games. In 1937, he landed a contract with Warner Brother's Studio in Hollywood, California.

Three years later, he married his first wife, actress Jane Wyman. As Jane's career advanced and Ronald's stagnated, friction developed and the couple divorced in 1948. He was elected president of the Screen Actors Guild, serving from 1947 to 1952 and again from 1959 to 1960. Reagan married actress Nancy Davis in 1952. In 1954, he became host for the

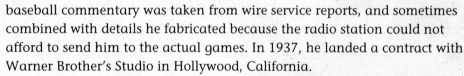

1982
Andrew Lloyd Webber's
Cats opens on Broadway

1982
Dr. Robert Jarvik implants an
artificial heart in a human subject

General Electric Hour on television and was their public relations representative as well. As he traveled around the country, Reagan developed a pro-business posture, becoming increasingly more conservative in his political views. He believed that the Democratic Party had philosophically changed from state's rights and individual freedom to centralized federal government and redistribution of wealth.

In 1964, he established his Republican credentials when he gave a televised speech in support of the Republican candidate for president. Convinced that he could win California's governor's seat, he ran and won in 1966. Voter satisfaction was clear at the ballot box in 1970 when he won a

Reagan, often called the Great Communicator, gives a televised address outlining his plan for tax-reduction legislation in July 1981.

Ronald Wilson Reagan was a surprisingly vigorous and relatively youthful looking president. He spoke in a clear baritone voice, developed during his years as a sportscaster and spokesman. Called the "Great Communicator," he effectively used television to present his administration's programs. He took the nation by storm with the Reagan Revolution, Reagan Democrats, Reaganites, Reagan Doctrine, Reaganomics, and the Evil Empire and Star Wars—a space age anti-ballistics system designed to take down any incoming Soviet nuclear missile. He was a gifted raconteur with a seemingly endless store of anecdotes and great "one-liners." For example, after being shot he quipped to emergency doctors, "Please assure me that you are all Republicans" and to his wife, "Honey, I forgot to duck." His quick wit and strong mind gave testimony to his literal "courage under fire."

Perhaps the most famous saying of all, and one that will ensure President Reagan's place in history, was his world-shaking challenge to Soviet leader Mikhail Gorbachev. Referring to the long gray line of concrete dividing the city of Berlin since 1961 and symbolizing freedom versus Communism, Reagan stood at its gate and said simply, "...if you seek peace, if you seek prosperity for the Soviet Union and Eastern Europe, if you seek liberalization, come here to this gate, open this gate. Mr. Gorbachev, tear down this wall."

President Reagan and Soviet Union General Secretary Gorbachev sign the Intermediate-Range Nuclear Forces Treaty in 1987, the same year Reagan implored Gorbachev to tear down the Berlin Wall.

Reagan's farewell address to the nation in January 1989 was not his last. In an open letter to the American people, he disclosed he had been diagnosed with Alzheimer's disease. He wrote, "I now begin the journey that will lead me into the sunset of my life." Nancy said the journey was a "tortuous long goodbye."

1985
Live Aid concerts in Philadelphia and London raise millions for African famine relief

1985
An expedition takes the first film footage of the wreck of the *Titanic*

Rancho del Cielo near Santa Barbara, California.

The Ronald Reagan Presidential Library, Simi Valley, California.

second term. Reagan lost his bid for the Republican Party presidential nomination in 1976, but four years later he was the frontrunner, going on to win the presidency handily. In his inaugural address he declared, "...government is not the solution to our problem, government is the problem." In Reagan's first term, he advocated supply-side economics, whereby money returned to businesses and consumers is theoretically reinvested in the economy, spurring growth and raising revenues. He also oversaw government deregulation, fired 11,000 striking air traffic controllers, faced down Communism around the world, intervened in Middle East conflicts, and ordered the successful invasion of Grenada. During this time, Reagan survived an assassination attempt by John Hinckley, Jr. who was infatuated by a movie about a deranged man who tries to kill a presidential candidate.

Reagan's second term was characterized by foreign policy challenges. One such challenge became known as the Iran-contra affair, involving the illegal sale of missiles to Iran in exchange for Americans kidnapped and held hostage by pro-Iranian groups in Lebanon in 1984. Reagan initially denied the allegations, and even as details unfolded, he never completely accepted the reality of what had happened. Reagan overcame the scandal partly due to an improving economy, but mainly because of the success of summit meetings he held with the Soviet Union on the reduction of nuclear weapons. Reagan's tactic of combining negotiation with pressure is credited for significant arms control, the end of the Soviet empire, and the termination of the Cold War.

When Ronald Reagan left the Oval Office in January 1989, just shy of his seventy-eighth birthday, his poll ratings were the highest ever for a retiring chief executive. As he and his wife Nancy, who said her life began when she married "Ronnie," flew over Washington on their last day, he said, "Look, honey, there's our little shack." Years earlier Reagan described Washington as he truly saw it, "The shining city on the hill."

My 2 cents
What would you nickname this president?

_____

The Author's Idea: The Life Guard

1988
Andrew Lloyd Webber's *The Phantom of the Opera* debuts on Broadway

1989
Successor president:
George H. W. Bush

225

TBM Avenger Bomber Aircraft
US Navy pilot George H. W. Bush was shot down over the Pacific Ocean by a Japanese fighter plane while flying a mission in a TBM Avenger.

GEORGE H.W. BUSH
41st President of the United States

POLITICAL PARTY: Republican
ELECTION OPPONENT:
  1988: Michael Dukakis, Democrat
  1992: William Jefferson Clinton, Democrat
         Ross Perot, Independent
TERM OF OFFICE: January 20, 1989 to January 20, 1993
VICE PRESIDENT: James Danforth (Dan) Quayle

Fun Assignment!

George H. W. Bush was named for his maternal grandfather.
What nickname did he also inherit from him?

"Poppy"

*Marker at the George H. W. Bush birthplace
on Adams Street in Milton, Massachusetts.*

Personal Profile

BORN: June 12, 1924, Milton, Massachusetts
SIBLINGS: Three brothers and one sister
RELIGION: Episcopalian
EDUCATION: Yale University; graduated 1948
CAREER: Oil field sales; oil executive

MILITARY: United States Navy, commissioned
  ensign, discharged lieutenant junior grade
MARRIAGE: Barbara Pierce
  January 6, 1945, Rye, New York
OFFSPRING: Four sons, two daughters (first
  daughter died at three years of age)
DIED: Still living

*Barbara Pierce
Bush*

1989
Previous president:
Ronald Reagan

1989
The first of twenty-four satellites of the Global
Positioning System (GPS) are sent into orbit

Visiting the President

BIRTHPLACE:
173 Adams Street, Milton, Massachusetts
(marked at site)

VACATION HOME:
Walker's Point, Kennebunkport, Maine

LIBRARY/MUSEUM:
The George Bush Presidential Library and Museum
1000 George Bush Drive West, College Station, Texas

Walker's Point,
Kennebunkport, Maine.

WIKI, Zollernalb

College Station, Texas

Tell me more!

Planes

On November 22, 2004, along with former presidents Ford, Carter, and Clinton, Bush was named an honorary member of the board overseeing rebuilding at the World Trade Center following the September 11th terrorist attacks. That same day, a plane en route to pick up Bush crashed in Houston, Texas.

Political Profile

- Member, United States House of Representatives
- United States Ambassador to the United Nations
- Chairman, Republican National Committee
- Chief of the United States Liaison Office to the People's Republic of China
- Director, Central Intelligence Agency
- Vice President of the United States
- President of the United States

1989
A Cornell University student is indicted for releasing the first computer worm virus

1989
A 6.9 Richter scale earthquake hits San Francisco

The Bush Administration Highlights

- The administration bans the import of semiautomatic rifles (1989)
- The Whistleblower Act is signed, protecting workers reporting fraud or abuse in federal programs (1989)
- The Fair Labor Standards Amendment is signed, raising the minimal wage to $4.25 per hour (1989)
- The Americans with Disabilities Act is signed (1990)
- The Clean Air Act is signed (1990)
- The Senate confirms Supreme Court nominee Clarence Thomas (1991)
- The Civil Rights Act, calling for the provision of damages in cases of deliberate employment discrimination is signed (1991)
- The 27th Amendment to the Constitution, originally proposed in 1789, is signed; it mandates that no congressional pay raise shall take effect before an intervening election has occurred (1992)
- The North American Free Trade Agreement is signed (1992)

At Yankee Stadium, Bush, captain of the Yale baseball team, receives Babe Ruth's autobiography, which he donated to Yale in 1948.

George H. W. Bush was raised amid wealth and privilege in a family known for leadership in private and public service. He grew up to be a versatile athlete and was fiercely competitive. A high school senior, Bush met his future wife, Barbara Pierce, the daughter of the publisher of Redbook and McCall magazines. It was love at first sight, but Bush turned his sights on another prize -- the defense of his country after Japan attacked the United States at Pearl Harbor. He deferred his college education and joined the navy on his eighteenth birthday. In June 1943, he was granted his wings and was the youngest pilot in the Navy at that time. Bush flew fifty-eight combat missions in the Pacific Theatre before being shot down over the ocean by enemy fire. He was rescued by a United States submarine on September 2, 1944.

George Bush on the carrier USS San Jacinto in 1944.

While home on leave from the navy, Bush married Barbara. Following graduation from Yale University, he struck out on his own, some say to escape his family's shadow, and accepted an

1989
Tom Clancy publishes
Clear and Present Danger

1990
Media giants Time, Inc. and
Warner Communication, Inc. merge

229

opportunity at an oil drilling business in west Texas. In 1953, he and a friend co-founded a petroleum business. In the mid-1960s, Bush sold his stake and became a self-made millionaire at the age of forty-one. In 1964, Bush lost his first attempt for political office, but bounced back to win election to the United States House of Representatives in 1966. From there he built an impressive political resume. Bush sought the Republican nomination for president in 1979, but was placed second on the ticket. He was a team player and as vice president, he traveled to all fifty states of the Union and sixty-five countries.

When President Reagan was shot in 1981, Bush was a reassuring presence; he remained calm in a potentially chaotic situation. With typical decorum, he refused to work out of the Oval Office or sit in the president's chair at cabinet meetings. Again in 1985, when Reagan needed surgery for a cancerous polyp, Bush served as acting president for eight hours. Reagan had transferred presidential powers to him before going into surgery.

In 1987, after eight years as a loyal vice president, Bush announced his candidacy for the party's presidential nomination. The defining moment of the Republican National Convention was Bush's acceptance speech; he predicted that when he was president he would not raise

Bush appointed Clarence Thomas, the second African-American justice to the Supreme Court, in 1991.

George H. W. Bush has an impressive heritage. Collateral relatives include Franklin Pierce, Theodore Roosevelt, Abraham Lincoln, Gerald Ford, even Winston Churchill and Marilyn Monroe. During his twenties and thirties, Bush was a classic Type A personality, but he changed his lifestyle after being warned that he was headed for an early grave. He is witty, warm, and easygoing, maintaining many friendships from his wartime and college days. Under Ronald Reagan, Bush was perceived as deferential, but he emerged as a tough, tenacious campaigner; the same traits that won him the Distinguished Flying Cross for bravery in action during World War II. Even on his seventy-second birthday, he demonstrated his adventurous and courageous nature by parachuting out of an airplane as a birthday celebration gesture.

President Reagan and Vice President Bush in 1981.

Bush brought to the White House a dedication to traditional American values and a determination to direct them toward making a "kinder and gentler nation." More than fifteen years after leaving Washington for his hometown of Houston, Texas, Bush declared, "After thirty years in politics, I don't miss it."

George H. W. Bush has two historical distinctions: he is the first incumbent vice president to become president since Martin Van Buren in 1836 and, in 2000, he became the first former president since John Adams to have a son who became president.

Bush noted in his diary on his last day in office, "I've tried to serve here with no taint or dishonor; no conflict of interest; nothing to sully this beautiful place and this job I've been privileged to hold."

1990
The 1990 census estimates the U.S. population at 248.7 million people

1992
Microsoft releases the Windows 3.1 computer operating system

President Bush visits "Operation Desert Storm" Gulf War troops in Saudi Arabia in 1990.

CONNECTIONS
The ruptured tanker Exxon Valdez spilled 11 million gallons of crude oil into Alaska's Prince William Sound on March 24, 1989. It had run aground on Bligh Reef, creating an ecologic disaster.

taxes and emphasized his remarks with, "Read my lips; no new taxes." Despite this pronouncement, less than two years in office, he did just that.

One of Bush's striking foreign policy achievements was bringing the 41-year-old bitter Cold War to an official end. His management of the transition to a new international arrangement proved that his foreign policy experience was his greatest strength. His presidency was not without crisis though; in the summer of 1990, Iraq invaded oil-rich Kuwait. Bush built a complex coalition to support the use of force against Iraq, a diplomatic tour de force. He was determined to win the war quickly and forcefully, sending 550,000 troops to the Middle East. This was more than had fought in Vietnam. The one hundred-hour land battle, dubbed Operation Desert Storm, routed Iraq's million-man army. On February 27, Bush proclaimed an end to the war.

In 1992, Bush was renominated for a second presidential term without opposition. Bush's ending of the Cold War on essentially American terms, his leadership in the Gulf War, and a public approval rating of ninety percent appeared to be solid indicators for him to win a second term. Yet, eighteen months later, Americans had turned away from foreign policy concerns and were focused on domestic issues, which were perceived as ignored by the Bush Administration. In a three-way race, Bush finished with the lowest percentage of popular votes for an incumbent president since William Howard Taft. With good humor, he quoted Winston Churchill who had said, upon being turned out of power in 1945, "I have been given the Order of the Boot."

The George Bush Presidential Library and Museum, College Station, Texas.

My 2 cents
What would you nickname this president?

_____
The Author's Idea: Read My Lips

1992
David McCullough publishes *Truman*

1993
Successor president:
William Jefferson Clinton

231

IMPEACHMENT

Impeachment is the process that enables a legislative body to remove a public official from office. This includes the president, the vice president and all civil officers of the United States. Impeachable offences are treason, bribery, and other high crimes and misdemeanors. Impeachment is comprised of two parts: an accusation or indictment and a trial. Under this two-part procedure, the House of Representatives initiates the process by bringing articles of impeachment against an accused official. The Senate tries the accused on the charges provided by the House of Representatives.

The House votes on each charge and any charge that gets a majority of votes is sent to the Senate for final judgment. The Constitution gives the Senate entire power to decide on the impeachment. If the President has been impeached, the Chief Justice of the Supreme Court is designated to preside, the Vice President presides in all other instances. A two-thirds vote of the Senate is required to convict and remove the official from office.

Only two presidents in the history of the United States have been impeached: Andrew Johnson and William Jefferson Clinton; neither were convicted nor removed from office.

WILLIAM JEFFERSON CLINTON

42nd President of the United States

POLITICAL PARTY: Democrat
ELECTION OPPONENTS:
  1992: George H.W. Bush, Republican
         Ross Perot, Independent
  1996: Robert Dole, Republican
         Ross Perot, Independent
TERM OF OFFICE: January 20, 1993 to January 20, 2001
VICE PRESIDENT: Albert Gore

Clinton's boyhood home, Hope, Arkansas.

Personal Profile

BORN: August 19, 1946, Hope, Arkansas
SIBLINGS: two half-brothers and a half-sister
RELIGION: Baptist
EDUCATION:
  Georgetown University; graduated 1968
  University of Oxford; Attended 1968-1970
  Yale University; graduated 1973

CAREER: Law professor; lawyer
MILITARY: None
MARRIAGE: Hillary Rodham
  October 11, 1975, Fayetteville, Arkansas
OFFSPRING: One daughter
DIED: Still living

Hillary Rodham Clinton

1993
Previous president:
George H. W. Bush

1993
The U.S. Holocaust Memorial Museum
is dedicated in Washington, D.C.

Visiting the President

BOYHOOD HOME:
Clinton's First Home Museum
117 South Hervey Street, Hope, Arkansas
LIBRARY/MUSEUM:
William J. Clinton Presidential Center
1200 President Clinton Avenue
Little Rock, Arkansas

The William Clinton Presidential Center in Little Rock, Arkansas.

Hope, Arkansas

Tell me more!

Road to Washington, D.C

After his election, Bill and Hillary Clinton rode the last 120 miles to Washington on a bus from Charlottesville, Virginia. The bus was a reminder of the campaign, but the route was the same Thomas Jefferson had taken on his way to his own inauguration. It seemed appropriate to Hillary that William Jefferson Clinton should follow in his namesake's footsteps.

Fun Assignment!

During his first presidential campaign, Clinton appeared on the Arsenio Hall Show in 1992 and performed his rendition of Heartbreak Hotel. What instrument did he play?

Saxophone

Political Profile

- Attorney General of Arkansas
- Governor of Arkansas
- President of the United States

1993
John Gray publishes *Men Are From Mars, Women Are From Venus*

1996
A ewe named "Dolly," the first mammal to be cloned from an adult cell, is born

The Clinton Administration Highlights

- "Don't ask, don't tell" policy is announced (1993)
- A bomb, planted by terrorists, explodes in the garage below the North Tower of the World Trade Center (1993)
- Family and Medical Leave Act is signed (1993)
- Janet Reno becomes the first female Attorney General of the United States (1993)
- Ruth Bader Ginsburg is confirmed as associate justice of the Supreme Court (1993)
- The Brady Bill is signed into law, establishing a five-day waiting period and background checks for handgun purchases (1993)
- The North American Free Trade Agreement (NAFTA) is signed, calling for the gradual elimination of tariffs and trade barriers between Canada, the United States and Mexico (1993)
- Stephen Breyer is confirmed as associate justice of the Supreme Court (1994)
- A car bomb destroys the Murrah Federal Building in Oklahoma City, Oklahoma (1995)
- The "line item veto" bill is signed (1996)
- Madeleine Albright becomes the first female Secretary of State (1996)

Bill Clinton (center) takes the oath of office on January 20, 1993. To his left is his daugther Chelsea, and to his right is his wife Hillary.

William Jefferson Clinton's original name was William Jefferson Blythe, IV. His father died at the age of 29 before Clinton was born. Clinton would say later that his father's untimely death made him impatient for success early. His mother married Roger Clinton in 1950. His stepfather was an abusive alcoholic; yet, despite his troubled environment, Clinton was a strong student. At the age of sixteen, he officially changed his name from Blythe to Clinton for "family solidarity." In high school, Clinton had already made up his mind to run for president someday. His mother, whose world revolved around her bright son Bill, also believed he was destined for greatness.

Clinton applied to only one college, Georgetown University in Washington, D.C. He wanted to be close to the country's political center, and subsequently he immersed himself in the politics on Capitol Hill. He won a Rhoads

1996
An anonymous author
publishes *Primary Colors*

1997
The Mars rover *Sojourner* begins its
exploration of the planet's surface

scholarship to England's Oxford University in 1968. During this time, he also was subject to the lottery system that selected men to be drafted into the army. Although he signed a letter of intent to join the Army Reserve Officers Training Corps (ROTC), he did not follow through when his high lottery number made it unlikely that he would be drafted. After two years at Oxford, Clinton accepted a scholarship to Yale University Law School, where he met his future wife, Hillary Rodham, a fellow law student.

Two years after graduating, Bill and Hillary Clinton settled in his home state of Arkansas. Clinton entered politics, and after serving as attorney general, he easily won the election for governor, becoming the youngest governor in the country at the age of thirty-two. He lost his bid for a second term, which transformed him into a more cautious politician. He made it a habit to pay more attention to public polls.

In 1983, he reclaimed the governor's seat and remained at the state capitol for the following nine years. In 1991, he was voted the country's most effective governor by his peers; that same year he announced his candidacy for president. During Clinton's presidential campaign, he was confronted with public revelations about his behavior, from draft avoidance to marital infidelities. Clinton overcame these challenges, dubbing himself the "Comeback Kid" while others dubbed him "Slick Willie." He won his party's nomination, with Albert Gore as his running mate. The team of two

Bill Clinton said, "Buy one, get one free." His wife, Hillary Rodham Clinton, is quoted as saying: "If you vote for him, you get me." They were political partners and competitors throughout their marriage and their White House years.

As First Lady, Hillary Clinton stirred controversy with the role she assumed in her husband's administration, especially as head of the Task Force on National Health Care. During the presidential transition, she established an office for herself in the West Wing and took part in deliberations for the appointment of cabinet members and other high-ranking officials. She was visible and outspoken, in some cases performing like an elected official. She became the most traveled First Lady in history, inside the United States and abroad. Hillary defended her husband during the impeachment ordeal, withstanding the firestorm with grace and personal courage.

Independent and a public figure in her own right, she announced her candidacy for senator from the state of New York, nearly a year before the end of her husband's term.

Hillary spent most of her life as Bill's advisor and sounding board; now, the Clinton machine focused on the other half of the Clinton-Clinton ticket. Bill Clinton went back on the campaign trail for his candidate wife -- the public stage he finds so invigorating and where he remains immensely popular with the people.

Daughter Chelsea, Bill, and Hillary on inauguration day, January 20, 1997.

1998
The government files an antitrust suit against Microsoft Corporation

1998
Tom Brokaw publishes
The Greatest Generation

Yitzhak Rabin, Bill Clinton, and Yasser Arafat at the Oslo Accords signing ceremony in September 1993.

youthful Southerners proved attractive to the electorate, and Clinton became the first baby boomer president.

Clinton's domestic policies addressed gays in the military, health care reform, gun control, deficit reduction, the environment, and welfare reform. With no military experience and little interest in world affairs beyond economic and trade concerns, Clinton oversaw the expansion of the North Atlantic Treaty Organization (NATO), the signing of the Oslo Accord between Palestine and Israel, humanitarian missions in Somalia, missile attacks on Afghanistan, and military involvement in Bosnia.

Clinton's presidency was bogged down with unprecedented assaults on his personal and business affairs, starting almost immediately. In 1994, an independent counsel investigated a controversial land deal, Whitewater, involving the Clintons. Their deposition was the first for a sitting president and first lady. That same year, a sexual harassment lawsuit was brought against Clinton and then, in 1997, allegations of inappropriate behavior in the Oval Office came Clinton's way. In another unprecedented event, Clinton was forced to testify before a grand jury concerning the charge of lying under oath in the sexual harassment suit and for obstructing justice.

Independent counsel cited impeachable offences and the House Judiciary Committee adopted two articles of impeachment. The Senate impeachment trial of Clinton failed to capture the two-thirds majority required for removal from office.

Clinton's complicated personal life and his questioned moral character was in sharp contrast to his intelligent, articulate, politically agile public persona, leaving "a big, permanent stain on his record." However, as Clinton himself said, politics was the "only track I ever wanted to run." His first press secretary summed it up: "If only this good president had been a better man."

Surgeon General C. Everett Koop and First Lady Hillary Rodham Clinton promote universal health insurance in 1993. The universal plan failed, but in 1997 the State Children's Health Insurance Program (CHIP) was approved.

Former presidents Bush and Clinton joined forces for charity in 2005.

My 2 cents
What would you nickname this president?

_____

The Author's Idea: The Man from Hope

1999
The Dow Jones reaches 10,000 for the first time, March 29

2000
The 2000 census reveals a U.S. population of 281.4 million people

2001
Successor president: George W. Bush

237

The Texas Rangers Ballpark
George W. Bush was one of a group of investors that purchased the Texas Rangers major league baseball team.
He was managing general partner and the public face of the team.

GEORGE W. BUSH

43rd President of the United States

POLITICAL PARTY: Republican
ELECTION OPPONENTS:
2000   Al Gore, Democrat
        Ralph Nader, Green Party
        Patrick Buchanan, Reform Party
2004   John Kerry, Democrat
        Ralph Nader, Independent
TERM OF OFFICE: January 20, 2001 to January 20, 2009
VICE PRESIDENT: Richard Cheney

The Bush childhood home in Midland, Texas. In this photo the home was dedicated as a presidential historic site.

A young George W. Bush, second from left, in the 1960s.

Personal Profile

BORN: July 6, 1946, New Haven, Connecticut
SIBLINGS: Eldest of six children
RELIGION: Methodist
EDUCATION: Yale University; graduated 1968
    Harvard University; graduated 1975
Career: Oil executive, part owner and managing partner of the Texas Rangers baseball team

MILITIARY: Fighter pilot, Texas Air National Guard; rank of lieutenant
MARRIAGE: Laura Lane Welch November 5, 1977, Midland, Texas
OFFSPRING: Twin daughters
DIED: Still Living

Laura Lane Welch Bush

2001
Previous president:
William Jefferson Clinton

2001
The first spacecraft lands on an asteroid

239

Visiting the President

BOYHOOD HOME: George W. Bush Childhood Home
   1412 West Ohio Avenue, Midland, Texas
LIBRARY/MUSEUM: George W. Bush Presidential Library and Museum
   Southern Methodist University, Dallas, Texas
   (groundbreaking late 2010, anticipated completion date in 2013)

Southern Methodist University in Dallas Texas, Laura Bush's alma mater, will be the home of the George W. Bush Presidential Library and Museum.

Tell me more!

Petigree

The Bush family moved into the White House with their aging English springer spaniel, Spot. The family pet had been born there to Millie, the pet dog of Bush's parents, George and Barbara Bush.

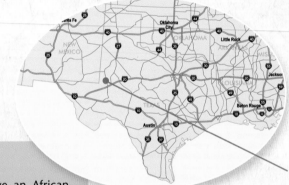

Midland, Texas

Fun Assignment!

George Bush became the first president to have an African-American serve as secretary of state and the first president to have an Hispanic serve as attorney general. Can you name them?

Condoleezza Rice and Alberto Gonzales

Political Profile

• Governor of Texas   • President of the United States

2001
Timothy McVeigh is executed for his role in the Oklahoma City bombing in 1995

2001
Enron files for Chapter 11 bankruptcy protection

The Bush Administration Highlights

- The Economic Growth and Tax Relief Reconciliation Act is signed (2001)
- The USA-PATRIOT ACT, granting government new authority to investigate and obstruct terrorism, is signed (2001)
- The No Child Left Behind Act is signed (2002)
- The McCain-Feingold campaign finance bill, banning the contribution of soft money to candidates campaigning for federal positions, is signed (2002)
- The Department of Homeland Security is established (2002)
- The U.S. Medicare Prescription Drug, Improvement and Modernization Act is signed (2003)
- Supreme Court Justice Sandra Day O'Connor announces her resignation (2005)
- John Roberts Jr. becomes the 17th Chief Justice of the U.S. Supreme Court (2005)
- Samuel Alito is confirmed as Associate Justice of the Supreme Court (2006)

Born in Connecticut and raised in Texas, George W. Bush inherited wealth, prestige, and an impressive political lineage. Following his father's footsteps early, Bush attended Phillips Academy in Massachusetts and Yale University. Also like his father, he played baseball, joined Delta Kappa Epsilon, and was a member of the secretive Skull and Bones Society. Graduating in 1968, and eligible for the draft instituted to provide troops for the war in Vietnam, Bush joined the Air National Guard. Once again following the example of his father, he trained as a fighter pilot. Between military assignments, he campaigned for Republican Party candidates, including his father.

In 1975, unsure of a career direction, Bush attended Harvard Business School. After securing his MBA, Bush returned to Texas and entered the oil business, as his father had done years earlier. In 1978, he flirted with politics, unsuccessfully running for Congress. During his campaign, Bush met Laura Welch, a librarian, and after a three-month courtship, the couple married. Ten years later, Bush sold his interest in the oil business, becoming financially independent for the first time in his life. He then moved his family to Washington so he could serve as senior advisor to his father's presidential campaign.

George W. Bush in the Texas Air National Guard.

2001
Laura Hillenbrand publishes
Seabiscuit: An American Legend

2002
Rick Warren publishes
The Purpose Driven Life

241

In 1989, Bush bought the Texas Rangers major baseball team with the help of a group of partners. Following his father's loss for reelection in 1992, Bush felt pressure to keep the family name in the political spotlight. He ran for governor of Texas and, with the support of his father, large campaign funds, skilled advisors, and a firm platform, Bush was elected with more than 53% of the vote. After a successful first term, Bush became the first Texas governor to be elected to a second consecutive term.

The Bush Cabinet was the most ethnically diverse to its date.

After five years as an elected official, Bush was ready for the White House and handily won the 2000 Republican presidential nomination. Not since the 1876 presidential race between Rutherford B. Hayes and Samuel J. Tilden had there been an election as controversial and bitter. On the night of the election, Bush and his Democratic opponent, Al Gore, had their eyes on Florida -- the

President Bush signs into law the No Child Left Behind Act in January 2002. The Act was an attempt to close the gap between rich and poor student performance.

George W. Bush was lively and outgoing, walked with a casual and jaunty gait, wore his favorite clothes till they were threadbare, and had an off-hand demeanor. When he was seven years old, his younger sister died of leukemia. He felt it was his job to take care of his mother. To distract her from her grief, he would crack jokes and tease. The use of humor stuck with him. When he was in elementary school, his mother said, "You don't want the class clown, you want a kid who's going to do his best." It took up to thirty years for Bush to change his attitude and channel his energies.

A bachelor until he was thirty-one years old, marriage was a turning point in his life, but his lack of success began to affect him. He started to drink heavily. Bush seemed to be "on the road to nowhere" and his wife Laura warned she would leave him. After getting intoxicated at his fortieth birthday celebration, he vowed to quit, and he did. He and Laura had twin daughters, Jenna and Barbara.

The Bush family in 1990.

The George H. W. Bush and George W. Bush legacy is sealed as Bush 41 and Bush 43. They are the first father-son presidential combination since John Adams and John Quincy Adams. The Bush legacy was attained within eight years while the Adams legacy took twenty-four years. An elder Bush friend said of George W., "He is always anxious to please his father and he has done it by emulation... In his way, he tried to relive segments of his father's life." When it comes to the presidency, though, George W. Bush is quoted as saying, "I never dreamed about being the president. When I was growing up, I wanted to be Willie Mays."

2003
Dan Brown publishes
The Da Vinci Code

2004
NASA lands two rovers to search for proof of
the past presence of water on the red planet

WIKI Michael Foran

The September 11, 2001 attack on the World Trade Center in New York City led the Bush Administration into a war against al-Qaeda in Iraq and Afghanistan.

state with the pivotal electoral votes. Because of the slim margin in the popular vote, Florida law mandated recounts. After numerous lower court suits, Florida Supreme Court suits, and two appeals to the United States Supreme Court, George W. Bush won the election with one electoral vote to spare.

Mindful of their candidate's campaign promise of "prosperity with purpose," the Republican Congress quickly passed the largest tax cut legislation in American history, but the direction of the Bush Administration changed dramatically on September 11, 2001 when terrorists attacked the World Trade Center in New York City and the Pentagon. Bush had to respond to the worst attack on United States soil since Pearl Harbor. He initiated a full-scale war against terrorism, starting in Iraq and expanding into Afghanistan. Against this backdrop, Bush's domestic agenda continued, including "No Child Left Behind," a student testing program, campaign finance reform, and a Medicare prescription drug program. The 2004 presidential election saw record turnout, with Bush capturing 286 electoral votes and fifty-one percent of the popular vote. His inauguration was marked by unprecedented security measures. Bush saw his win as a referendum on his handling of the economy and the war; he believed the voters had given him "political capital." Few of Bush's initiatives were implemented in his second term. Bush remained steadfast, his strategy on the war on terror never wavered and he spoke to the "spreading of democracy" as America's noble mission.

CONNECTIONS
On April 28, 2001, Dennis Tito, a billionaire California businessman, became the first "space tourist" when he blasted off from Kazakhstan to spend eight days aboard a space shuttle. Tito paid $20 million for his trip.

Bush with New Orleans Mayor Ray Nagin following Hurricane Katrina in 2005.

My 2 cents
What would you nickname this president?

The Author's Idea: Forty-One's Son

2004
Ronald Reagan is laid to rest

2004
Martha Stewart is sentenced to five months in prison for obstructing an investigation of insider trading

2009
Successor president:
Barack Obama

243

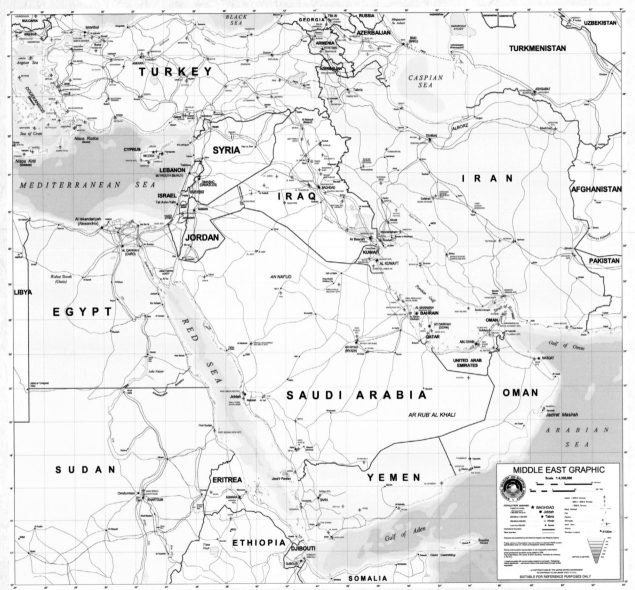

The Middle East has been politically and militarily significant since the terrorists attacks of September 11, 2011.

BARACK OBAMA

44th President of the United States

POLITICAL PARTY: Democrat
ELECTION OPPONENT: John McCain, Republican
TERM OF OFFICE: January 20, 2009
VICE PRESIDENT: Joseph Biden

Barack Obama Portrait: WIKI, Pete Souza

Fun Assignment!

President Obama authored two best selling books. Can you name them?

"Dreams from my Father" in 1995 and "The Audacity of Hope" in 2006

Punahou School, a private college prep school in Honolulu, Hawaii, that Barack Obama attended from the fifth grade through high school graduation in 1979.

Personal Profile

BORN: August 4, 1961, Honolulu, Hawaii
SIBLINGS: Eight half-siblings
RELIGION: Christian
EDUCATION: Occidental College (1979-1981)
    Columbia University; graduated 1983
    Harvard Law School; graduated 1991

CAREER: Community organizer, lawyer, law professor, and author
MILITARY: None
MARRIAGE: Michelle Robinson
    October 3, 1992, Chicago, Illinois
OFFSPRING: Two daughters
DIED: Still Living

Michelle Robinson Obama

Visiting the President

HOMESTEAD: 5046 Greenwood Avenue
Chicago, Illinois
CURRENT RESIDENCE: The White House
1600 Pennsylvania Avenue, Washington, D.C.

Tell me more!

Meeting Michele

Obama met his future wife, Michele, when
he was employed as a summer associate at a
Chicago law firm and she was
his advisor at the firm.

Senators Barack Obama
and Tom Coburn sponsored
the bill for the Federal
Funding Accountability and
Transparency Act
of 2006. Above,
President George
W. Bush signs
the act
into law.

WIKI, Ari Levinson (Autumnfire)

Senator Obama, recognized as a
gifted orator, delivers a speech at the
University of Southern California
in 2006.

Chicago, Illinois

Political Profile

- Member, Illinois State Senate
- Member, United States Senate

- President of the United States

2009
H1N1 virus, named the Swine Flu,
is deemed a global epidemic

2009
United States unemployment
reaches 10.2%

The Obama Administration Highlights

- Lilly Ledbetter Fair Pay Act (2009)
- Sonia Sotomayor appointed associate justice of the Supreme Court (2009)
- American Recovery and Reinvestment Act is signed (2009)
- Elena Kagan appointed associate justice of the United States Supreme Court (2010)
- Health Care Reform Bill is signed (2010)

Supreme Court Associate Justice Sonia Sotomayor.

Supreme Court Associate Justice Elena Kagan.

Ann Durham, a Kansas-born anthropologist and Barack Obama, Sr., a Kenyan economist, were the parents of Barack Obama. After two years of marriage, the couple divorced. Obama, now six, moved to Indonesia with his mother and new stepfather. Four years later, Obama returned to Hawaii. He lived with his maternal grandparents while his mother pursued her anthropological work in Indonesia. She, too, returned to Hawaii in 1994 and died a year later. His biological father died in 1982.

Barry, as he was called in his youth, attended a private preparatory school, graduating in 1979. He attended Occidental College in California for two years and then transferred to Columbia University in New York City, where he majored in political science. During these years, Obama reverted to his given name. Following graduation, he worked as a community organizer in Chicago.

In 1988, Obama entered Harvard Law School. While there, he was elected the first black president of the *Harvard*

President Obama signs the Lilly Ledbetter Fair Pay Act, January 2009.

Law Review. He gained media attention and earned a publishing contract, producing a personal memoir, *Dreams From My Father*. Obama met Michelle Robinson, a fellow lawyer, in 1989; the couple married in 1992.

From 1996 to 2004, Obama served as an Illinois state senator. He resigned that post upon his election to the U.S. Senate. His unexpected landslide victory in that race, combined with his delivery of the keynote address at the 2004 Democratic National Convention, made him a rising star within his political party. On February 10, 2007, Obama announced his candidacy for president at the Old State Capitol in Springfield, Illinois -- the same spot where Abraham Lincoln delivered his historic

2009
Senator Edward
(Ted) Kennedy dies

2009
Hillary Rodham Clinton is the first former First Lady
ever appointed to a federal government position

Barack Obama has joined the select group of forty-two men given the honor of occupying The White House. Most of these men called The White House home for either four or eight years, with two extreme exceptions: Franklin Delano Roosevelt for an astounding 4,432 days and William Henry Harrison for only thirty-two days. The father of this country, George Washington, was the only president who never slept in The White House. However, he did select its site, gave approval to the design submitted by Irish architect James Hoban in an open competition, and was present at the laying of the cornerstone on October 13, 1792. Washington preferred calling the future home of the presidents "The President's House," but by any name, it is not a palace or a fortress -- it's a dwelling of democracy. Barack Obama is the people's current choice to reside at 1600 Pennsylvania Avenue, and his legacy is yet to be written.

President Obama signs Health Insurance Legislation into law, March 2010.

"House Divided" speech in 1858. Against all odds, Barack Obama defeated his Democratic primary election opponent and went on to defeat his Republican opponent in the general election, becoming the first African-American president of the United States.

The Deepwater Horizon oil rig explosion, the country's worst environmental disaster, occurred in April 2010.

As chief executive, he has appointed two women to the Supreme Court, signed a $797 billion economic stimulus package, and a bill to overhaul the country's health care system. Barack Obama has a full plate of foreign and domestic initiatives. Critics argue he is taking on too much and is creating too big a federal government. History and his constituency will be the judge.

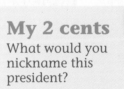

My 2 cents
What would you nickname this president?

_____

The Author's Idea: To Be Determined

2010
A British Petroleum deep water oil
rig explodes in the Gulf of Mexico

Air Force One flies over Mount Rushmore.

The White House

While Barack Obama is the current resident at The White House, this very special building that graces Pennsylvania Avenue in our nation's capitol has housed nearly all of our presidents and their families. As our country has changed and evolved, so has this stately symbol of freedom and democracy. It has survived fire and water, political upheaval, serious renovation, and whimsy. Through it all, it has remained the heart of a nation.

The White House sits on eighteen landscaped, tree-shaded acres at 1600 Pennsylvania Avenue in Washington, D.C. Its first occupant, John Adams, moved into the unfinished home on November 1, 1800. Over the years, the house has undergone a series of upgrades, additions, renovations, and demolitions. Running water arrived during Andrew Jackson's term and electric lights were installed during Benjamin Harrison's term. Modern day conveniences appeared, such as the telephone, during Rutherford B. Hayes' administration and the television during Truman's.

The White House improved and expanded over time. The first serious overhaul came at the end of the War of 1812, after a fire set by British troops roared through The White House, leaving only the four outer walls. James Madison insisted on rebuilding the residence to its original specifications. White paint was used to hide the charred stone exterior. The project was completed in 1820 when James Monroe was president. Subsequently, the following changes have taken place:

- In 1824, Monroe added a rectangular portico to the north side of the home.
- Andrew Jackson added a curved portico on the south side.
- During Theodore Roosevelt's administration, interior partitions were removed to create open space. Also, a public entrance was added to the east colonnade and a new one-story building was constructed on the west side.
- During the Coolidge administration, a third floor was added to the house, providing eighteen rooms for guests, servants, and storage. In addition, an electric elevator was installed.
- William Howard Taft converted a rectangular room into an ellipse in 1909, emulating the grand oval rooms of the south side of the home.
- Franklin Roosevelt renovated the West Wing, including a new second floor. He transferred Taft's Oval Office to the extreme southeast corner of the West Wing. After Pearl Harbor, an air raid or naval bombardment against the White House was considered a real possibility. In response, a bomb shelter was constructed east of the main residence and covered by a two-story addition with a large foyer and office space. The bomb shelter is currently referred to as the Presidential Emergency Operations Center (PEOC) and was used on September 11, 2001 by several members of the executive branch of the government.
- Age and inherent structural weaknesses led to a major demolition of the main residence of the White House, taking almost all of Harry Truman's second presidential term to complete at a cost of six million dollars. Thirty million viewers watched Truman conduct a televised tour of the completed project.
- Rosalyn Carter officially established the east wing as the office of the First Lady, a role it has retained ever since.

The White House is a symbol of our national heritage. It is the People's House. Over one million visitors a year pass through its portals. It serves many purposes, but it is primarily the home of the President of the United States. The décor and personality of the residence changes with each new occupant, and it is, as Grace Coolidge said, "a home rich in tradition, mellow with years, hollowed with memories." John Adams wrote, "I pray Heaven to bestow the best of blessings on this House. May none but honest and wise men ever rule under this roof."

BIBLIOGRAPHY

Aiken, Lonnelle. *The Living White House*. Washington, D.C.: White House Historical Association, 1982.

Baily, Thomas A. *Presidential Greatness*. New York, New York: Appleton Century, 1966.

Beschloss, Michael. *American Heritage: The Presidents*. New York, New York: Byran Press, 2003.

Blodgett, Bonnie and D. J. Tice. *At Home With the Presidents*. New York, New York: The Overlook Press, 1988.

Boller, Paul F., Jr. *Presidential Wives: An Ancedotal History*. New York, New York: Oxford University Press, 1988.

Boyd Caroli, Betty. *First Ladies from Martha Washington to Michelle Obama*. New York, New York: Oxford University Press, 2010.

Cunningham, Homer. *The Presidents' Last Years*. Jefferson, North Carolina: McFarland & Company, INc., 1989.

Davis Melick, Arden. *Wives of the Presidents*. Washington, D.C.: Hamond Incorporated, 1972.

De Gregorio, William A. *The Complete Book of U.S. Presidents*. New York, New York: Gramercy Books, 2005.

Hamilton, Neil A. *Presidents: A Biographical Dictionary*. New York, New York: Checkmark Books, 2004.

Harris, Bill. *First Ladies Fact Book*. New York, New York: Black Dog & Leventhal, 2009.

Kelly, C. Brian. *Best Little Stories from the White House*. Nashville, Tennessee: Cumberland House, 2005.

Lamb, Brian. *Who's Buried in Grant's Tomb?* New York, New York: BBS Public Affairs, 2003.

O'Brien, Cormac. *Secret Lives of the U.S. Presidents*. Philadelphia, Pennsylvania: Quirk Books, 2004.

Matuz, Roger. *The Presidents Fact Book*. New York, New York: Black Dog & Leventhal, 2009.

Smith, Carter. *Presidents: All You Need to Know*. New York, New York: Hylas Publishing, 2005.

Whitney, David C. *The American Presidents*. New York, New York: Doubleday & Company, 2005.

ABOUT THE AUTHOR

Walter Eckman, a native of Chester County, Pennsylvania, is a graduate of Pennsylvania State University and served with the United States Marine Corps. He has been active in the insurance, banking, and real estate industries. In 2001, he published his book, Retirement and Your Living Quarters, a guide for Baby Boomers' housing choices.

Mr. Eckman's expertise on the personal lives of the presidents of the United States is the result of years of interest and study. He and his wife JoAnne have traveled thousands of miles visiting presidential libraries, birthplaces, homesteads, and gravesites. In addition, Mr. Eckman is a professional speaker on the lives of the men who occupied the White House, and enjoys escorting his two daughters and three grandchildren to presidential destinations.

Notes:

Notes:

"You are not here merely to make a living. You are here in order to enable the world to live more amply, with greater vision, with a finer spirit of hope and achievement. You are here to enrich the world, and you impoverish yourself if you forget the errand."

– Woodrow Wilson
28th President of the United States of America